Policy Studies Institute

REPRESENTATIVE GOVERNMENT AND ECONOMIC POWER

Policy Studies Institute

REPRESENTATIVE GOVERNMENT AND ECONOMIC POWER

David Coombes

 Heinemann Educational Books·London

Heinemann Educational Books Ltd
22 Bedford Square, London WC1B 3HH
LONDON EDINBURGH MELBOURNE AUCKLAND
HONG KONG SINGAPORE KUALA LUMPUR
IBADAN NAIROBI JOHANNESBURG
EXETER (NH) KINGSTON PORT OF SPAIN

British Library Cataloguing in Publication Data

Coombes, David
    Representative government and economic
    power.—(Policy Studies Institute series)
    1. Industry and state—Great Britain
    I. Title   II. Series
    338.941   HD3616.G73

    ISBN 0-435-83180-1
    ISBN 0-435-83181-X Pbk

Phototypesetting by Georgia Origination, Liverpool
and printed by Biddles Ltd, of Guildford

Contents

Acknowledgements

This book is the result of a study on government and industry made in 1979 and 1980 by David Coombes, a senior research fellow in the European Centre for Political Studies at the Policy Studies Institute. The study was made possible thanks to financial help from Imperial Group Ltd, The European Cultural Foundation and the Joseph Rowntree Memorial Trust. An advisory group to the study was chaired by Lord Roll of Ipsden KCMG, CB and composed of leading figures from management, trade unions, the Civil Service and politics. Although the book expresses the author's own views and not necessarily those of the advisory group or of PSI, the author is indebted to those members of the advisory group and others who gave considerable time to discuss the study with him and to read and comment on earlier drafts of the book. He was also greatly assisted by participants from industry, government and elsewhere who attended occasional seminar discussions at PSI as part of the Institute's continuing programme of research on government and industry.

Part One
The Nature of the Problem

1 Introduction

This book sets out to attack a problem that exercises both academic students of the social sciences and practitioners in government, politics, business, trade unions and elsewhere. The problem is, in effect, that of how an advanced, industrialised society like Britain can be governed and it has arisen as a problem from the way three trends in Britain seem to be inter-related. These trends may be introduced in summary as:

- a growing dependence of those engaged in industrial activity on a whole range of decisions by government for the effective performance of their different functions;
- a growth in importance of organisations acting on behalf of particular social and economic interests based on industrial activity, above all employers' organisations and trade unions;
- an apparent decline in the status and influence of Parliament.

There is already a substantial and diverse literature on both general and particular aspects of these trends. Some writers have put them together under the collective name of the problem of 'corporate power' but it will be suggested here that the problem cannot be pinned down so easily. It is all too common in this subject to suggest some scapegoat – such as the economic power of trade unions or that of large business corporations – and to fall back on special pleading for some one-sided or otherwise predisposed view.

In fact, in making the study of which this book is the result I have not been convinced of any straightforward solution to the problem or even of the possibility of solving it. The study was certainly prompted by a feeling among both academics and practitioners that at least some practical proposals for improving the way we are governed should be sought. The present book hopes to fulfil that purpose by showing more clearly the obstacles to, and likely consequences of, applying different proposals. It ends with a strongly expressed view that the nature of the problem, at least as it appears in Britain, is not such as to be resolved by short-term or partial measures, but rather that it points to the need for major changes in the British system of government. In this way, the book raises more questions than it settles, but to be less ambitious would have been to allow a false sense of security and so to do a disservice to those for whom the book is especially intended – students of the social sciences and those responsible for, and affected by, major decisions in both government and industry.

The study set out, therefore, with a more simple remit than that with which it ended. It was thought that what related the three trends mentioned earlier, in such a way as to create a practical problem for governing Britain today, was essentially the means by which the relationship between government and industry was conducted. The aim was not to examine the economic shortcomings and possibilities of that relationship, relevant as these might be in their own right, but to see how far there was a political dimension on which useful changes could be recommended ('political' not just in the sense of party politics but also in that of the institutions and machinery through which government and industry communicate and deal with each other).

The main possibility to be considered was that changes in our representative institutions should be admitted more readily and extended further, in order to develop means of giving industry more direct representation at the level of central government. Such an approach certainly seemed to be suggested by the growing academic literature in political science on 'corporatism' and functional representation. It was also made relevant by the recent popularity, especially among industrialists themselves, of the idea (by no means new) of a national forum, chamber or council in which representatives of industry would be consulted by, and advise, government directly.

As the study progressed, however, it became obvious that such an approach, whether at a theoretical or a practical level, raised a whole host of questions that made it necessary to re-think, not only certain aspects of the government/industry relationship itself, but also the role of Parliament. Industrialists, civil servants and others advising on the project agreed (and some actually proposed) that such a wider remit was inevitable. The result, in what follows, is an attempt to set different past attempts and present proposals to adapt the means of conducting the government/industry relationship into their wider context, and thereby to see where they lead in terms of practical measures and possibilities. The present introductory chapter is intended to serve as a means both of indicating why a broader approach was thought necessary and of explaining the use of certain key terms and concepts that will recur in the rest of the book. The arrangement of the book's theme will also be summarised.

Government and industry

One reason why the subject of this book cannot be narrowed down to the working relationship between government and industry is the difficulty of finding a satisfactorily limited definition of what is meant by 'industry'. What is so special about industry that it can be considered worthy of study in relation to the general government of a country like Britain? When we speak of the representation of 'industrial interests', what other interests are we intending to exclude and why?

We are already familiar with the use of the term 'industry' to refer to a branch of manfacture or trade – as in 'coal industry', 'textile industry' or even 'tourist industry' – though we are prone to forget that its use in that way is often no more than an artificial one invented by economists or administrators to group together for some special reason different firms engaged in a similar activity. As in this book so far, the term is also commonly used to refer collectively to all such branches – as in 'industrial policy' or 'Confederation of British Industry'. There is, however, a risk of reading too much into such a concept, since in reality there are not always clear boundaries between what is industry and what is not, nor always that much identity of interest in industry as a whole.

In view of the history of industrial development in Britain and of the nature of the British economy in this century, it is obvious enough that in such a study one is dealing for the most part with manufacturing industry. It would not usually be denied (though it may not be adequately recognised in practice) that in Britain the economy depends ultimately on manufacturing industry and its associated activities and services such as banking and finance, transport, energy and distribution. It does not depend in the same way, as some other countries do, on agriculture, the export of raw materials or the provision of services such as tourism.[1] It might even be said that in view of the interdependencies created by industrialisation, it would be difficult to find any major economic activity in Britain that is not in some way vitally related to manufacturing industry – from finance and banking to the retail trade. There is a very important sense, therefore, in which a study of the government/industry relationship must also be a study of the role of government in the economy.

It is, indeed, when examining the impact of government on industry

[1] If we take the Central Statistical Office's index of gross domestic product for 1975 'manufacturing' accounts for 283 out of 1000, but added (as it should be) to 'mining and quarrying', 'construction', 'gas, electricity and water', 'transport and communication', 'distributive trades', and 'insurance, banking, finance and business services', the total weighting is 669 out of 1000. See: Central Statistical Office, *National Income and Expenditure* 1980 Edition, (HMSO, London), p. 107.

that the difficulties of delimiting the latter concept become most apparent. The significance of public policy and administration for industry would be under-estimated, if we narrowed our concern to those measures and procedures specifically directed at manufacturing industry. Industrial policy itself, in the sense of measures of direct intervention or procedures of consultation and departmental 'sponsorship', does not go widely enough. As Chapters 2 and 3 below will try to explain, there is a much longer history and a much more complex web of interdependence between government and industry than the relatively recent emergence of a distinct Department of Industry might otherwise suggest. Not only are there the traditional functions of the Board of Trade, but also, growing since the middle of the last century, the variety of departmental responsibilities falling generally under the description of social policy, especially where this concerns the pay and conditions of those in employment and the treatment of those unemployed, who are no less dependent on industry, in whatever sense, for their welfare.

In fact, as we shall see, governments' attempts to manage the economy as a whole, whatever form these have taken, not only provide the continuing background against which industrial decisions have to be made, but may also impinge directly by setting explicit limits to what those decisions can be. Obviously a wider range of interests and of people are affected by all such public policies and their application than are denoted by the concept of manufacturing industry or even of industry in a wider sense, but for our purposes a rather indefinite concept of industry is both permissible and necessary.

Interest groups and economic power

One way of indicating that we should encompass more than manufacturing industry might have been to use the term 'business' instead of 'industry'. But that would have narrowed our perspective in another important way, since many of the activities and interests with which we ought to be concerned in terms of our brief cannot be adequately described as commercial in nature.

Not only is industry in practice diversified and difficult to define on account of different structures and scales of operation and different kinds of output, it also includes different categories or groups claiming their own distinct identity and interest, sometimes cutting across firms and sectors, sometimes distinguished within them. We must take account, in other words, of the growth in importance, especially in the relationship between government and industry, of organisations representing separately the interests of employers and labour, both at the level of specialised trades, occupations or sectors and at the national level. The term 'industry' is often used to refer only to employers, but we shall use it here to comprise also trade unions, whose activities and interests would have been excluded by the use of a term such as 'business'. Increasingly, other groups of interests have also been recognised, though the basis of their organisation is much less established, such as management and consumers. In later chapters of this Part we shall see how the role of the public sector and of public intervention in privately-owned industry provide additional reasons why the term 'business' would have been misleading.

The role of organisations representing group interests in industry has special importance for our theme, and it is a major reason why industry has such significance for the study and practice of British government today. When we speak of the consultation of industry by government we invariably mean not those actually engaged in production or trade, but the spokesmen and officers of employers' organisations, trade unions and other bodies set up to represent different categories of interest. Political scientists are familiar with the role of more or less voluntary organisations, known as 'interest groups', which defend and promote in the political sphere some special social or economic category. Interest groups in general are now acknowledged to be a vital element in representative government. In industry, employers' organisations and trade unions are significant for their social and economic functions in, for example, collective bargaining. That in itself gives them a wider political significance, in view of the extension of government responsibilities in social and economic policy. But such bodies should also be seen more widely as performing a function like other interest groups, whether or not industrially-based, in articulating and promoting their members' interests in relation to government. The question of industrial representation, therefore, inevitably leads to wider and more complex issues about the nature of representative democracy itself.

The significance of the role of interest groups in relation to government can be illustrated briefly by comparison with that of political parties, which in many ways they have come increasingly to challenge, if not altogether replace. First, whatever their ideological or other differences, political parties usually seek to represent the general interest; although their members and voters may be largely confined to some special category or class of people, they usually claim, and also to some extent need, to be able to act for people in general, regardless of social and economic differences. Secondly, indeed, parties usually aim at taking responsibility for government and are not just concerned with pressing claims and defending interests. Finally, although some parties may be identified with a particular economic interest and rely on it for financial and other means of support, their power normally depends on their ability to win electoral support and not on the availability of sanctions of a social or economic kind.

Interest groups also often purport to seek the general interest, and with some justification, especially in view of their role in relation to government. However, they cannot make the same claims in this respect as political parties, since almost by definition their membership is exclusive. Similarly, interest groups often get themselves into a position where they are not just pressing claims on government but also assisting in the administration of policies and even taking some measure of responsibility, and this is an important function that will be discussed at length in later chapters. But too close an association with government will make their functions of defending and promoting their members' special claims more difficult, and their participation is usually limited to aspects of administration in which they have some special knowledge or interest (though the experience of the 'social contract' between the Labour Government and the trade unions presents an exception that will need particular attention in this book). Finally, interest groups are usually considered useful by government because of some specialised knowledge they can uniquely provide or because the support of their members is seen as essential for the effective performance of some public measure or objective. Some groups, and this is especially important for our theme, are capable in an advanced, industrialised society of proving even more necessary to government, since their power rests on an ability to disrupt some vital part of the economy. In other words, the political significance of interest groups may derive, unlike that of political parties, from their economic power.

It has been above all the economic power of industrial interest groups that has made the relationship between government and industry a problem with a wider political dimension. By the 1970s public concern with the problem in Britain had come to a head mainly with respect to the role of trade unions, especially in the events leading to the general elections of February 1974 and May 1979 and in relation to the 1974-79 Labour Government's 'social contract' . It is true that employers and other industrial interests have not had a similar impact nationally. However, the tendency for Parliament to be by-passed by a direct and close relationship between government and employers' organisations and other groups representing particular trades and occupations has long been cause of concern to students of representative democracy. The question of how to bring industry's needs and interests more effectively to the attention of government is complicated, therefore, by what role should be afforded in a representative democracy to organised groups based on social and economic interests. What is at stake is not only some theory of government but also the effective practical operation of the relationship between government and industry and, therefore, the economic health of the country as a whole.

Politics and consensus

One reason why there should be concern about group influence backed by economic power is the need to see to the welfare of less powerful groups as well as to protect the public interest. However important industry may be to the British economy and however inclusive it might be in an advanced society, there will always be vital interests that are not adequately catered for by means of the government/industry relationship. Even interest groups based on industry itself would not always want to be seen as exclusively industrial in nature or purpose, and this is especially true of trade unions. The central problem of this book, therefore, is an age-old one of how to find the right balance among different interests in society – whether these are highly organised or not. In an advanced, industrialised society, where certain groups wield economic power, this may be a highly complex problem.

As we have seen, the focus on industry must be to some extent blurred in any event. These days it may not even be clear, for example, that the duties of the judiciary and the police in maintaining law and order, or those of the armed forces in providing defence of the realm should be excluded. The first of these functions, for example, may today include intervention in industrial disputes and the second the procurement of weapons and materials leading to a close interdependence with particular industrial undertakings. However important in Britain industrial employment and output may be, we would normally exclude from our definition such vital professional and other services as those of the law, medicine, social administration, education and so on. But even these nowadays have some significant overlap with industry. We might, above all, regard industry as clearly distinguished from the political activity of MPs or the administrative activity of civil servants, but in this respect too, industrial issues are continuously and pervasively on the agenda.

The question is less one of drawing clear boundaries of occupation, vocation or interest than of getting the purposes of the government/industry relationship into perspective.

A major reason why the role of industry is thought to be crucial to the central problem of this book is that the development of an industrialised society has been associated with an increasing need for consensus embracing industrial interests. The use of the term 'consensus' in this respect, which has become increasingly common for the whole process of government, itself suggests some special condition for the effective exercise of political authority. 'Consensus' – and the term will be used recurringly in the rest of this book – implies both a measure of agreement that is especially inclusive (more so than what is usually suggested by mere majority decision) and also a kind of agreement that is reached essentially with the active consent of those involved rather than by compliance with the orders of some established authority (however legitimate and freely acknowledged). In an advanced, industrialised society like Britain, with all its social and economic interdependencies, there are obvious reasons why a minimum of consensus among different industrial interests and between industry and government should be considered of particular importance. But there are reasons, nevertheless, why consensus must have a vital political dimension and why the very concept needs much closer examination than it usually gets.

The emphasis on consensus, especially through the direct intercession of representatives of industrial interests, arises partly from misgivings about the political process based on elections, political parties and Parliament. At an academic level it has even led to attempts to revise the whole conception of representative government and to the revival, for example, of notions of corporatism, to which we shall need eventually to return. Such trends of thought reflect the concern of practical men in government and industry with the problems of adapting parliamentary institutions to the circumstances of government in an advanced, industrialised society, with the need to find new ways of exercising political authority in the face of the economic power of certain organised groups, and with the apparent divisiveness, and dislocation from industrial reality, of the main political parties. The problem remains, however, of how far a notion of consensus reached by some means other than the traditional methods of political competition and political obligation can be effective.

That problem is kept to the forefront by the persistence of political differences not only about the particular measures and actions that should result from the government/industry relationship, but also about the very nature of that relationship itself and the principles, including the economic reasoning, on which it should be based. Indeed, an apparently broad measure of agreement about the ends of public policy in economic affairs in general, lasting in the postwar period to the middle of the 1960s, has given way to a renewed contrast in the attitudes of the two major parties towards the role of the state. At the time of writing, in fact, a new challenge to the preponderence of the Conservative and Labour Parties has been launched in the shape of a new political party, the Social Democrats, pledged to defend the mixed economy against both the state socialism that has become increasingly influential in the Labour Party and the revival of *laissez-faire* in the Conservative Party. Obviously, we cannot attempt to resolve such issues in the present book, and that was never its purpose. What is significant for our present theme, however, is that such political differences imply different conceptions of what consensus entails.

On one side, for example, consensus, in the sense of widespread agreement voluntarily arrived at, will be possible only after a decisive change in the distribution of income and wealth and in the ownership of property, both requiring extensive public intervention. On another side, such consensus is seen as attainable or meaningful only as the result of a free interaction of the forces of supply and demand, which the mediation of public authorities with the help of organised interests is thought usually only to impede. Between these extremes there are varying shades of opinion in both Labour and Conservative Parties, and the Social Democrats and Liberals regard both sides as misled and unrealistic. But political reality does not offer a single view of what consensus means or of how it should be sought. Therefore, it is not enough to answer the extreme views on either side simply by positing a need for consensus as an alternative to them.

This book will examine more closely how and why such a need for consensus came to be seen as so important to the government/industry relationship and to British government in general. It will be led in so doing to question wide-ranging aspects of the British political system, beyond the operation of the government/industry relationship itself. Moreover, since the very nature as well as the operation of that relationship are in question we shall need to re-examine its foundations and purposes and its more recent application, even though studies of these already abound, in order to come to grips at all respectably with those who would maintain that the problem we are confronting here is either not a problem at all or is one to which the application of political science is largely inappropriate.

Plan of the book
In Part One, which is intended generally to state the nature of the problem, we shall re-examine, in Chapter 2, the foundations of the government/industry relationship and, in Chapter 3, trace the causes of the growing interdependence between government and industry culminating in the postwar mixed economy. The purpose of these chapters, which cover ground already amply mapped in numerous other historical and economic texts, is to try to indicate how far a relationship exists in spite of party political differences in the past or at present. They will also consider to what extent broader issues of economic and social policy are involved. Chapter 4, which is of necessity more theoretical in its approach, tries to explain why the government/industry relationship has a wider political dimension, whatever particular view is taken of its nature and purposes, especially in view of the role of organised interest groups and the emergence of a

'corporate economy'. Chapter 5 then deals mainly with political institutions and behaviour and is intended to retrace ground fairly well-trodden elsewhere in order to explain why central features of the British political system make it ill-adapted to fill the political needs which are identified.

Part Two examines how our problem has been approached by successive governments during a period roughly of the past twenty years. It is not an historical account, but one that breaks down what has in effect been a search for consensus into three main approaches: devolution to different kinds of public agency and official of responsibility for applying the public interest (Chapters 6 and 7); the direct involvement in economic policy making of industrial representatives, or 'tripartism' (Chapter 8); and more de-centralised approaches to 'concertation' by wider and more specialised participation of those engaged in industry (Chapter 9). We shall not only be concerned in that Part of the book with what has actually been practiced but also with the reasoning behind it, as well as with other possible approaches in the same spirit. The analysis is intended to show how the attempt generally to compensate for features of the political system has usually succeeded, if at all, only partially and for short periods.

In Part Three we shall be concerned with possible alternative remedies, beginning in Chapter 10 with an account of the view that traces the problem to adversary politics and of the various attitudes to political reform that have become prevalent as a response to the nature of party politics in Britain today. The next two chapters examine in some detail the possibilities of reinforcing the direct representation of industry. Chapter 11 deals with different proposals to that end, including the idea of a 'House of Industry', while Chapter 12 takes a more theoretical approach to the whole question of corporatism in relation to representative government, finding that it has certain fundamental limitations both as a method of explaining the central problem and as a way out of it. By this stage of the account, the nature of the problem will itself have been somewhat re-defined, being traced to underlying causes in British political life. Chapter 13 accordingly turns to the record and prospects of the reform of Parliament, interpreting that in a wider sense to include such issues as electoral reform. The final chapter tries to bring the argument back to the government/industry relationship itself and to show how some of its more typical problems might be easier of solution if political circumstances changed. It also indicates, though it does not attempt to resolve, some of the major constitutional issues such a change would imply.

Britain has not been alone among advanced, industrialised countries in experiencing the trends considered in this book, nor in finding them problematical. But, with the exception of some foreign comparisons made in Chapter 12 and some other references, the study has been concerned with Britain's own reaction and approach. Much of what is said should, however, prove relevant to those interested in the subject on a comparative basis or in other countries. Similarly, the book does not seek to pay special attention to international influences or the effects of British membership of the European Community, though the relevance of these is pointed in the final chapter. These omissions do not make any substantial difference to the argument of the book and have been allowed for the sake of greater brevity and clarity of argument as well as because comparisons not based on an equally thorough investigation into the circumstances of the country or countries concerned may be highly misleading. The subject certainly needs to be developed on a comparative dimension and in an international context, especially that of the European Community. As is pointed out in the final chapter, fuller consideration of the international circumstances and relationships of British government and industry would undoubtedly tend to strengthen the general line of argument made here.

2 The Foundations of the Government/Industry Relationship

What functions are suitable or desirable for government in the economic sphere has been a central issue in every British general election since 1945. However, in spite of the continuing conflict of party manifestoes, it seemed in the mid-1950s that a broad basis of agreement had emerged that governments (of whatever party composition) accepted certain economic responsibilities. The seeds of consensus were supposed to be in the commitment made in the war-time coalition's famous 1944 White Paper, *Employment Policy After the War* (Cmd 6527) to maintain 'a high and stable level of employment after the war'. As historians have been ready to point out, there were important qualifications to that commitment even at the time, since price stability, rising living standards and protection of the balance of payments were to be conditions of full employment. Nevertheless, the general commitment to maintaining full employment was undoubtedly the most significant transformation in the expectations of politicians and electorate alike brought about during the war (Middlemas, 1979; Lee 1980).

By the end of the 1970s, however, even the priority of that objective has come to be questioned, opening up again fundamental differences about the role of government in economic affairs. It is still not clear, in spite of the rising unemployment of recent years, whether full employment in the long term has ceased to be the universally-accepted yardstick of a government's economic performance. It is possible to argue, in other words, that current differences about economic policy concern means rather than ends. Even so, present differences about economic policy are significant enough. From the perspective we now have of the period since 1945 the all-party commitments made in the 1944 White Paper can no longer be regarded as the basis of a social and economic consensus, as they were in earlier accounts of the economic responsibilities of British government (Grove, 1959; Chester & Willson, 1957).

Nevertheless, it would be equally wrong to assume that the relationship between government and industry depended entirely, or even mainly, on fluctuations in political ideas about the role of government. The aim of this chapter is to look beneath the outer layers of the government/industry relationship, as we have known it in its varying forms over the last twenty years or so, and to recall its deeper and more lasting foundations.

The chimera of laissez-faire

The theory and practice of political economy in Britain is sometimes supposed to take as its main assumptions – the normality from which all other arrangements are held to be a departure – those of the economics of *laissez-faire*, in which the unhindered play of self-interest is meant to work to the benefit of all. However, the political economy of the English liberals of the nineteenth century was inspired, not by a normality of *laissez-faire*, but by one of government intervention, which was seen in its mercantilist form as impeding efficiency and enterprise and as unduly restricting individual freedom. Those thinkers most closely identified with Anglo-Saxon liberal economics (such as Adam Smith, Jeremy Bentham and J. S. Mill) took for granted, in their attempt to reveal the advantages of self-interest as a social and economic mechanism, an over-arching moral and cultural order that was supposed in effect to temper self-interest. Indeed, the end of their design was not some universal abandonment to individual wants, but rather a fuller achievement of certain moral values, in which self-realisation and self-development of the individual ranked among the highest (Coats, 1971; Plamenatz, 1973).

In British experience there has never been, in fact, a *laissez-faire* government, since all governments have found themselves, whatever their instinct to the contrary, with some responsibility for economic intervention (Dell, 1973). Certainly, if economic freedom is seen as the nineteenth century liberals saw it, that is, as a means rather than as an end, then the connection between economics and politics cannot be avoided. In other words, the free play of market forces was acceptable only to the extent that it promoted the wider moral values on which society was seen to depend and in which human beings were thought to achieve fulfilment. It was the purpose of government to promote these values. The role of government in the economy, though it may still be impossible to define satisfactorily or reach complete agreement about, has flowed, therefore, from something far more profound than an economic methodology.

To a large extent it may be seen in Britain and elsewhere as being quite separate from the form of government – the basis of its authority, its composition, its relationship to those subject to its rule. Throughout history, be they authoritarian, oligarchical, democratic, or whatever, governments have found themselves exercising economic intervention as a consequence of their need to provide security against external attack and to maintain internal order. Economic responsibilities have also flowed inevitably from the less clearly recognised need of governments of different kinds to look to the welfare of their subjects. In fact, of course, these primary functions of government are interdependent, though they may be treated separately.

Nationalism

In industrialised societies the rise of nationalism has itself been a prime cause of a large amount of public intervention in economic affairs. Protection of domestic industry has been a recurrent and widely accepted aim of such intervention. It is now realised that protection may take various forms and not only that of restrictions on imports by means of customs duties or quota restrictions (as the difficulties of the European Economic Community in dealing with non-tariff barriers to trade illustrate). Even before industrialisation, the defence and promotion of native production and manufacture in the interests of external security were common among European governments. To a large extent protection has been found necessary to ensure supplies of materials essential to armed defence. It has been repeatedly demonstrated just how much of the close involvement between government and domestic industry in peace time has been a legacy of the extensive regulation and control of industry that proved necessary for national defence in two world wars (Chester, 1951; Grove, 1962; Pollard, 1973; Middlemas, 1979). In times of peace, economic has often replaced military competition between nations. Domestic manufacturers and traders are subsidised, given special internal privileges and defended from foreign competition for the sake of national prestige as well as for reasons of economic or defence policy. To a considerable extent industrial policy as practised by British governments since 1945 can be shown to have flowed essentially from protectionist motives, reflecting among other influences those of the imperial tradition (Dell, 1973).

In all industrialised nation-states such intervention has as often as not been sought by industry itself. It has been encouraged not only by a regime's self-interest in defending its right to rule the territory concerned but also by the people's own consciousness of a common identity of interest. Indeed, today a call to 'buy British' in times of domestic economic hardship goes almost unquestioned in this country. The development of international organisations such as the General Agreement on Tariffs and Trade (GATT) has clearly restricted the use of many protectionist devices for nationalist ends. Above all, Britain's accession to the European Communities in 1973 has placed policy on international trade, and even domestic trading and industrial policy, in an entirely new context of Community law, shifting many key decisions to the Community institutions. But the ties between national government and industry are not thereby loosened nearly as much as might be supposed. In some ways they have had to be strengthened, in view of the need for representation through the national government in international negotiations and within the Community institutions (Hansard Society, 1977).

Internal law and order

In the midst of contemporary political debate about the proper extent of government, it is also often overlooked just how much the economic intervention of British governments is, in fact, an extension of their functions in maintaining law and order. Just as in other forms of social activity, traditional rules of contract and of private or civil wrong have had to be adapted to the economic sphere following the impact of industrialisation. It is, of course, a matter for some dispute just how far the maintenance of internal law and order requires governments to intervene as legislators, administrators or arbiters in economic affairs, as has been seen in recent times with such questions as labour law, consumer and environmental protection, and restrictive trade practices. Also disputed is the balance of responsibility between central and local authorities, as well as that between public and voluntary private bodies. But, whatever the outcome in terms of public policy, primary government responsibility for ensuring that standards of law and order extend to economic activity by some means or other is not denied (Grove, 1962, Pollard, 1973).

Social welfare

With respect both to external defence and to internal law and order, it is often difficult to disentangle as a separate cause of economic intervention, concern for the welfare of the subject. Wise rulers have invariably assumed both that a well-fed and healthy people is necessary for the external defence of the realm and also that poverty and un-employment breed disaffection and rebellion within. But, for whatever reason, governments have rarely dispensed with all responsibility for the supply of material necessities to their people, agriculture being the prime and probably earliest example of public intervention to this end. Industrialisation has extended that responsibility, however, not least by introducing new conceptions of necessity and by creating new interdependencies. Furthermore, it has brought with it a new social order and new technologies, both of which have created problems, expectations and possibilities that in their own right have changed the way the role of government is viewed.

It would, therefore, hardly be denied in Britain today in any part of the political spectrum that government also has responsibilities assumed under the name, broadly speaking, of social welfare. These responsibilities have further increased the need for a relationship between government and industry. They take the concern of governments beyond the supply of material necessity to include such matters as: the protection of those outside the market economy or possibly exploited by it (such as children, the sick, the unemployed, the handicapped and so on); the distribution and the security of income and wealth; the human consequences of conditions of work; and equality of opportunity for those able and willing to participate in economic activity but otherwise prevented, either by the effects of market forces themselves or by discrimination on grounds such as sex, religion or race. Vital responsibilities of modern government for industrial health and safety – as regards both producers and consumers – date back to the early nineteenth century, when public intervention was already far more extensive than is commonly supposed (Parris, 1965,1969).

Public intervention was obviously boosted by the growing strength of certain political movements in the latter half of the nineteenth century and into the twentieth. The new functions thus acquired by government are generally attributed above all to the effects of two great reforming administrations – the Liberal Government elected in 1906 and the Labour Government of 1945-50. It is tempting for that reason to see the influence of social policy, unlike the other causes of economic responsibilities of government that we have considered so far, as being closely related to the form of government itself: as a consequence, in other words, of representative democracy in the shape of universal suffrage and the growth of popular political parties.

Too close a connection is belied, however, by the much longer history of public intervention for ends of social welfare. It has now been widely recognised by scholars of British social administration that many of the major legislative and other measures of social welfare have been not only accepted, but actually introduced, by Conservative Governments, in a way that suggests a tradition of 'Tory paternalism' (Beer, 1965; Gilmour, 1979; Smith, 1979).

Effects of industrialisation

In fact, a fundamental reason for the great influence of social policy on economic intervention by governments in Britain and elsewhere over the last hundred years is to be found in the consequences of industrialisation itself. It is well known that many, if not most, of the social responsibilities now placed on government were in a predominantly agrarian society entrusted to private organisations – the family, the church, or the feudal system. Moreover, where public administration of social services was considered necessary (invariably for reasons mainly of public order or the supply of necessities), it was highly decentralised and personal, leaving much to the discretion of local notables.

The social and political effects of industrialisation have been so often described by sociologists that no more than a selection is required here. The movement of population to towns, or urbanisation, broke down the traditional social ties and the self-sufficiency of the countryside. The growth of population, as well as its geographical concentration, created for public order the new problem of the urban masses, while the appearance of markets for labour created a new scale of problems of poverty and unemployment. The sense of community, based on a relatively stable notion of status gave way to the impersonal and more fluid relationships of a contract-based society, epitomised eventually in the modern corporate business enterprise (see p.37). Specialisation and the division of labour, together with the dependence on machines, also increased interdependence and encouraged a larger and more impersonal scale of organisation. Particularly important for the main theme of the present study, the authority relationships developed within industry itself made it a venue for the exercise of power, in which decisions could be taken, whether consciously or not, affecting vital aspects both of the individual's welfare and of the wider social order. Industry came, meanwhile, to include in its workforce a substantial majority of the adult population of both sexes (Burns, 1969; Kumar, 1978).

How far public intervention can deal effectively with all the social demands thus generated is, of course, a matter of dispute. But no government of an advanced, industrialised country has been able to avoid ultimate responsibility for the social consequences of industrialisation.

Influence of organised labour

Well before the Labour Party entered government, industry had learned to accept legislative restriction and public inspection of such matters as the conditions of employment of certain categories of workers, safety for employees and consumers, and in the case of some services (such as railways and waterways) even of competition and the conditions of supply. The role of public authorities was greatly extended not only in the field of social administration (including education, public health and care for the aged) but also in the provision of a much wider range of essential services (such as gas, electricity and water supply) (Grove, 1962; Parris, 1965, 1969). In the years immediately before and during the first world war the foundations were laid for public intervention in labour markets.

However, the growth of organised labour was itself an influence leading to public intervention, first, in the legal recognition of trade unions and, subsequently, in providing services of arbitration in industrial disputes and even, for certain categories of work, machinery for regulating wages and conditions (Middlemas, 1979; Martin, 1980). The influence obtained by trade unions through political representation was clearly important in this respect even before and during the first world war. The role of trade unions within the Labour Party clearly had an impact on the role of government during and after the second world war. Although as a movement it has always been ambivalent about the relevance of pursuing wider social ends by political means, the concern of British trade unionism with general aims of social welfare, and not only with the particular interests of its members, has undoubtedly been an important factor in its own right. However, even without direct influence from organised labour for expanding the responsibilities of government (and it was weakened during the inter-war years of unemployment), the economic importance of organised labour since 1940 would have been enough on its own to make governments actively concerned with the results of collective bargaining. The economic and political power of organised labour is clearly of major significance for the main theme of this study and we shall return to its wider implications at length.

The machinery of government
At the same time, within public administration itself there has been since the 1870s a cumulative transfer of responsibility from both private, voluntary organisations (often sponsored by public legal and financial protection) and from local authorities to the central government. Two main influences seem to have been at work here.

First, given especially the increasing need for central government to bear the growing financial burden of services, centralisation has been encouraged in the interests of greater administrative and financial efficiency. Secondly, there has been the pressure to ensure uniformity of standards.

The process has contributed greatly to the expansion of the size and scope of the central government, and, therefore, both to the responsibilities of ministers and to the role of the Civil Service. A host of new ministerial departments of state grew up in the course of this century under various titles, concerned with the provision of services to individuals and with economic activity of different kinds as British central administration had not known before: education, health, housing, pensions and national insurance, supply, transport, labour and so on (Chester and Willson, 1957). Much of this expansion was prompted directly by the needs of government during the first world war, but the growth of a centralised public administration did not abate in its assumption of functions bearing directly on the day-to-day lives of people, forming nowadays an essential aspect of the way they gain and dispose of their livelihoods.

One notable feature of the growth of central government, however, has been the retention by the department traditionally responsible for housekeeping and budgeting, the Treasury, of vital powers of central co-ordination and control. Indeed, while the number of new departments with economic responsibilities was increased and new responsibilities were added to the old Board of Trade, probably the most significant transformation in terms of economic policy was that in the role of the Treasury. A major influence was the importance that came to be placed during and after the second world war on the government's own financial activities as a means of influencing economic activity as a whole. As a result, the budget itself was transformed after the 1930s from an instrument simply for controlling the financial activities of central government into a complex mechanism for managing fluctuations in the domestic economy. The Treasury's relationship with the Bank of England (formalised rather than substantially altered by the latter's nationalisation in 1945) added vital responsibilities for the supply of currency and credit (including substantial power to influence rates of interest) and for the exchange rate. More flexible instruments of fiscal policy have since been evolved under the Treasury's aegis, enabling central government to intervene outside the normal budgetary cycle in an attempt to influence aggregate demand in the economy (Roll, 1968; Brittan, 1971; Clarke, Sir R., 1978).

Management of the economy

Four main developments made it possible for governments to assume these critical economic responsibilities. First, as has just been explained, there was the growth as a proportion of gross domestic product of public expenditure itself, caused both by the expansion of governments' traditional functions, such as defence, and by the influence of social policy. Secondly, the application of science, especially during the second world war, made available the statistical knowledge with which the behaviour of different components of economic activity could be measured (and later even predicted). Thirdly, new significance came to be given to economic science in public policy making, so that economists, as the professional operators of a new technology, serving both government and industry, came to exercise their own substantial influence, if in different ways, on both public and private decisions. Fourthly, another lasting change has been the firm conviction among electorates, politicians, public administrators and industrialists that government is responsible for seeking to manage the main aggregate economic variables – employment, prices, incomes, investment and the balance of payments. Indeed, the past performance and future promise of governments in exercising this responsibility came after the war to be the major issues in general elections and even in day-to-day political life (Beer, 1965; Brittan, 1968; Butler and Stokes, 1971).

The most significant political outcome was probably, as already suggested, the commitment of all major parties towards the end of the war-time coalition to maintaining full employment. This commitment has, of course, proved extremely difficult to reconcile in most circumstances with other ends of macroeconomic policy. Much of the history of British politics since the war can be explained in terms of the search for an elusive means of so managing the economy that the different variables could be kept in a satisfactory relationship to each other.

The impact of the economic theories of J. M. Keynes on public policy making led in the 1930s and 1940s to what has been described as an 'intellectual revolution' by suggesting that governments were capable, by the use of macroeconomic analysis in relation to the management of their own income and expenditure, to induce stability in economic activity seen as a whole, avoiding both extremes of under-employment and those of inflation (Roll, 1968; Winch, 1969; Brittan, 1971; Meade, 1975). The influence of Keynes was to encourage the belief that full, or almost full, employment could be ensured by public intervention. And it led postwar governments, backed by vastly improved statistical resources, to use a variety of instruments, especially fiscal measures, to seek to manage aggregate demand in the national economy. Industry thereby found itself, not only obliged to furnish the information on the basis of which government could seek to manage the economy, but also increasingly dependent on government for the economic conditions in which its own decisions about investment, production and pricing would have to be taken.

One important effect of the influence of Keynes was to restore confidence in the economic system of industrialised democracies after the shocks left by the Great Depression. A basically free market, it seemed, could after all be made compatible with full employment and stability. In other words, a major attraction of economic policy using Keynesian principles was that it sought not to transform the economic system but to make it manageable, without such a change in the power of public authorities as would make representative democracy impossible. The responsibility of government was to be increased, but not at the expense of the market economy itself nor of the basic freedoms of private ownership and choice (Hirsch, 1977; Skidelsky, 1977).

Subsequently, that confidence has been much less easy to sustain on the basis of economic theories and techniques associated with Keynes. In conditions of full employment the application of Keynesian techniques came to be directed not at curing problems of depression but at managing demand in an attempt to avoid inflation (Trevithick, 1977). The doubtful record of British governments in both these respects has increasingly brought to the surface doubts about the very feasibility of management of the economy in existing economic, political and social circumstances. At one extreme, there is the view that objectives such as full employment and economic growth are at best marginally influenced by the conscious actions of governments and should be left to depend largely on trade. At another is the conviction that much greater changes in the relationship of state to society are required (and particularly in the extent of public ownership and regulation) than have yet been envisaged by any governing political party. One may even doubt how far the apparent consensus expressed at the end of the war did more than paper over underlying fundamental differences about the role of government in the economy (Bogdanor and Skidelsky, 1970; Middlemas, 1979).

The scope available to governments for managing the national economy is also limited by international commitments and by the effects of international monetary and trade fluctuations. British governments have found themselves especially vulnerable in these respects, given Britain's declining economic and political status since the war. Membership of the European Community, which entails substantial limitations on sovereignty in the economic sphere, was itself an attempt to find a more secure defence against the effects of world economic disorder. In fact, the need to respond to international influences is itself a reason for domestic industry to become more dependent on government.

It would, in fact, be extremely hard for any government nowadays to deny all responsibility for the behaviour of the major economic variables, whatever range of instruments it may choose to influence them. For all its complexity and uncertainty as to methods, public intervention to manage the national economy must now be seen as a natural extension of government's primary responsibilities, associated with defence of the realm and internal order, and its functions in relation to social welfare. It is not necessary to maintain that public authorities have some special aptitude, let alone a distinct purpose, for achieving economic ends, in order to recognise the economic responsibilities of governments and the foundations of a government/industry relationship.

3   A Growing Interdependence

The last chapter sought to describe certain lasting and generally accepted foundations of the government/industry relationship in Britain today. However, we have not yet obtained a complete picture of the degree of interdependence between government and industry since the second world war. For most of the time since 1945, that interdependence has been widely accepted in both politics and industry. The co-existence of public and private sectors of industry provided the basis of an apparent convergence between the main economic policies of the Labour and Conservative Parties that reached its high point during the 1950s in the years of 'Butskellism'.[1]

Nevertheless, the durability and the extent of that convergence were never certain. It has never really been possible to present the government/industry relationship in terms of unequivocal or generally agreed principles. A variety of sometimes conflicting influences and factors have had to be taken into account. Different interpretations of the role of government have always been possible. In both of the two major political parties there have continued to be influential elements for which the existing government/industry relationship was an unsatisfactory compromise. In the 1970s, those elements came increasingly to the surface and, as a result, the pattern of politics clearly became one of divergence rather than convergence.

All the same, it is important to recognise, as we shall try to do in this chapter, the extent to which government and industry have grown increasingly interdependent regardless of differences of party-political doctrine.

Public ownership

Perhaps the most politically controversial method of public intervention in industry has been the transfer of major undertakings to public ownership in the name of 'nationalisation'. It was one of the major objectives and results of the immediate postwar Labour Government from 1945 to 1950, after which roughly twenty per cent of industrial and commerical enterprises had been brought into public ownership

[1] The term was coined by *The Economist* in 1954 from the names of the then Chancellor of the Exchequer, Mr R A Butler, and the then Oppostion spokesman on Treasury affairs, Mr Hugh Gaitskell (Smith, 1979, p. 209).

(Smith, 1979). Significant later additions have been made, so that statutory public corporations now own and take responsibility for most of the energy and inland transport sectors, steel production, national airlines and airports, posts and telecommunications, and the aerospace and shipbuilding industries. They now account in total for roughly eleven per cent of gross domestic product and eight per cent of employment. Other forms of direct public participation in the ownership and operation of industrial undertakings, such as through partial share ownership, state holding companies and government representation on company boards, have been used less in Britain than in some other West European countries. But the last twenty years have seen a substantial increase in such forms of intervention, so that public participation now extends to major parts of the oil industry, mechanical engineering (mainly motor cars), electronics and some other sectors.

The extension of public ownership can, in many of its aspects, be traced uniquely to socialist influences within the Labour Party both before and after the war. However, as has been frequently pointed out, the precise aims have been at best ambivalent. An ideological commitment to public as opposed to private ownership has not been the over-riding motive. In fact, public ownership has invariably followed a history of public intervention in different forms, including centralised public regulation, subsidy or direct participation introduced by Conservative Governments or coalitions, rather than by Labour Governments (Coombes, 1971; Foster, 1971). In retrospect at least, the 1945–50 Labour Government's acts of nationalisation were restrained, certainly in the eyes of observers from some other West European countries (Leruez, 1967). With the exception of road transport and steel they were accepted by later Conservative Governments. Not until after the general election of 1979 were serious attempts made to return parts of other basic nationalised industries to private ownership.

Public ownership of industry came to be regarded, even in the Labour Party, as only one means among others, and by no means always the most effective means, of achieving social and economic ends of public policy. This was, of course, one of the main themes of Crosland's highly influential re-assessment of socialist policy in his *The Future of Socialism* (Crosland, 1956). Towards the end of the 1960s it was possible to claim realistically:

'The significant fact is that in nearly all the major industrial countries the ideological context over the ownership of business enterprise is now at a very low ebb. I find it hard to believe that it will break out again in full force in the foreseeable future, though this cannot be ruled out. It seems more likely that questions of the most effective administration of the public and private sectors (mainly in regard to particular areas such as public utilities) will provide the primary source of intellectual debate and political controversy.' (Roll, 1968, p. 47)

As a prediction, such a view has suffered from subsequent political developments, at least in Britain. But there has remained a very wide spectrum of opinion in both politics and industry in this country that would accept the sentiments expressed.

In fact, what had emerged by the 1950s in Britain was what has now come to be known as a mixed economy. That concept is difficult to define with any clarity or consistency and it has been used to encompass what are in effect different approaches to public intervention. We shall discuss its complex political implications in the next chapter. Basically, a mixed economy is characterised by the co-existence of public and private ownership in industry, with public ownership confined largely to public utilities and industries occupying a vital position in the economy (Rogow, 1955; Roll, 1968, 1978; Smith, 1979). We shall return in Chapter 6 to the problems of operating such a substantial public sector, which have involved governments in, among other things, decisions similar to those required by the management of any large-scale industrial undertaking. But a mixed economy may also be taken to include an indefinite but significant degree of public intervention in industry by means other than outright public ownership. In this respect there has also been an interdependence between government and the private sector of industry.

The private sector

Since the second world war, British industry and business in the wider sense (including finance and banking, and services) have been made subject to many new forms of general legal constraint designed to achieve economic ends in the public interest. Probably of longest duration in this category are laws intended to prohibit certain restrictive trade practices, control monopoly and promote competition. In addition, legislation dealing with conditions of employment and workers' rights and with environmental and consumer protection has in recent years greatly extended the incidence of public intervention on grounds of social welfare, while also refining concepts of what is legitimate conduct in business activity. More detailed and direct regulation of prices, incomes, rents and dividends has from time to time even further restricted the scope of business decisions.

Governments' concern with economic efficiency has led to various measures to promote mergers and other methods of rationalisation, particularly in manufacturing industry, and to encourage technological innovation, labour mobility and regional development. Subsidisation of particular undertakings has been practised in Britain, most notably since 1960, in relation to shipbuilding, aircraft, textiles and aluminium. In addition, it has become normal for governments to adopt a variety of measures making general financial assistance available to industry on certain conditions and designed to promote particular economic ends. Both fiscal methods (such as investment incentives or special taxes) and direct financial grants have been used (Vernon, 1974; Young, 1974; Hayward and Watson, 1975). It is estimated that in 1970/71 government expenditure, including indirect tax reliefs, on financial assistance to British industry already amounted to £923 million (Corden and Fels, 1976).

The growth in importance of large-scale industrial undertakings has tended to produce a coterie of leading businessmen who can be said to enjoy privileged access to Whitehall and to ministers themselves (Turner, 1971; Ionescu, 1975; Smith, 1979).[2] In much of what follows we shall be concerned with the functions of consultation, advice and persuasion that the government/industry relationship now includes, often on a personal basis, and involving the boards and management of individual large private corporations.

The legacy of the second world war itself did much to influence the working relationship between government and industry in peacetime. By the end of the 1940s, the bulk of the instruments of the centrally planned and closely regulated war economy had been dismantled. But the repercussions of economic administration during the war lasted in the experience of politicians, civil servants, professional economists and industrialists, if only in the personal contacts that had been established. Furthermore, the growth in scale and importance of those parts of the public administration dealing with economic affairs never reverted to pre-war conditions (Smith, 1979).

During the war, individual 'production' departments had been given particular responsibility for 'sponsorship' of private undertakings in their particular sector. This meant and has continued to mean, though on a much less intensive scale, not only administering whatever legislative and financial provisions apply to the sector, but also maintaining regular contact with representatives of industry in a two-way process of consultation and advice, sometimes through the machinery of advisory committees, more often on an informal basis. The departments involved during and just after the war included the Board of Trade and various ministries for supply, food, agriculture, fuel and power, public works and transport (Chester, 1951; Rogow, 1955; Grove, 1962). The system has been retained, even without the physical controls and the extensive regulation of the war economy,

---

2 It has been estimated that in 1968 the 100 largest corporations in Britain accounted for over 50 per cent of all profits and about one-third of total employment in all industrial and commercial companies (Bannock, 1971 p. 31).

in spite of the fact that there have been successive re-allocation of functions among government departments. The operation of the system was described in the mid-1970s as follows:

> 'There is now almost certainly somewhere in government a little unit of people whose job it is to acquaint themselves with what is happening in each industry and, as far as they can, watch over its interests – not only in connection with government controls but also more generally.' (Sir Ronald Mackintosh in Lethbridge (ed.), 1976, p. 84)

In fact, private enterprise has come to depend in all sorts of ways on the public sector as supplier and consumer. As the development of social and economic policy has caused government to grow even beyond what is required by modern armed defence, so government itself in its own operations has become a major employer, consumer and in many respects producer. By this means it has become a major competitor with private industry for resources and also a major customer, sometimes with a decisive influence on its suppliers' commercial prospects. Estimates of the size of the public sector vary, and there is controversy about methods of estimation. But in the 1970s, something approaching fifty per cent of the gross domestic product in Britain could probably be accounted for by public expenditure of one kind or another (Wright, 1977). British governments have come to realise the potential of this economic power, not only for further reinforcing macroeconomic policy, but also for seeking to influence the behaviour of sectors, industries and individual enterprises. For example, they have required special standards on the part of suppliers, obliged suppliers to employ special productive factors, and purchased particular products as an act of hidden subsidy. It is, in fact, common for industrial undertakings in countries comparable to Britain to look to government for basic support in matters such as research and development, industrial training and labour mobility, and help with certain kinds of investment (Vernon, 1974; Hayward and Watson, 1975; Zysman, 1977). The decisions of large scale industrial undertakings impinge on a government's responsibility for a whole range of 'public goods' in fields such as employment, social security, education, the environment and the supply of necessities.

Economic planning
Towards the end of the 1950s, the role of government in the economy was widely seen as providing grounds for optimism about the prospects of economic growth not only in Britain but in the West generally. The key instrument was central planning of the economy by public inter-

vention suitably adapted to the conditions of a basically capitalist market economy.

That, in turn, implied adapting political institutions and behaviour to a more positive role for government in the economy. As with the earlier impact of Keynesian economics, the aim was essentially to protect, and even turn to better use, both the principles of a market economy and those of representative government. Students of the history of economic policy in Britain show how the conception and application of economic planning in Britain in the 1960s can be traced to the influence of those prewar politicians and intellectuals who, individually, had already seen planning as the answer to the social and economic problems of democracy. However, they also reveal that planning has had almost as many different meanings as there have been authors (Leruez, 1975; Smith, 1979). And there continued to be as many potential differences as there were unarticulated assumptions behind the conversion to planning in the 1960s.

The British approach in practice drew on three vital elements in the mixed economy. First, it sought to extend government's responsibility for management of the economy to include a positive commitment to targets of national economic growth. It would then be up to governments themselves to deploy the different instruments of economic management in accordance with such a commitment and up to industry to make its own plans on the assumption that a government's commitment was both realistic and genuine. But the authority of official projections was expected to flow partly, like government's fundamental role in management of the economy, from the application of scientific techniques and access to information supplied by industry itself. In other words, there was to be an important element of technocracy in the approach to planning. Secondly, government would make use of the existing public sector for promoting growth in accordance with its plan, and would also be endowed with new forms of selective intervention in the private sector. But public ownership would not necessarily have to be extended, and at least not on the model of complete nationalisation of industries. What mattered above all was establishing the right kind of relationship with privately-owned industry backed by suitable powers, especially those of giving financial support, designed to meet particular needs. Thirdly, governments would make use of the increasingly centralised and well-defined organisations set up to represent social and economic interests, such as trade unions and employers' organisations, both to improve its own intelligence of industrial realities, and to infuse industry with a greater sense of common purpose, without the need for extensive public regulation and physical controls. In this respect, earlier corporatist

methods practiced during the war would be developed,[3] while attention
was drawn in particular to the French postwar experience with a
'concerted economy'[4] (Shonfield, 1965).

As we shall discuss further in Part Two of this book, attempts to
apply this approach to planning in the 1960s were largely frustrated, so
that 'planning' itself became something of a dirty word. But, in spite of
all the subsequent chopping and changing of policies, measures and
institutions, it left a lasting impression on the government/industry
relationship. A mixed economy thus became associated with the
dependence of governments on elaborate means of economic intelligence and technical advice, the deployment of a whole variety of public
agencies and measures of selective intervention and the development of
departmental 'sponsorship' into an elaborate web of regular
communication with industry, especially by means of trade unions and
employers' organisations.

Intermediary organisations

The rise in importance of economic interest groups such as trade
unions and employers' organisations is now seen as part of a general
trend towards greater collective organisation in all aspects of life in an
advanced, industrialised society (Marris, 1974; Bell, 1976; Kumar,
1978). In Britain, trade unions now include new categories, such as
white-collar workers, and have increasingly emphasised a concern with
wider public issues, such as care for the aged and unemployed or
industrial training. Similar principles and methods of organisation

---

[3] Tied into the central machinery for economic planning of the war economy (co-
ordinated by the powerful Lord President's Committee at Cabinet level) was the
National Production Advisory Council, set up to advise the Ministry of Production and
including representatives of employers and trade unions, as well as other economic
interests. Attached to the same Ministry were regional councils and prominent
industrialists employed as regional production controllers, together with joint production
committees at the level of firms. Control of prices by the Board of Trade depended
largely on voluntary machinery operated by means of private trade associations. In the
national Joint Advisory Council attached to the Ministry of Labour trade union
representatives played a vital role.

The system has since been described as 'corporatist', because of the extent to which
public responsibilities were devolved on private individuals and bodies (Leruez, 1975).
Such arrangements were retained, and in some ways developed, by the postwar Labour
Government in its partial attempt to establish peacetime planning between 1945 and
1947 (Smith, 1979).

[4] A widely-quoted definition of the concerted economy is that given by Bloch-Lainé: 'A
regime in which the principal options in matters of investment, production, and
exchange do not entirely depend on the heads of business or on the public departments in
their respective spheres, but proceed from a permanent collaboration, so that there are
not two series of autonomous and separate acts with no link between them, corresponding to the division between the public sector and the private sector.' (Bloch-Lainé, 1963,
pp. 5–6).

have been extended to religious, cultural and other primarily non-economic groups, as well as to such broader economic categories as consumers or even the 'middle classes' (Smith, 1979). In their relations with government, trade unions, employers' organisations and other such bodies play a role in promoting coherence and even discipline among their own memberships. Their activities are partly directed at bringing a view of the general interest to bear on the sectional and particular concerns of the manufacturing, trading or other activities they represent.

A recent detailed history of the relationship between government and industrial organisations in Britain since Edwardian times has gone so far as to designate trade union and business associations as 'governing institutions', given the extent to which governments have devolved functions on them, especially with the object of promoting consensus in economic policy (Middlemas, 1979). Indeed, the authority such private bodies have been able to acquire owes much to the positive support of government itself, both in giving legal and official recognition and in various forms of encouragement to organise on a national scale.

Their essential duty, therefore, straddling, and even acting as an essential link between, the private, individualist and competitive sphere of commercial activity, on the one hand, and the public, collectivist and co-operative one of civil society on the other – justifies the use of the rather clumsy term used here of 'intermediary organisations' (Parry, 1969).

Although such organisations do not even overtly have as an essential aim the commercial exploitation of resources for their own profit (though some trade associations began as agreements formed in restraint of trade), they do have as an essential purpose protecting the economic interests of their members. They also have, or at least claim to have, explicit social purposes designed to benefit not only their own members, but also, to some extent, society as a whole. Not only did they emerge largely as voluntary bodies designed to provide common services of a collective nature (trade unions, for example, as friendly societies), but their development has owed a great deal both to the need of their members for representation towards government at central and local levels and to the need of government for spokesmen of different categories of workers, employers, producers, traders and so on.

The significance of intermediary organisations in Britain can be seen in their growing inclusiveness, large scale and centralisation. In the years after the first world war trade unions set about strengthening their central organisation based on the Trade Union Congress (TUC), the membership of which has grown from between $3\frac{1}{2}$ and 5 million between the wars to 8 million in 1944 and 11 million today, accounting now for nearly half the working population. The Parliamentary Committee of the TUC, which had previously been entrusted with representing the trade union movement at the level of central government, gave way in 1921 to the newly-appointed General Council. This latter body proceeded during the inter-war years with the help of its own growing administrative organisation, not only to acquire increasing discretion in acting on behalf of organised labour at government level, but also greater internal authority. Members and officials of the TUC General Council were in contact with ministers of the war-time coalition between 1940 and 1945 on a daily basis. Peacetime saw only a slight decline in the intensity of the relationship. The second world war brought about the TUC's aim of being recognised as an 'equal partner' in the government/industry relationship alongside employers (Middlemas, 1979; Martin, 1980).

Business itself, in fact, has been slower to develop a unified, national organisation. Since the end of the first world war, distinct 'peak associations' were established to represent employers' organisations – the British Employers' Confederation and large companies and trade associations – the Federation of British Industry (FBI), while a third body – the National Association of British Manufacturers represented mainly smaller businesses. It was not until 1963 that, with active government sponsorship, the Confederation of British Industry (CBI) was established to replace these three organisations, though chambers of commerce, small businesses and the retail trade were to continue to maintain their own separate collective organisation (Blank, 1973; Grant and Marsh, 1977).

Nevertheless, since 1940 it has been possible to speak of a 'tripartite' arrangement of government, employers and unions based on collective representation. The central organisations on both employer and union sides have been seen by all postwar governments in Britain, not only as a means of conducting a dialogue with their respective memberships, but also as convenient instruments of mediation in conflicts between different sectional organisations and generally in times of social and economic difficulty.

In fact, the role of intermediary organisations in relation to government has been both negative and positive. Acute problems have been posed not only by the influence of organised economic interests on government, but also by their effects on the relationship between prices and costs in industry through oligopoly and collective bargaining. On the other hand, most British governments since the war have found it necessary to devote substantial effort to encouraging intermediary organisations and their members to act in a positive way to promote the general interest. The critical areas have been, first, the economic effects of strikes and other forms of industrial unrest and, secondly, the need for restraint in the fixing of prices and incomes. Legislative means have been tried in both these areas, more particularly since 1965, but with very limited success in affecting industrial relations and success for only very limited periods in controlling the general rate of increase of prices and incomes. More often governments have relied on direct persuasion, influence and pressure with the aim of voluntary agreement. In this, personalities on both sides have often been crucial, involving leading ministers including the Prime Minister (Barnes and Reid, 1980).

Both government and industry have changed, therefore, in ways that create a new interdependence between economic activity of all kinds and the role of public authorities. Fundamental responsibilities of government, such as those described in Chapter 1, have to be exercised in new circumstances arising from the development of an advanced, industrialised society. Public authorities face pressures of a new scale and type from organised interests with the possible sanction of economic power, as well as those from political parties claiming to act on behalf of mass electorate with often exaggerated expectations of what government can and should achieve. New methods of obtaining consent, settling conflict and identifying the public interest have had to be sought by governments. Indeed, although their functions may have grown in scope and complexity, governments do not necessarily find themselves better equipped to achieve the ends of public policy, especially in view of the complexity of the issues and the resistance of organised groups, not to mention the constraints imposed by international pressures.

By the same token, it has not been enough simply to extend the responsibilities of government. As the public sector has grown, intricate problems of public administration have emerged, not least regarding the control of public expenditure. The transfer of parts of industry to public ownership does not by itself solve the major problems of management that exist in the private sector, and it adds new ones. In their relationship with industry in both public and private sectors governments have to countenance the power of organisations based on sectional economic interests, but claiming in addition essential social purposes. The distinction between public and private interests has thus itself become blurred. In practice, the most difficult decisions have arisen from trying to reconcile general ends with particular means in relation to industry as a whole whether publicly or privately owned. In the end, as defenders of a mixed economy have had to stress increasingly, what matters is the enterprise and efficiency of those immediately responsible for industrial activity – the managers and workers of the undertakings themselves, however owned and organised (Dell, 1973; Mackintosh, 1978). The interdependence of government and industry, however, has produced a new order of problems of an essentially political nature.

4 The Need for Consensus

R. K. Middlemas in his historical account of the relationship between government and industry from 1911 to the end of the second world war suggests that there has been a general, cumulative tendency towards collectivism. He argues that a greater measure of continuity was possible in British government than in other European industrialised countries largely through successful attempts at government by consensus. That success was possible because literal party-political attitudes tended to be diluted in government and because national representatives of social and economic groups were persuaded to commit themselves to a 'fundamental national aim' – one that comprised 'social harmony, economic wellbeing and the avoidance of crisis'. One consequence of collectivism, however, according to Middlemas, was that a 'new order' of British politics emerged, which by 1945 had replaced 'for all practical purposes classical democratic theory as that had been understood in 1911' (Middlemas, 1979, p. 371–4).

Trevor Smith's study of political attitudes towards economic planning since the first world war goes further and indicates that, when the significance of political ideas is taken into account, the collectivist tendency must be seen as raising vital arguments about the nature of government. The 'great debate' on planning, as Smith calls it, conducted virtually since the first world war across the whole spectrum of British politics, has reflected a deep concern to reconcile the collectivist implications of planning with traditional ideas and practices of representative government. But it has failed to get to grips effectively with the real political consequences of collectivist approaches. As a result, we are still faced with '*the* fundamental political conundrum that man has had to ponder down the ages . . . the fundamental question as to the proper role of the state in relation to the freedom of the individual' (Smith, 1979 p. 86).

A major question for the present study is whether or not the collectivist tendency is inevitable. Certainly, the increasing signs of divergence in British politics, especially since the general election of 1979, suggest that it is by no means universally accepted. Middlemas himself admits that during the 1960s and 1970s the governing consensus was breaking down, so that his historian's search for continuity could not be sustained (Middlemas, 1979). If collectivism is not, therefore, a universally acceptable or perhaps even a feasible approach, what are the alternatives? Some might conclude that consensus is simply no longer attainable – a conclusion that would be profoundly depressing both for Britain's future economic wellbeing and for the prospects of representative government. Others might conclude rather that the methods of obtaining consensus have been lacking or have been misapplied. In later chapters of this book we shall be directly concerned with the recent evidence for both sorts of conclusion. We shall, however, seek to pay special attention to an aspect of the problem that most previous authors have tended to put on one side – the possibility that the political system itself has failed to adapt to the consequences of the growing interdependence described in the previous chapter. The relevant developments in the political system will be considered in the next chapter. In this we shall attempt to take further account of some of the complexities that an advanced, industrialised society presents for government. First, we need to review briefly the reasons why the consensus promised by the mixed economy of the 1950s proved so fragile in practice.

Political reactions to the mixed economy
The British approach to the mixed economy in the 1950s did not in fact settle traditional political differences. Nor did it give stability to the government/industry relationship by reducing it to a matter of finding the right technical instruments and using appropriate procedures and structures of decision making.

For advanced, industrialised democracies in general, an 'end of ideology' was being predicted in the mid-1960s and even a trans-formation beyond industrialisation to a 'post-industrial society', in which many older problems would have withered away (Aron, 1967; Bell, 1971, 1974). But in Britain, at least, the promise of economic growth did not prove anything like sufficiently attainable to overcome old discontents and divisions. Meanwhile, industrial conflict proved more durable than was assumed in the more optimistic days of the 1950s. Whatever their true cause, conflicts between employers and labour, and between all sorts of different groups of employees and other economic actors have had their own profound impact both economically and politically (Stewart, 1977; Barnes and Reid, 1980; Caves and Krause, 1980).

In politics not only have prewar or even earlier attitudes proved resilient but seem now even to have been reinforced as the two major parties have reacted to what are seen as failures of the mixed economy. The general election of 1979 resulted in a new style of government designed to make a radical departure from the main policies and methods of public intervention employed since the war, just as a similar departure was attempted in 1970. Its chief hallmark is a far more sceptical view of what government can achieve, relying far more on industry itself to make necessary adaptations and suffer the consequences. On the other hand, in the Labour Party more traditional views of state socialism seem to have increasingly gained the upper hand, with their own radical implications for the responsibilities of government in the economic sphere.

It is possible to account for the disappointment partly by factors beyond the concept of a mixed economy. Undoubtedly, international circumstances have been highly unfavourable, above all with the effects of world economic disorder and those of the world recession growing throughout the 1970s. It is also likely that the approach to planning was mismanaged and that subsequently the potential of a mixed economy has been wasted through misapplication or neglect (Shanks, 1977). Planning was itself turned to in the 1960s as a welcome alternative to the 'stop-go' effects of management of the economy during the years of 'Butskellism' with their emphasis on demand management mainly by fiscal means. But British governments have continued to sacrifice medium or longer-term objectives in favour of measures to deal with short-term contingencies, especially when these have arisen from international fluctuations. Management of a sizeable public sector has itself proved to be a continuing burden, especially with regard to the control of public expenditure in general and the running of nationalised industries in particular. Selective intervention in industry has brought its own problems, the dynamic intentions of public support invariably being frustrated and public involvement extending to new areas only in order to rescue firms from bankruptcy and to prevent redundancies. Finally, in spite of the survival of new machinery for a concerted approach with industrial representatives (as in the National Economic Development Council and other bodies to be considered later), governments have proved unable or unwilling to use such machinery to achieve the results attributed to French *concertation* (Ionescu, 1975). The relationship of governments with employers and trade unions at national level came to be engrossed with the need to restrain earnings, and the emphasis has been on prices and incomes policies when intervening on the supply side of the economy. Attempts to concert organised social and economic interests have thus tended to drag governments into further and more complicated responsibilities than either they or their interlocutors on the industrial side have been equipped to undertake.

All these explanations, however, themselves suggest that a more profound adaptation of political institutions and behaviour was demanded than advocates of planning in the early 1960s were willing to recognise – even those few who paid special attention to the need for political and constitutional reforms (for example, Shonfield, 1975). The outcome may suggest that what was attempted was in effect incompatible with representative government, leading some to believe that the role of government should for that reason be far more modest (Jay, 1976; Brittan, 1978; Buchanan, 1978; Hayek, 1979), and others to look for alternative meanings and forms of democracy (Milliband, 1973; Holland, 1975, 1978). It has, indeed, contributed to the new polarisation of British politics.

The fact remains that the interdependence of government and industry has given differences of political doctrine in Britain, and many of the policies and measures based on them, a distinct air of unreality. The political implications of government's role in the economy are by no means simple. They cannot be reduced to a straightforward choice between libertarian and collectivist approaches. In order to grasp the full complexity of what interdependence means for politics, and to get an adequate measure of the challenge to political institutions, we need to pay some attention to certain wider aspects of an advanced, industrialised society.

The corporate economy

One major respect in which the party-political treatment of the government/industry relationship has been misleading is the way it has thrown such emphasis on the issue of nationalisation. We already noticed in the previous chapter that public ownership of a sizeable industrial base came to be accepted as part of the mixed economy. But, in spite of what seemed to be an earlier consensus, there has in practice been continuing uncertainty about the extent of public ownership as a consequence of doctrinal differences between the two major parties. Not only has that uncertainty adversely affected the ability of the existing private sector to plan effectively and with confidence, but shifting policies and attitudes towards the nationalised industries have hampered their management's ability to reconcile the needs of economic efficiency with other, social obligations, statutory or otherwise, in the public interest. What doctrinal conflicts have tended to overlook is, on the one hand, the limited relevance of ownership to many of the major decisions entailed in running a large-scale industrial undertaking and, on the other, the extent to which interdependence enlarges the area in which industrial activity has an impact beyond the immediate concerns of profitability of the enterprise.

First, there is the fact, widely discussed over the years, and painfully apparent to those responsible for running nationalised industries, that nationalisation did not resolve some of the major problems of the industries concerned (Edwards, 1967; Coombes, 1971; Foster, 1971; NEDO, 1976; Parker, 1977). One of the main problems is how to assess the Boards' performance. Successive governments have in practice seen no alternative to applying criteria - in theory, if not always in practice - of commercial operation. For the most part, therefore, the Boards have been expected to make a surplus and have been treated as if they were operating in market conditions, at least where supply of and demand for their products and services are concerned. This is not the place to go into the reasons for the ambivalence of such criteria in relation to nationalised industries or for the inconsistency with which they have been applied. There are general difficulties in applying criteria of economic efficiency to large-scale monopolistic undertakings. Moreover, the nationalised undertakings provide goods and services that are essential for the economy as a whole.

It has been suggested that, in view of the difficulties of applying commercial criteria, ministerial control of the industries should be increased. But it remains far from clear how ministers and departmental officials employing standards of social and economic policy politically determined would be any more effective at managing large-scale industrial enterprises than the existing Boards and their staff. (We shall return to this question in Chapter 6.) In fact, a whole variety of structural and other changes in the organisation of nationalised undertakings is conceivable. But there is still the problem of reconciling the needs of efficient commercial operation with those of handling the wider social and economic consequences of the way such vital industries are run. The sectarian party debate with its appeal to public or private ownership as the decisive element has done nothing to help disentangle the complex problems involved.

Secondly, indeed, account should be taken of the growing trends towards separation of ownership and management in larger scale private enterprise. These trends have, on the one hand, weakened arguments that private ownership is by its very nature uniquely designed to ensure enterprise, efficiency and flexible decentralised structures. They have, on the other hand, further weakened claims that only by an extension of public ownership can responsiveness to the public interest be ensured.

Already in the 1930s, economists were trying to grapple with the challenge to their science, and in particular to the theory of competition, of the existence, indeed the apparent necessity in some circumstances, of monopolistic or oligopolistic market structures. But it is the growth of the modern business corporation, or at least the evidence of its spread from the USA to Britain and other parts of Western Europe, that has been especially important in the last twenty years in altering the assumptions on which the relationship between government and privately-owned industry has to be based (Shonfield,

1975). Above all, economists have had to consider the fact that functions traditionally associated with the individual entrepreneur have come to be exercised in practice by managers employed by the artificial, legal structure of the corporation. At the same time, the internal organisation of an enterprise has had to be treated as a factor at least as important as market forces in determining economic behaviour.

The top and middle managers of the modern business corporation are said to represent 'an entirely new class of businessman' (Chandler, 1977, p. 3), whose functions are not only those of responding to price and other market mechanisms but also exercising administrative co-ordination and control of the varied operating units making up the enterprise (Shonfield, 1965; Channon, 1973; Chandler, 1977). Responsibility for the key operating choices in private enterprise carries with it power to make economic decisions that in classical economics were seen as virtually automatic consequences of the free play of market forces. The development of such economic power can be seen to lead, in connection with the corporations' close relationship to government, to what Galbraith calls 'the planning system' (Galbraith, 1967, 1974).

The typical structure of the modern business corporation is large in scale, containing 'many distinct operating units', acquired by various forms of expansion and diversification. These characteristics have been justified by many economists, even though they encourage monopoly, because they take unique advantage of economies of scale, given especially management's ability to achieve results by administrative rather than competitive means, and in view of increasing dependence of efficient production on capital-intensive technology (Chandler, 1977). On the one hand, the large scale centralised structure of the modern business corporation gives it discretionary power that has wider economic, social and political significance (Mason, 1960; Galbraith, 1967; Ionescu, 1975; Lindblom, 1977). It also, on the other hand, makes the corporation in some ways more easily accountable to central economic policy makers and more available to public intervention.

Thirdly, the capacity of both private and public industrial corporations to make and carry out decisions with an impact not only on their own suppliers, employees and consumers, but also on all sorts of groups in society, has made them all the more important to government. The prognostications contained in the growing literature on the modern business corporation, mainly as it has evolved in the USA, may not all be applicable in Britain (Ionescu, 1975; Bell, 1977; Lindblom, 1979). However, to the extent that the large industrial corporations are able to make decisions having a major impact on investment, employment, the location of industry, market structures and research and technology, they are clearly using economic power to influence matters bearing on the public interest in potentially vital ways.[1]

The fundamental problem is that markets do not take care of many of the economic problems that arise in an advanced, industrialised society. The 'increase in the extent to which the actions of individuals in society directly impinge on other individuals has greatly broadened our sense of the public interest as it has the capacity of corporate organisations to affect it' (Marris, 1974 p. 87). The decisions of individual industrial undertakings impinge on a government's responsibility for a whole range of 'public goods' in fields such as employment, social security, education, the environment and the supply of necessities. And the dependence of government on industrial corporations exists in the public sector itself, where the nationalised industries are vast corporations with the power to make decisions impinging on various aspects of social and economic policy (Parker, 1977).

The challenge of the corporate economy is, therefore, political in nature, in the sense that a wide range of people become dependent on the decisions and actions of large-scale industrial undertakings. The problem is how to make the management of such undertakings responsive to the needs of those affected without impairing enterprise and efficiency – in other words, a new and especially intricate problem of finding consensus. As a consequence of attempts to resolve that problem, the responsibilities of government have become stretched far beyond what was considered normal in the heyday of theories of representative government, while the scope for taking economic decisions by competitive, decentralised methods has been increasingly restricted. That is one reason why many feel that it is the growth of corporatism in its different forms, rather than problems associated with ownership, that presents the real challenge to the government of an advanced, industrialised society.

'Social justice' and economic power
The pressure on governments to accept increasing responsibilities for the consequences of economic activity is reflected also in the efforts of academic theorists to re-define the functions of governments and the conditions of public order. Attempts have been made in particular to

[1] Where undertakings are part of multinational corporations, as is often nowadays the case, then the challenge to government is especially acute. One does not need to follow the more alarmist literature on the subject to recognise that multinational corporations are in a position to escape forms of public accountability applied at a national level (Vernon, 1971; Dell, 1972).

develop and refine notions of 'social justice', in order to include limitations on inequality in the conditions for individual liberty and political obligation. By far the most influential work in this respect has been Rawl's attempt to resurrect the idea of the social contract[2] (Rawls, 1971). Such efforts to reconcile political ideas of 'distributive justice' with those of liberal democracy have satisfied neither Marxists nor 'neo-liberals' (Hayek, 1973, 1976, 1979; Birnbaum et al, 1978). Profound doubts remain, on the one hand, about the validity of any defence of the market economy, and, on the other, about that of extending the notion of justice to economic and social welfare at all rather than confining it to concerns of public order and individual freedom. All the same, the quandary of theorists who seek to justify collectivism in terms of representative democracy should alert those concerned with the practical problems of government and industry that neither traditional nor commonplace ideas are likely to be of much help in handling the political complexities that arise from interdependence.

Nevil Johnson has aptly described the result as a form of 'providential government' (Johnson, 1977). The range of concerns of government has become, in fact, so extended as to make the allocation of resources political rather than economic. Representative democracy has itself contributed to this, and earlier theorists of democracy from J. S. Mill to Schumpeter foresaw what have since been depicted as 'the economic contradictions of democracy' (Brittan, 1979). But the 'public household', in which economic activity now largely takes place, is the result of more than the demands of a mass electorate for public provision of social security: 'it not only has to provide for *public needs* in the conventional sense, but it has also become, inescapably, the area for the fulfilment of *private and group wants*' (Bell, 1976, p. 232).

In terms of the British economy in the last twenty years the influence of these changes has been seen most vividly in their contribution to inflation. The differences about how best to deal with such inflationary pressures by means of public policy is well known. Our concern here will be with the contribution of political institutions, which cannot be ignored in any serious attempt to resolve economic and social problems of direct concern to industry. For one thing, the pressures are themselves the result of political attitudes and forces that will not be diverted by the natural play of economic activity (or even by the electoral competition of political parties in Britain, as we shall see in the next chapter).

---

[2] The term in this use should not be confused with the use of the same term in British political practice, as in the recent agreement between the Labour Party and the TUC, which will be discussed in Part Two, though the connection has sometimes been suggested to lend intellectual respectability to particular political strategies.

All governments are subject to, often conflicting, pressures from sectional groups to bend fiscal and monetary policies to favour some special interest. In Britain, these pressures have been evident in recent years, mostly in the demands of organised labour. But the problem is a wider one than the power of one particular set of sectional organisations such as trade unions. Britain has experienced a general decline of traditional attitudes of deference which, in an earlier time, helped to sustain consensus. There has instead been a growing resort to collective bargaining and acceptance of it, even when backed by crude use of economic sanctions, as a legitimate method of determining economic rewards (Hirsch and Goldthorpe, 1978). Moreover, we have already remarked in Chapter 3 on the spread of the organised defence of sectional economic interests to an ever wider range of groups, willing, moreover, to justify the use of whatever social and economic power might be available.[3] Some interpret this as a general acceptance of the right to exploit economic power engendered by the very market principles retained by the mixed economy (Hirsch, 1978; Hirsch and Goldthorpe, 1979). But the inflationary and other socially disruptive consequences can be tempered only by some general exercise of self-restraint and a reinforced sense of social and political obligation.

At the same time, monetary rewards have themselves been supplemented, and even substituted in some respects, as legitimate objects of organised group demands by concerns such as security of employment, status at work and so on. Consequently, the issues of group conflict are extended to include such questions as worker participation in management and power relationships in industry generally. And people look to government to secure the provision of various kinds of public goods and amenities. Public authorities are therefore presented not only with the responsibility of providing minimum standards, but of ensuring somehow an equality of standards, at least in recognising the right of groups to demand and press for such equality (Marris, 1974; Bell, 1976; Hirsch, 1978). As a result, the economic performance of a government tends to be judged in relation to a whole range of already extended responsibilities for maintaining social welfare – education, health, housing, environmental protection and so on. The group demands that in this way lead to greater public intervention are, like the inflationary pressures of claims for higher monetary rewards, political in origin as well as social, if not predominantly political. The satisfaction of claims on scarce resources, and the necessary arbitration of claims, involve negotiation among organised groups that do not hesitate to threaten and use the

---

[3] Most noticeable in the 1970s was the extension of such attitudes to nurses, policemen, firemen and other employees in professional or public services.

sanction of political redress, which may mean economic or social disruption as much as withdrawing electoral, or other conventional, forms of political support.

The problem of 'governability'

To the extent that they have political as well as social causes, the results of interdependence therefore challenge existing political institutions. If the response to that challenge is made only in terms of a straight difference between collectivist and libertarian approaches the prospects are certainly forbidding.

Those who have tended to take a more or less collectivist approach do not normally go into any detail about the consequences for political order. Short of an abandonment of democratic principles it is far from clear where the logic of collectivism is meant to lead, yet:

> 'If the objective of universal participation is not abandoned, the constraints set by social limits will inexorably make society more dependent on collective provision and collective orientation.' (Hirsch, 1977, p. 189)

Beyond vague calls for a stronger sense of community, a new 'social morality' or what seems to be a new stoicism of self-restraint, it is not clear from the collectivists what precise changes in political procedures and institutions might be required to achieve the necessary consensus (Hirsch, 1977). In other words, politics is treated by those who take a collectivist approach essentially as secondary, as if rendering representative democracy or any other basis of political rights and obligations compatible with expanded public authority were simply an instrumental problem once the appropriate moral regeneration had been achieved. Might it not be more realistic to question whether political instruments of the right kind are available at all? The limits to growth could be explained by the failure of the existing political order to contain the demands and expectations that it has itself generated.

Indeed, there has recently been great interest in problems of 'governability' in industrialised democracies (Crozier *et al*, 1975; Dahrendorf, 1980). The diagnosis is, roughly, that while representative democracy has increased expectations of what governments can and should do, it has also reduced their capacity to respond effectively. In Britain, this condition has been identified particularly in some of the reasons for failure in economic policy, above all an apparent increase in the willingness of private groups to challenge the authority of government (King, 1975). The symptoms are described most often as the many examples of 'industrial anarchy' during the last fifteen to twenty years, and of successful resistance to attempts to prevent such anarchy by legislative means (Ionescu, 1975). During the same period the trade union movement was suspected of twice being the effective cause of a fall of government – Conservative in 1974 and Labour in 1979. Certain vital developments in industrialised society, in particular the critical interdependencies it creates, have changed the potential significance of organised labour out of all recognition.

'Society is directly vulnerable to the pressures of specialised workers because their skills, be they of the least prestigious order in the chain of production, cannot be replaced as in previous phases of the industrial society when contingents of unskilled workers could be replaced by other similar contingents. Moreover, insofar as the national economy is more enmeshed than ever before – and more enmeshed with the international economy – any refusal to deliver goods or services will sooner or later bring the affected economies to a halt. To this, of course, must be added the formidable political and social strength of organised labour through its unions, and to some extent, through working class parties.' (Ionescu, 1975, p. 26).

The forlorn struggle of successive British governments to contain the rate of inflation while responding to various group demands has, in fact, tended to sharpen the ideological basis of political conflict and preserve conditions favourable to class and group antagonisms. The libertarian approach has tended to become one of seeking to confine the scope of politics by means of a withdrawal of government into what is regarded as a more realistic sphere of responsibility. The tendency of public expenditure to absorb any increases in productivity has encouraged the view that only a drastic re-appraisal of the functions of government can both ensure economic survival and preserve representative government (Rose and Peters, 1979). There is, indeed, nothing especially new in recent doubts about the impact of democracy on economic management. It was foreshadowed in Schumpeter's warning that 'the effective range of the political decision should not be extended too far' (Schumpeter, 1943, p. 291). But there is now a new energy in the conviction that the functions of government have been allowed to expand at political costs that are far too great. The return of a Conservative Government in 1979 may be attributed to wider support for that view.

It still remains to be seen how far there has been a genuine change in group and electoral expectations of full employment and of 'providential government' in general. If a break with the attempt to govern by consensus is genuinely being made, then the viability of the system may certainly be tested in a very practical way and at no little risk. Marxists or others who see collectivism as fulfilling social and economic prerequisites, may not count the risk of representative government as very costly. Indeed, if the libertarian pathologists turn out to be right about 'governability', then they might simply be seen as confirming the Marxist prophecy that the liberal capitalist system would destroy itself.

Faced with such stark choices, we may well feel that the mixed economy needs a much more adequate positive justification than its defenders have usually provided. One approach is to examine how far the infection and the remedy lie in the existing condition of representative government itself. If we take a political standpoint, rather than a purely economic or social one, we might find that there are ways of controlling the various effects of interdependence without assuming that there are somehow ineluctable forces foreclosing political choice or reducing it to a collectivist/libertarian dichotomy. We cannot expect to find a political solution that embraces all or most of the demands on government in the economic sphere. Such demands tend to be self-defeating and are sometimes made with deliberate unconcern for the political outcome. But we might be able to find out what trends and practices in our politics worsen the problem and increase the risks of decline.

It will be argued here that there are particularly severe negative factors in this country's political system that threaten to make the problem far worse than it might be. We shall now, therefore, turn to the question of how our political institutions of elections, political parties and Parliament have responded to the problems of adaptation thrown up by the development of industrialised society. In Part Three the underlying and essential causes of failure will be traced to fundamental aspects of British politics – the fall of Parliament in public esteem and effectiveness, and the nature of political party and electoral competition. It will be argued that it is not enough, when considering the limits to growth, to treat those political aspects as immutable, all the more so since they have become highly disputable in their own right as we are about to see.

5 The Decline of Parliament

Concern at the economic and social results of the government/industry relationship, as witnessed in Britian during roughly the last twenty years, has been accompanied by fundamental questioning of the political order. In fact, radical proposals for change in the very structure and process of British government became topical in the 1970s, and claimed the time of governments, far more than at any period since before the first world war. Many of the pressures, like demands for regional devolution and the assertion of particular social and economic interests, seemed to indicate widespread centrifugal tendencies, which challenged representative government with a need to respond with new political methods (Smith, 1972; Ionescu, 1975).

What has been at work essentially, however, is a fundamental change in the role of Parliament as viewed in constitutional theory, leading in the 'collectivist era' of British postwar politics (Beer, 1965) to the final demise of the House of Commons as both the centre of national life and the essential source of government. Thus, along with the growth of collectivism in social and economic affairs, it is possible to trace a collectivism in politics, discernible to some even as far back as 1914 in the first steps towards creating the apparatus of a 'managerial state'. From that time on, it has been alleged;

> 'Great areas of national policy tended to become the prerogative of ministers and civil servants, acting within the curtilage of "government", rather than of political leaders and MPs in the House of Commons.' (Middlemas, 1979, p. 309).

In this development, not only has Parliament itself tended to be ineffectual as governments have claimed their own direct relationship with the electorate, but an alternative basis of 'functional representation' has emerged in the role of intermediary organisations, with the effect above all of endowing the spokesmen of business and trade union interests with their own direct access to ministers.

Two related aspects of Parliament's role have been of vital importance for the operation of the government/industry relationship in practice. The first is the way the House of Commons is composed and prompts the question whether Parliament can, under modern circumstances, be regarded as an adequate forum for the representation of social and economic interests:

'It would now be hard to find in the House of Commons men sufficiently prominent in industry, either on the management or the union side, to be accepted as the spokesmen or as the mouthpiece of these interests.' (PEP, 1974, p. 80).

The second aspect is Parliament's essential detachment from the decisions that effectively determine the way the vital government/ industry relationship is conducted:

'It can, indeed, be argued that in many important aspects of economic affairs . . . the parliamentary dimension is of little importance and is characterised by more or less automatic procedures to approve government policies when required, while the real power and influence are exercised elsewhere.' (Coombes and Walkland, 1980, p. 30).

After considering both these aspects in turn we shall look critically at the newer constitutional theories that have come, in effect, to justify for many the decline of Parliament as the centre of national life, for industry as for social and economic interests in general.

The composition of the House of Commons
It is disputable whether the elected chamber needs to, or should, be in its composition a 'microcosm' of the social and economic character- istics of the nation. Nor can we take it for granted that the Commons should go out of its way to perform the function of expressing particular social and economic interests. Moreover, there is no necessary relationship between Parliament's composition and its behaviour: MPs do not have to come from a particular background to be able to act as spokesmen for the interests of those who share that background and they may conversely have special experience without being influenced by it in their parliamentary functions (Birch, 1971). Nevertheless, it is significant for our main theme that the proportion of MPs with a genuine industrial background or with authority to speak for commerce and industry seems to have declined.

It is impossible, without much more research than could be under- taken as part of the present study, to give an adequate account of relevant changes in the character of the Commons' membership. Existing data are derived from information (usually supplied by Members themselves) about MPs personal education and backgrounds and about their occupations.

The social background of MPs has some bearing on the question of industrial representation in that only about 14 per cent of Members elected in October 1974 or in May 1979 were defined as having occupations as 'workers' (Butler and Kávanagh, 1975, 1980). That category has steadily declined since the last war. Indeed, one of the more noticeable differences of the House today from that at the beginning of this century is the relative absence of a sizeable group of MPs who can claim backgrounds as industrial workers. In the early part of this century, in fact, working-class representation in the Commons was a major objective of the trade union movement. The proportion of trade union sponsored MPs in the Labour Party has actually increased in recent years (to nearly 50 per cent), but about one-fifth of the Members concerned come not from working-class, but from professional and other middle-class, occupations (Butler and Kavanagh, 1979). The growth of white-collar unionism is not the only explanation; there has also been a change in the overall composition of the Parliamentary Labour Party towards 'professional politicians' from backgrounds in local government, education, journalism and even full-time employment by the Party itself[1] (Walkland, 1979; Walkland and Ryle, 1981).

MPs described in the surveys as having occupations in 'business' may well not have had direct experience that could be considered truly industrial. Even so, the proportion of MPs with such backgrounds seems to have declined from just over 30 per cent on average for the first 70 years of this century to 19 per cent in October 1974 and 22 per cent in May 1979 (Walkland, 1979; Butler and Kavanagh, 1975, 1980). An occupational background described as 'professional' has thus tended to become preponderant in both major parties. That category may, of course, include people with industrial experience as managers, accountants, engineers and so on. But it would seem safe to assume that the Commons has undergone a transformation during the present century from a preponderance of industrial, commercial and financial interests to one of professional interests of various kinds, often only marginally associated at best with the world of industry. This transformation has been at least as important as that which took place after the 1832 Reform Act from a preponderance of the landed interest to one of business and manufacturing interests (Walkland, 1979).

More important than such quantitative estimates is the generally accepted observation that those with prestige in industry no longer find it desirable or possible to pursue a parliamentary career. The reasons are not difficult to find in view of the nature of Parliament today. There has been an increase in 'professionalism' even in the sense that the MP's job is more time-consuming and specialised. Politics itself has increasingly been seen as a career in its own right. Other parliamentary systems in advanced, industrialised countries have experienced similar trends, but in Britain it is significant that the House of Commons has come to expect an especially severe work load from its Members. At the same time, individual British MPs have

---

[1] It has been estimated, however, that over 80 per cent of all MPs hold trade union membership cards (Ellis and Johnson, 1974).

found it necessary to spend an increasing amount of time on constituency work and, with the expansion of the social and economic responsibilities of government, to perform vital functions as 'welfare officers' for individual citizens in relation to public authorities (King, 1974; Mackintosh, 1978; Walkland, 1979).

But a major factor is also the influence of the political party on parliamentary careers. Not only is substantial service to one of the two major parties (for example, in local government) now usually required before selection as candidate in a winnable constituency, but the power of the parties in the electoral process (especially at local level) means that a loyal Member can expect to be long serving. The lack of occupational mobility that characterises so much of contemporary British society certainly seems to have affected Parliamentary politics (Walkland and Ryle, 1981). The very fact that political activity can be regarded as a career in its own right (as it now usually is) emphasises the changing character of the Commons. For most Members ministerial appointment at some level is the chief aim, and an increasing number can now be successful, given that modern governments normally include appointments for at least one-third of the governing party (King, 1974). Prestigious and successful trade unionists, businessmen or managers, therefore, simply could not have devoted the necessary time over a sufficient period of years to becoming and remaining MPs. At the same time, of course, industrial occupations themselves have tended to become more professional.

Of course, the House of Commons probably never has been particularly representative in any 'microcosmic' sense and it does not need to be (Birch, 1971). There are several means by which individual MPs are able to take account of the views and interests of industry without necessarily having an industrial background themselves. These means include both contacts at constituency level and relationships with private representative organisations at national level (Barker and Rush, 1970). Both these are important channels of communication between MPs and industry, though a more important question is how MPs make use of the information.

In this last respect, it is well known that within the two main parties, backbench MPs belong to specialised subject groups that meet regularly within the Palace of Westminster and may be attended by ministers in the area of specialisation concerned. The party Whips regard such groups as important sources of information on the way backbenchers are feeling on particular issues. In the Conservative Party specialised party committees are believed to have become increasingly influential. Those dealing with industrial and wider economic questions include a number of Members with relevant qualifications and experience (King, 1974). In the Labour Party the significance of industrial representation lies chiefly in Members with trade union experience and these meet as the trade union group. Individual unions undoubtedly consider MPs sitting under their sponsorship as a valuable additional agency, especially on matters that affect the union particularly.

When a particular industrial interest finds itself the object of legislative or other measures that it finds unfavourable, a group of backbench MPs in either main Party, and sometimes cutting across both, can usually be found to put its case, and even to fight off a challenge (King, 1974; Mackintosh, 1978). Backbench MPs have been known to organise in this way to resist proposals of their own party when in government. A famous, if unsuccessful, attempt was that by Conservative MPs to resist, and subsequently to amend, legislation to abolish resale price maintenance in 1962 and 1963 (Butt, 1967). Another more successful one in the Labour Party led to the abandonment of the Industrial Relations Bill in 1969, though the trade union group seems to have been less influential here than opposition across the whole of the Parliamentary Labour Party and from trade union leaders outside Parliament (Heffer, 1973; Barnes and Reid, 1980). But the trade union group as a whole does not seem to have been so important as other groups within the Party set up for political reasons (such as the Tribune Group). In general, the images of both major parties, as respectively the party of business and the party of organised labour, have become less realistic. The influence of industrial interests within both has tended to diminish in favour of the more ideological attitudes of party professionals and constituency activists (PSI, 1978; Grant, 1980).

In general, however, the composition of the House of Commons, to the extent that it reflects the willingness of people to enter it, must surely be a function to a large extent of the powers available to the MP once elected (Dell, 1973; PEP, 1974). The significance of the individual MP also affects his value to those who might want to persuade or simply to educate him.

The role of the individual Member of Parliament
The shortcomings of Parliament as a means of representation must be explained largely by the way the realities of power give individual MPs so little influence on the course of government. Indeed, complaints against Parliament as such are often misdirected.

'Parliament is wrongly blamed for bad government because Parliament does not govern. To put it baldly: the government governs; Parliament is the forum where the exercise of government is publicly displayed and is open to scrutiny and criticism. And the Commons does not control the executive – not in any real sense;

rather the executive control the Commons through the exercise of their party majority power.' (Walkland and Ryle, 1981, p. 13).

A recent study (Coombes and Walkland, 1980), indicated the extent to which Parliament is now by-passed: by ministers taking discretionary measures under delegated legislation or committing sizeable funds leaving Parliament with at best a limited opportunity of review after the event; by ministers' direct relationships with statutory public corporations or local authorities; and by ministers' direct relationship with bodies representing organised private interests – both general, like the TUC and CBI, and particular, representing different sectors. One obvious implication is that, in order to influence public policy and its administration, it is better for the affected interests to take a direct route to the Executive than to bother too much with the House of Commons. It is probably safe to surmise that, to the extent that bodies representing industry do seek to influence individual MPs, the purpose is less to use Parliament to affect public policy directly than to improve the knowledge and alter the attitudes of those who will eventually hold executive office themselves.

It has never been true (nor have prudent parliamentary reformers ever claimed) that the party organisation has become so monolithic as to reduce Parliamentary proceedings entirely to predictable routine. At all periods since the last war there have been famous examples of backbench rebellion spilling on to the floor of the House and even into the division lobbies. Moreover, even party unity in formal proceedings is often the result of hard-fought persuasion and compromise behind the scenes. Private Members' independent views can find expression not only in such formal ways as signing motions, putting down questions or submitting amendments to Bills, but also, as we have seen, in private meetings of their parliamentary party and its subject committees. Managing the House is not only a strenuous and unrelenting task for ministers in terms of time, but also for both sets of party managers in terms of the substance of business (Butt, 1967; Crossman, 1976). What is significant, however, is the stress placed on management of the House of Commons.

The problem that has been uppermost in procedural reform and that has also been the source of most criticism of parliamentary activity is that of congestion of the House of Commons timetable. Balfour's procedural reforms of 1902 virtually excluded the opportunities for private Members, acting individually or in groups, to make effective use of tactics of obstruction or delay (Walkland, 1979). The official Opposition can still make organised use of such tactics and from time to time does so. But its aim is essentially not to use time for its own proposals, or even to make amendments to government measures, but to embarrass and frustrate the party that happens to be in office.

It is not any increase in influence by backbenchers, but the vast expansion of the activities of government, including especially the growth in legislation (in terms of complexity even more than quantity), that accounts for the unprecedented pressure on time in the House of Commons today (Hansard Society, 1979). The increased work load has not been accompanied by any reduction in extra-parliamentary consultation by the Executive prior to legislation, or of ministers' powers to make delegated legislation.[2] The problem of congestion is, indeed, both symptom and cause of the irresistible attraction of belonging to a political party that can form a government. The attraction is less for Members who may for whatever reason feel themselves excluded from the promise of ministerial office or for those who are sceptical about the value of such office within the present political system. For a large majority of Members, however, there would seem to be little point in trying to play a constructive role in legislative or budgetary proceedings; not only are the opportunities limited but the prospects of power from having one's party form the government are seen to be so much greater. This is not a criticism of the personal ambition of MPs. In view of the procedures and customs of the House, and the facilities now afforded to the Executive, it is hardly surprising that our political life should be dominated by the belief that incomparably more can be achieved if one can get one's party into office than if one seeks to make independent use of the procedures of the House of Commons.

The role of Parliament today is, in fact, the result of certain crucial developments in the nature of electoral and party competition. These developments have been extensively analysed and documented elsewhere, and no more than a summary will be given here. But they provide the essential background to any serious attempt to reappraise the workings of representative democracy in modern conditions.

The theory of the mandate

Since the last war the primary end of electoral activity in Britain has been that of returning the Labour or the Conservative Party to office. The individual MP, and parliamentary activity itself, are considered significant chiefly as a means of supporting one of those parties in government, or supporting it in the hope that it will eventually enter government by electoral means. It is now usually considered both undemocratic and irresponsible for a governing party not to get its electoral programme implemented.

Most parliamentary and other public criticism of a government, in

---

[2] The number of general statutory instruments made annually was 1,508 in 1948, falling to 657 in 1955 and 685 in 1958, but rising again to 1,168 in 1977 (HC 588, 1977–78). Most ordinary decisions affecting industry are taken by ministers under such powers.

fact, focusses on the validity of its actions in terms of its 'electoral mandate', as set out in the party manifesto presented during a general election campaign. Behind this attitude lies the assumption that electors can exercise meaningful influence only if they are offered a clear choice between alternative programmes and if the successful party endeavours to carry out its own programme when in office. The result is what the late John Mackintosh described as a 'plebiscitary' system of representation, in which the individual MP is obliged, in the interests of democracy, to support whichever party platform he identified himself with at the election (Mackintosh, 1978). The mystique attaching to this theory of representation (which some in other countries have actually sought to copy from British experience) has been repeatedly debunked by political scientists and found wanting as a description of reality. The following lengthy quotation serves to summarise the main arguments:

> 'The parties do not usually present coherent programmes of action in their election manifestoes. They outline their general objectives, but they rarely commit themselves to more than two or three specific proposals. Secondly, surveys of the attitudes and motives of voters suggest that these policy statements influence the voting behaviour of only a very small proportion of the electors. People are influenced by traditional loyalties, by the general image that each party presents and by the record of the government of the day, but not to a great extent by election promises. Thirdly, the record of history shows that election promises are a poor guide to the actions of the successful party after it has taken over the government: circumstances change, and plans usually have to be modified accordingly. For all these reasons, it would be inaccurate to portray the British system of government as one in which the electors, by preferring one set of policies to another, give the successful party a mandate to translate its policies into practice during the ensuing five years.' (Birch, 1971, pp. 99–100)

In more recent years it has become increasingly evident that party leaders have tended to exaggerate the authority granted to them by electoral success, however marginal that success may be over the other party and even though in British experience successful parties do not usually win the support of an overall majority of voters. There has also been excessive expectation of the scope of action available to one of the parties when in office. In view of what we know about electoral behaviour and the vagaries of the electoral system, there are no grounds for assuming so much moral authority simply from 'winning' a general election; there are quite understandable limits to any government's practical ability to carry out any sort of programme.' (Finer, S. E., ed., 1975; Johnson, 1977)

Party government

The fact remains, however, that British government is no longer best described as Parliamentary Government, or even Cabinet Government, but as 'Party Government' (Rose, 1976). The crucial development has been the growth to supremacy of two mass, national parties, with organisational means that are essential for contesting elections successfully and with the capacity to demand between them the allegiance of the bulk of the Members of the House of Commons. It is certainly true that both the Conservative and Labour Parties include divergent views and interests, and to some extent they have played a role in 'aggregating' these into some sort of consensus. But, as shown in S. H. Beer's classic description of the history of party politics in Britain, there has been, since the second world war, a growing concentration of the two major parties. In this 'collectivist era' of British politics, the process of government has rested essentially on the competition between monolithic party structures *bidding* for the votes of the electorate, and *bargaining* for the support of organised economic and social groups, both mainly in economic terms (Beer, 1965).

Furthermore, there is a sense in which public opinion is itself influenced or 'manufactured' by the parties themselves. As S. H. Beer again has explained:

> 'Party does not merely aggregate the opinions of groups, it goes a long way towards creating these opinions by fixing the framework of public thinking about policy and the voters' sense of the alternatives and the possibilities. In turn, of course, the party may find itself under pressure from such opinion. And when in its competition for votes it responds to this pressure, the flow of influence seems to be in only one direction, from voters to party. But by taking a wider view we will see that the parties themselves, backed by research staffs, equipped with nation-wide organisations, and enjoying the continuous attention of the mass media, have themselves in great part framed and elicited the very demands to which they then respond.' (Beer, 1965, p. 347)

Within the parties, there is a corresponding tendency to believe that, to be legitimate and effective, policy need be inspired and developed only by some internal process in the party concerned.

The tendency to obligarchy and the need for consensus

Government and industry have become increasingly interdependent, therefore, against a background of increasingly collectivist modes of organisation not only in industry and in the direct representation of economic interests but also in electoral and party representation. Traditional institutions of representative democracy, in particular the House of Commons, have played a declining role. Both the process of defining the public interest in economic affairs and that of reconciling the various interests, attitudes and demands relevant to economic policy have come largely to by-pass Parliament.

The decline of Parliament in this sense is fairly well acknowledged among those directly concerned with the government/industry relationship. They may not even consider it particularly important, having adjusted to other centres of power and influence and accepted the consequences of Party Government. Indeed, the prevailing tendency has been to treat the government/industry relationship as a matter primarily for small leadership groups on both sides – party leaders, on the one hand, and the spokesmen of corporate industrial organisations, on the other. This obligarchical tendency may even be seen as making the relationship more manageable for both sides. In many respects, as we shall see in Part Two of this study, there has certainly been a general inclination to take the relationship out of politics, above all in an attempt to find a consistent view of the public interest that is both technically sound in terms of economic viability and sufficiently broad to obtain the commitment of major economic interests, including especially those of employers and trade unions. The shift in balance of power from Parliament to the Executive has thus been justified in terms both of creating tolerable conditions for a public administration with incomparably more complex and delicate responsibilities in the economic sphere and of facilitating the essential process of bargaining among collective economic interests.

Nevertheless, the oligarchical tendency can be shown to carry its own risks of disruption and uncertainty. On the one hand, both the nature of competition between the two governing parties and the basis of the intermediary organisations that are meant to represent the different interests of industry may be inclined to exacerbate traditional class and group conflicts as well as ideological differences. On the other hand, the authenticity of the leaderships on both sides cannot be so easily ensured, in view of the very concentration of power that their positions entail – both in the sense of responding to diverse needs and interests and in that of carrying their followers in commitments of a peculiarly specific nature. The relationship comes, in other words, to be played for unnecessarily high stakes.

In recent years the government of Britain has been seen by many as especially prone to risks of this kind. The main response has been to regard a substantial degree of consensus as an over-riding, mutual need of government and industry. The structures and methods used to conduct the government/industry relationship have, in fact, been designed to play down potential elements of conflict and inconsistency – all of which have been thought to intensify in one way or another what might be called political limits to economic growth. In Part Two we shall examine in turn the three main paths that the search for consensus followed in Britian in the 1960s and 1970s, and we shall then consider attempts to re-appraise it in the face of the shortcomings that became increasingly apparent.

Our ultimate concern, however, will be to assess the wider implications of the search for consensus itself. It will be suggested that many of the obstacles it has met arise from the very tendency to treat the government/industry relationship in oligarchical terms.

Part Two
The Search for Consensus

6 Devolution of Responsibility

Attempts by different governments in the 1960s and 1970s to operate a relationship with industry took the form largely of a search for a wider consensus than that considered attainable through conventional electoral and parliamentary procedures. At certain times the search proved so frustrating that the government concerned resorted mainly to trying to impose its view by legislation or by appealing to the electorate through a dissolution of Parliament. In general, however, such resort has been considered only when other means of obtaining agreement on a common view of the public interest have failed.

Behind the search for consensus, lies the view that government has potentially vital functions in managing indirectly the economy as a whole and also in managing directly an extensive public sector of the economy. At the same time, government is expected to use its various powers of intervention to influence, support or direct major decisions in particular sectors, industries and even firms and undertakings. It has usually been recognised that to perform these responsibilities effectively government must call on the aid of special skills and aptitudes that neither political leaders thrown up by representative democracy nor the kind of public service established to support representative government are normally equipped to provide. Above all, government can be seen to depend ultimately on the co-operation of managers and workers in industry itself in both public and private sectors. Moreover, the time scales, complexities and uncertainties of economic decisions suggest the need for restraining the influence of political fluctuations and conflicts. There is also the conviction that government is responsible for helping to find that level and distribution of rewards and benefits, which, it is supposed, will satisfy the major different groups in the economy and so lay the basis of both social order and economic prosperity. The desire to limit the effects of competitive and acquisitive forces in the market economy by means of public intervention, flows from that conviction. So, however, does the desire to restrain the effects of party political competition along with the impact of personality, ideology or ambition, commonly assumed to be major factors in electoral and parliamentary politics.

The recent search for consensus has adopted two central approaches, which are closely related to one another. One of these, which we shall consider in Chapters 8 and 9 is to bring representatives of social and economic interests themselves into a kind of partnership with government chiefly through intermediary organisations of employers and trade unions. These 'partnerships' may cover the whole range of economic policy or deal simply with special aspects of it.

The other approach which we shall now consider in this chapter and the next, is to develop special machinery for defining and implementing a view of the public interest that can be protected from the transitory and partial effects of politics. The approach we shall consider in Chapter 7 implies a special view of the role of the public official and it is no accident that during the period we are considering administrative reform has been a repeated concern of government, especially in relation to economic affairs. A major characteristic of British central administration in economic affairs during the past twenty years, however, has been an eagerness to make use of a whole variety of more or less independent bodies outside Whitehall. The general aim has been to find means of determining and upholding the public interest without the pressures of short term or partisan political considerations and with a capacity for judgement and expertise that the conventional public service is thought unable to provide. This practice has been particularly important in the operation of the government/industry relationship and has led to the direct employment in the public sector of businessmen and others with an industrial background. In fact, it has a much longer and wider application than is sometimes supposed, though its record since 1960 is of special interest in illustrating the difficulties and the hazards of taking the relationship out of politics.

The industrial public corporation

A typical model of public intervention in industry in Britain is the 'Morrisonian' public corporation, so called because it is basically the type of organisation chosen, on lines first publicly propounded by the former Labour Minister, Herbert Morrison, for the major undertakings nationalised between 1945 and 1950 (Chester, 1975). The legacy of those acts of nationalisation remains, after various modifications in structure rather than principle, in the Boards that now run the publicly-owned coal, railway, electricity supply, gas and iron and steel undertakings. The undertakings are vested in a Board of public figures, now usually with mainly industrial or commercial experience and including some trade unionists, appointed by the sponsoring minister concerned. Each Board is set certain general obligations and objectives by its enabling statute, which also gives the minister concerned certain powers of direction, though these are rarely used and do not refer specifically to decisions about prices, wages or most commercial aspects of production and supply. The minister has the right to approve capital investment programmes, but otherwise in theory, the Boards are financially independent of government. In practice, however, ministers have never hesitated to concern themselves with the general pricing and other commercial decisions of the Boards, while the latter have for most of the time not only had a Treasury guarantee for any long-term borrowing from private sources but have also been dependent – either temporarily or endemically – on the Exchequer both for funding capital and for covering losses.

Given the enormous problems associated with this model of organisation, it is remarkable how little it has been altered by governments of either party and, perhaps even more remarkable that it has been frequently copied by subsequent Labour Governments. The postal and telecommunication services, formerly run as a ministerial department, were vested in a public corporation in 1965, as were the re-nationalised iron and steel, road haulage and passenger transport undertakings, while new measures of public ownership created the British National Oil Corporation, British Shipbuilders and British Aerospace. In addition, there have been a number of more specialised or regional public agencies of an industrial nature established roughly on the same model, at least in their relationship with ministers.

The fundamental – and seemingly intractable – difficulty of separating the activities of industrial public corporations, or at least of the larger and more economically important ones, from the influence of politics has been described in a whole host of official publications and academic studies (see especially Edwards, 1967; Coombes, 1971; Foster, 1971; Tivey, 1973; NEDO, 1976). Again and again their inherent political significance has obliged ministers to take a direct interest in the way the undertakings are run, above all when they have been seen as providing essential social services that cannot be self-financed on a commercial basis. Sometimes (as with the railways) the service is one to special types of consumer (such as rural branch-lines or commuter services). Sometimes (as has been the case with coal and steel in particular) it is simply one of providing employment for workers in particular categories or regions, thus saving government from having to pick up the pieces of unemployment itself. Increasingly sophisticated measures have been devised to treat 'uneconomic' activities of this type separately from an individual Board's commercial operations, usually by the payment of some kind of government subsidy or by 'writing off' debts to the Exchequer. But the whole issue is further complicated by government's responsibilities as 'shareholder' to the undertakings and increasingly also as their 'banker'. In fact, such descriptions are inappropriate, because ministers of neither party have treated these responsibilities consistently in any commercial sense.

One leading feature of the mixed economy is meant to be the way the public sector can itself be used to achieve general ends of economic policy. However, in British experience there has been a recurring vicious circle in this practice, which no government has been able to break. The fundamental problem is that the more the nationalised industries or undertakings are obliged to take certain decisions in the interests of a government's policy – say, to postpone increases in prices, modify plans to create redundancies in a particular sector or region, or protect a particular kind of consumer, supplier or worker – then the more the government concerned has to intervene eventually to bail the Board out of consequent financial difficulties. In some ways, the Boards of the nationalised industries seem to have the most unenviable task in either government or industry, subject as they often are to quite incompatible requirements. They have sometimes been expected to meet a fixed rate of return while also taking decisions at the behest of ministers about pricing, wages policy or methods of production that make such a return impossible. In the absence of an official prices and incomes policy, the nationalised undertakings have often been a major instrument of anti-inflation policy, as happened under the Conservatives between 1970 and 1972 (even though that government had the declared intention of applying more 'commercial' standards to the operation of the public sector).[1] In more recent years, with the introduction of 'cash limits' to restrain public expenditure, the Boards have been obliged to treat capital requirements financed externally as part of the 'public sector borrowing requirement' and thus as integral to the Treasury's operation of monetary policy. Since many of the Boards have inherited substantial losses incurred as a result of the policies of successive governments, this approach may be seen as an even more incisive encroachment on their ability to act as efficient industrial managers. Their position has increasingly become, in many ways, the invidious one of responsibility without power.

Another crucial element that has to be considered, and which is of central importance to our theme, is the role of trade unions with members in industrial public corporations. The autonomy of the Boards might be supposed to be designed to give greater scope for improving industrial relations, and also for limiting the direct involve-

---

[1] Alternatively, of course, a Board's pricing policy can be used as a form of indirect taxation when it is designed to exceed a fixed rate of return, as seems to have happened in the energy sector in the last few years.

ment of ministers in these. Yet some of the industries have, as is well known, from time to time been subject to some of the most disruptive political strikes (including the one that led to the collapse of the Heath Government in 1974). The more the Boards are known to rely on government supplies of finance, then the greater is the inclination on the part of the unions to treat them as 'test cases' of a government's nerve in economic policy and the greater is the temptation to assume that any commercial criteria may be overridden by political or social motives on the part of ministers.[2] Moreover, unions in some of the nationalised industries, given the latters' monopoly position in supplying essential goods and services, are able to wield exceptional economic power.[3] In other words, the Boards are often pincered not only between contradictory demands of ministers, but also between those demands and the unions.

In general, therefore, the industrial public corporation has not proved a particularly effective means of taking the public interest out of politics or of overcoming some of the major problems associated with public intervention in industry. They have certainly not made the responsibilities of ministers, and therefore the duties of civil servants, in the government/industry relationship any less complex or intractable on political grounds.

The use of public agencies for selective intervention
The use of public agencies has also been developed in other ways as an instrument of direct public participation in industry, as, since the mid-1960s, a variety of forms of public subsidy, acquisition and investment, and of partial shareownership, have been tried in efforts to influence the decisions of particular industries or firms. Such attempts fall roughly into three main periods, each marked by the recurring effects of the political cycle.

First, partly from a concern to modernise certain declining sectors and to provide more balance among regions, and partly inspired by the fashionability in some quarters of the 'industrial logic' of larger units, the Labour Government of 1966–70 embarked on a policy of selective intervention mainly on the basis of the Shipbuilding Industry Act 1967, the Industrial Expansion Act 1968 and the Industrial Development Act 1966. Departments, including the new Ministry of Technology created in 1964, intervened directly, though sometimes with the help of special expert inquiries (such as that into the aircraft industry), but in 1966 the

---

[2] If run commercially some of the Boards would have undoubtedly gone bankrupt some time ago.
[3] The most recent notable example has been the ability of the National Union of Mineworkers to breach the present Conservative Government's pay norm for the public sector during the winter of 1980/81.

Industrial Reorganisation Corporation (IRC) was set up. The Corporation, managed by a board of businessmen, was given the statutory remit of using funds made available to it from the Exchequer mainly for promoting plans to restructure industries with a view to increasing productivity. It was to undertake tasks growing out of the responsibilities of the Ministry of Technology but considered unsuitable for civil servants to perform (Young, 1974; Smith in Hayward and Watson, 1975).

The IRC was concerned primarily with promoting mergers and achieved a mixed reputation for high-level expertise (valuable to both government and industry) and irresponsible interference (it acted independently of ministers, but took no long-term financial stake in the undertakings in which it intervened). Many claim that a major weakness was its restricted perspective, and that it was too closely identified with the 'merger mania' to which certain ministers at the time were thought to be especially prone (Dell, 1973; Smith, 1979). It was not always clear how its methods related to other aims of industrial policy, themselves not always easily reconcilable, such as promoting competitiveness by controlling monopolies and restrictive practices, on the one hand, and protecting employment by supporting declining industries on the other. In other words, the IRC did not resolve underlying and essential political choices, as its short life tends to demonstrate; though it had won round the CBI's support, it was abolished by the new Conservative Government in 1971.

The second period really began in 1972 with the same Conservative Government's Industry Act of that year. This provided £500 million for direct financial assistance to industry, which could include obtaining a share in the equity of undertakings. However, that government had already found itself, contrary to its declared policy of 'disengagement', intervening to rescue two concerns in which a substantial amount of public finance had been committed by the previous Labour Government: Upper Clyde Shipbuilders and Rolls Royce Ltd. Rather than create public corporations on the Morrisonian model, the Conservative Government brought these undertakings under the direct control of the Department of Trade and Industry. The general powers subsequently provided by the Industry Act were also vested in that department, but were to be exercised by an Industrial Development Executive. Unlike the IRC, this agency was placed within a government department and made dependent on it. This approach in effect led to a substantial extension of the direct responsibilities of ministers in relation to industry and the involvement of civil servants. But the problems of reconciling different ends of industrial policy remained. Indeed, the Heath Government came to power with a studiously prepared programme of non-intervention and administrative reform. In November 1970, the Secretary of State for Industry, Mr John Davies, a former businessman and Director-General of the CBI, made his famous reference in a Commons speech to 'lame ducks'. This reference was to be turned against the government after 1972 when it found itself committed to rescue operations similar to those undertaken at considerable public expense by its predecessors (Bruce-Gardyne, 1974; Leruez, 1975; Stewart, 1977).

Finally, after the return of another Labour Government in 1974, much of the now growing collection of holdings acquired by governments in the name of industrial policy was once again vested in a largely independent public agency, the National Enterprise Board (NEB). This body was given powers and financial means to acquire further holdings under the Industry Act of 1975. Like the IRC before it, but in a much more flexible way, this body has succeeded in providing valuable expertise and enterprise that could not have been provided by the Civil Service itself. It has backed a number of 'winners', especially in the field of high technology. Its role, however, was still ambivalent and precarious, again under the influence mainly of party political attitudes. The majority of its holdings consisted at first of 'lame ducks' acquired under previous administrations and there was inevitably suspicion that in this respect its hands were somewhat tied, given the reluctance of the Labour Government to face further substantial reductions in employment in the sectors concerned. On the other hand, great stress was placed on its role as 'banker' in stimulating promising new enterprises or helping existing ones through temporary difficulties. In any event, this attempt to establish an effective state holding company was interrupted by the change of government in 1979. Disagreement with the government in the autumn of 1979 led to the unprecedented resignation of the Board's chairman and all its members.

The NEB's reputation with business probably suffered from its identification with the more interventionist policies of the Labour Party in opposition before 1974, which were still publicly professed in office by Mr Benn as Secretary of State for Industry. Its full potential as a means of managing different kinds of public holdings in industry largely of a short-term nature has, therefore, yet to be adequately tested. The present Conservative Government again seems more inclined to vest such holdings directly in ministerial departments. The Heath Government seems to have given some consideration to a wider use of state holding companies, even for the nationalised industries now run by public corporations, (Bruce-Gardyne, 1974) but, on the whole, neither Conservative nor Labour Governments have been able to establish a lasting arrangement capable of breaking new ground in the relationship between ministers and civil servants, on the one hand,

and industrial activities subject to direct public participation, on the other.

Public agencies with an adjudicative function

Yet a third method of shielding the public interest from political bias and competition is delegation to another type of public agency, one with a more or less quasi-judicial function. Such bodies have been used extensively in British economic policy during the last twenty years, predominantly in relation to monopolies and restrictive practices and prices and incomes policies.

The most judicial in form has been the Restrictive Practices Court established in 1956, assisted for most of its life by a Registrar of Restrictive Practices, a civil servant with independent status (like the Comptroller and Auditor-General). The Registrar was replaced in 1973 by a Director-General of Fair Trading with a wider remit. The Court combines features of an administrative tribunal with those of an ordinary court of law, and its decisions are final, subject to appeal on matters of law to the Court of Appeal. It has not, however, been popular with industry, which seems to prefer to deal directly with ministers than to be made subject to judicial arbitration (Dell, 1973).

The need to register agreements proved a check to restrictive business practices in itself and did much to remove the restrictive effects of many trade associations. However, ministers have still been able to follow their own policies towards competition in general and this has been far from consistent. The Monopolies Commission between 1956 and 1973 and the Monopolies and Mergers Commission since 1973 have been dependent on ministers who have had to decide whether to refer cases to the Commission and how to act on the latters' judgements. The extent to which either body has been effective has depended on the attitude towards competition of the government of the day. Invariably the public interest has taken on a different meaning, and often no clear meaning at all, in relation to particular cases of market domination arousing ministers to intervene (Dell, 1973).

A more hybrid form still was the National Board for Prices and Incomes (NBPI). This body was created by the then Labour Government in 1965 to apply the criteria of its prices and incomes policy, which was at first agreed on a voluntary tripartite basis with national representatives of employers and organised labour, though it replaced to some extent the National Incomes Commission which had been already created by the Conservatives in 1962. While the NBPI's main function could be described as adjudicative, its composition, like the reasoning it employed to justify its decisions, would be better described as expert. In this, the Board resembled to some extent the Monopolies Commission, as it did also in its dependence on ministers for making references and carrying out its judgements. The Board had no compulsory powers to require witnesses to appear before it or to impose its judgements and it was composed on a tripartite basis with the co-operation of employers and unions. The criteria it had to apply were essentially economic and it developed a great deal of flexibility in applying them to different cases. Related as it was in its origins to the Labour Government's attempts at economic planning, it assumed the responsibility of taking a longer-term view and offering technical prescriptions for achieving growth without inflation (Fels, 1972; Jones, 1973; Leruez, 1975). At the same time the NBPI's main function in practice, as its former chairman has stressed, was to apply a 'non-partisan' judgement in the short term to individual cases (Jones, 1973).

A regular feature of public intervention in labour relations in this country has been the use of impartial mediators from time to time, including judges and committees of inquiry chaired by members of the judiciary as well as individual 'trouble-shooters' with an industrial background (Barnes and Reid, 1980). There has always been a problem for ministers in deciding whether the aim of intervention should be conciliatory, in effect to avoid strikes, or to pursue wider economic objectives, such as restraining wage increases in the hope of containing inflation. The NBPI, however, clearly saw its duty as recommending pay and price changes in line with a policy to contain inflation. This role became preponderant during periods when the prices and incomes policy had to be imposed by statute. In general, however, it did not always make the Board popular or acceptable either to trade unions or to employers. Although both were represented on the Board, each of these interests had reasons from time to time to thwart attempts to apply the criteria of prices and incomes policy by voluntary means. Moreover, ministers were on the whole reluctant to explain their reasons for deciding whether or not to refer cases to it and whether or not to act on its judgements (Jones, 1973). Associated as the Board was with a particular government's policies, its influence tended to decline as the government's own commitment faltered towards the end of the 1960s (Smith, 1979). The Board was finally abolished by the Conservative Government returned in 1970. Many now believe that the Board suffered less from its own performance (though proposals have been made for improving that and for reviving this form of agency) than from its 'guilt by association' with the Labour Government's approaches to planning and to prices and incomes policy.

Most of the functions of the NBPI were, in fact, re-created by the Conservatives, when they themselves adopted a statutory prices and incomes policy in November 1972. Two new agencies were set up in 1973, the Pay Board and the Price Commission, to apply new powers vested in ministers to regulate prices, pay, dividends and rents according to a Prices and Pay Code to be established by the Treasury and intended to last for three years. In some respects, the Pay Board actually had greater power than the NBPI, in that its decisions stood unless expressly reversed by the Secretary of State for Employment. It had far more disadvantageous political associations, however, and the unions refused to participate (Leruez, 1975).

The Board lasted little more than a year, since the 'social contract' agreed between the Labour Party in opposition and the trade unions before 1974 meant that 'free' collective bargaining was restored with the return of a new Labour Government in March 1974. The Prices and Pay Code had itself been severely curtailed as a result of Labour opposition in Parliament and trade union obstruction in the country. Its political vulnerability was dramatically illustrated in the events leading to the general election of February 1974 (Ionescu, 1975; Stewart, 1977; Barnes and Reid, 1980). Although control of prices was retained by Labour Governments (and moved from the Treasury to a new Department for Prices and Consumer Protection), it was relaxed in 1976 following sustained pressures from industry that profits were being squeezed in a way that was severely damaging to the economy, and following also a change of direction by the government itself (Stewart, 1977; Barnes and Reid, 1980). The Prices Commission was in fact abolished in its turn by the Conservative Government in 1979.

It has been repeatedly explained that, if public agencies combining an adjudicative and an expert approach are to be successful, then security both in their existence and in government support for their judgements is essential. Both kinds of security have been vividly lacking in British experience of prices and incomes policies (Dell, 1973; Finer, S. E., 1975; Stewart, 1977).

The limitations of devolved responsibility
Other types of public agency, used recently to intervene in industrial relations, labour markets and industrial training will be considered in Chapter 9, since they were intended primarily for devolving executive functions to representatives of employers and unions. But there is a sense in which the same general problem faces all attempts to devolve responsibility for interpreting and applying the public interest in relation to particular economic circumstances. This problem is that, to be effective, the agencies concerned need clear and consistent guidance as to what ends they are expected to achieve or what rules they have to apply.

In British experience the public interest has turned out to contain such conflicting and changing elements that devolution has often proved self-defeating. Those entrusted with special technical, commercial or adjudicative tasks may have tried conscientiously to apply professional or other standards, but have time and again been frustrated by decisions taken at a political level. Sometimes they find their work being judged by criteria different from those they were originally supposed to apply. Moreover, the very creation of independent agencies of one kind or another has often been flavoured, deliberately or not, with party political considerations, so that genuine impartiality has been difficult to establish and the prospects of surviving changing political moods and outcomes poor. Both Conservative and Labour Parties in office have found it desirable or necessary to devolve functions in this way, but neither have been able to put them beyond the reach of the vicissitudes and predilections of partisan interests.

It is, of course, not easy to establish clear-cut or permanent rules for public intervention, especially in a representative democracy, nor is it always desirable. This in itself does not debar the use of independent public corporations and agencies, which clearly have a vital part to play in the government/industry relationship. To find suitable arrangements for such devolution, however, is a major task in the study and practice of modern public administration in the economic sphere as a whole. But if the political system fails to produce a sufficient measure of consensus and stability, or makes it impossible to allocate and exercise technical, commercial or adjudicative functions in the public sector effectively, then devolution of responsibility for the public interest is no substitute on its own. There is really no way of avoiding, therefore, the effects of the ultimate responsibility of political leadership in these matters. In its turn, that inevitably affects the attitudes and capacities of the 'classical' public service in the form of permanent career officials.

7 Technocracy and the Civil Service

Devolution to public corporations and agencies has itself been one way of reforming public administration, for example, by relieving ministerial departments of tasks for which they are considered to be unsuited. On the other hand, as we have seen, devolution does not on its own remove the need for ministers, the Civil Service and the machinery of central government to adapt to new problems thrown up by industrial, and wider economic policies, while in some ways it adds new problems of its own. There has been much discussion over the past two decades of reform of the Civil Service as well as of the machinery of government itself. Successive governments have given serious consideration to new methods of recruiting and training public officials, of organising their careers and of allocating functions among ministerial departments and providing for co-ordination and control of those functions. A number of practical measures of different kinds have been taken in an effort to respond to criticisms of the efficiency of public administration and of the capacity of the permanent government machinery to cope with its extended responsibilities. The needs of the government/industry relationship have been a major influence in these respects, and the role of the senior government official and the organisation and methods of central administration have in many ways been relevant to the continuing search for consensus in economic affairs.

The role of the Civil Service

Civil servants are often criticised for interfering in devolved functions and for being jealous of the role of technicians and others employed to perform special tasks outside usual departmental channels. Indeed, a major purpose of setting up independent or detached groups and agencies has often been precisely to counteract the influence of the career civil servant in ministerial departments, and, particularly in economic affairs (Hayward and Watson, 1975). Senior civil servants work essentially in the context of ministerial responsibility, which means in the present political system that it is their duty to protect the interests of their minister. It is not surprising if their reactions appear at times fastidious and at others deranging to those who are not expected to show the same sensitivity to political needs.

In all evaluations of the role of the Civil Service, the fundamental limitations of public administration in a political system like Britain's should be remembered. Certainly, there is a sense in which the established bureaucracy will be influenced by its ingrained loyalties and customs to act as a resistance to change and diversity. But there is also a sense in which the bureaucracy itself contains potentially disjointed and even conflicting elements, especially since individual departments have their own sectional perspective along with their own 'clientele' among interests outside Whitehall. Whatever its economic policies may be, any government must ultimately be concerned to achieve some kind of synthesis among the different sectors and objects of public intervention, including those it will have inherited from its predecessors. For one thing, it will want to make a coherent response to events beyond its control. For another, it has to see to its own internal 'housekeeping', not least the control of public expenditure. There are contrary pressures at work in all governments, therefore, between forces broadly speaking, of synthesis and those representing mainly sectional or partial views. The tensions that arise as a result seem to be endemic to public administration; they come to the surface most when attempts are made to contain the growth of public expenditure. They reflect inherent problems of reconciling different objectives and facing unforeseen contingencies not only at the level of civil servants, but also and above all, at that of ministers.

In short, too much should not be expected of the Civil Service, or of any set of agents operating under the aegis of ministerial responsibility. They are liable to reflect the inconsistencies common to government itself, when this is torn between the desire to respond to various special demands and the concern to respect certain general objectives and standards. The balance will be all the more precarious, of course, when a single party in government expects, and is expected, to outdo the other major party in terms of both the quantity of goods and services provided and the efficiency with which the public sector and the economy as a whole are managed.

Nevertheless, Civil Service reform has been an objective of most governments over the past twenty years. Technocractic ideas and tendencies have been influential in this respect too. A major aim has been to adapt the Civil Service, and the structures in which it works, to the expanded role of government in the economic sphere and to the particular needs of the government/industry relationship. Following on from the internal Plowden Report in the early 1960s there has been a growing stress on 'managerialism' in the public service (Smith, 1979). It is typical that the reforming trend has grown from a concern primarily with the way decisions about public expenditure are made and with the effectiveness in this respect of co-ordination from Cabinet level downwards.

Civil Service reform

The Fulton Report in 1968, (Cmnd 3638), recommended extensive changes designed largely to enhance both the managerial and technical capacities of the Civil Service. As is well known, however, these recommendations have had only a limited impact on the recruitment, training and careers of senior civil servants (Garrett, 1980). The Report expressed a 'preference for relevance' in the qualifications for recruitment. But there has been no general shift of emphasis from educational qualifications and it has remained far from clear what sort of 'relevance' can be read into these, even when they represent specialisation in one or other of the social sciences. Both as part of initial training and in mid-career there are greater opportunities for officials to gain some direct experience outside Whitehall, including secondment to industry. But attempts to recruit officials on secondment from industry seem to have made very little impact, while the career structure of the Civil Service remains essentially distinct and closed.

A fundamental separation of the public service from occupations in industry, therefore, continues to be a central feature of the government/industry relationship in this country. Many of those in industry and in other economic activities who have to deal with government find various ways in which this separation affects the relationship in practice (Dell, 1973; Abraham, 1974). For one thing, civil servants have their own career pre-occupations, strongly influenced by a desire for stability of employment, a regularised grading system and pension rights as by an emphasis on hierarchy, respect for formal procedures, and impersonal responsibility.

In contrast, the industrial manager, in spite of the growth of corporate organisation in industry, is far more exposed to the consequences of economic success and failure and is accustomed to a career structure that stresses personal responsibility, adaptability and initiative. Civil servants, whatever their particular function may be, work essentially in an elaborate framework of inter-departmental relationships; their career structure and working environment are designed to discourage particular or personal commitments and to encourage thinking in terms of the government service as having a common interest of its own distinct from other activities.

While mobility outside the Civil Service remains limited, the principle of mobility within seems entrenched, with the result that officials cannot expect to spend sufficient time in one post to build up specialised knowledge, commitment or personal contacts. Many examples have been given by those with direct experience of the government/industry relationship of the effects of the traditional 'arm's length' attitude of the Civil Service towards industry (Dell, 1973). This attitude is largely the consequence of a traditional concern to maintain the integrity and protect the public accountability of the administration, especially in the face of its growing involvement with economic interests. It has tended to encourage, however, a failure to understand or to respect the needs of industry.

Given the political pressures for expanding social and economic responsibilities, on the other hand, the conventions have not prevented a vast growth in public intervention and in the discretionary power of civil servants in relation to economic activities of all kinds. The system of 'sponsoring' departments may ensure relatively easy channels of communication between industry and the Civil Service (as explained in Chapter 3). But it has not meant that officials are necessarily sensitive to industrialists' own perceptions or that they are equipped to take account of the likely consequences of discretionary decisions affecting industry. Time and again departments have found themselves with unintended commitments and with embarrassing responsibility for the affairs of firms or for the welfare of the latter's employees or consumers (Dell, 1973; Brittan, 1973; Vernon, 1974; Hogwood, 1976).

Organisation and management in government

Certainly, however, the managerial element in the role of departmental officials has come to be much more readily acknowledged. It is said that Permanent Secretaries now tend to treat management of their department with at least the same importance as their traditional functions as ministerial advisers and departmental accounting officers (Clarke, 1978). Procedures for reviewing the allocation of functions among departments, the efficiency of the public service and the machinery of government in general have been strengthened, mainly by reinforcing the direct responsibilities in these respects of the Prime Minister and the Cabinet Office. One consequence over the last twenty years has been a whole series of attempts to re-organise departments and their functions, but with different objectives and little long-term effect.

Attempts to create more specialised departments, designed to press for particular objectives such as economic growth or industrial modernisation and to increase the influence of officials with specialised technical competence, have not usually survived either the resistance of traditional departmental interests or changes at a political level in the status of individual ministers or the direction of policy. The most notable example in the 1960s was the chequered career of the Department of Economic Affairs which finally disappeared in 1969 (Leruez, 1975; Shanks, 1977). On the other hand, the 1970 Conservative Government's experiment with large-scale departments, intended mainly, it seems, to facilitate central co-ordination and encourage rationalisation has been to strengthen collective responsibility and, in this sense, to reinforce the status of the party programme, on the basis especially of the Prime Minister's own authority. But the machinery of government has proved to be a poor defence against the instability of government policy or conflicts within a Cabinet. Indeed, much of the passion for re-organisation may seem in retrospect to have created an 'illusion of progress' while causing no more than 'confusion, inefficiency and demoralisation' (Cmnd 4641). The effect in the sphere of economic affairs, and therefore on industry, must certainly have been one of bewilderment and extreme frustration. But the fact remains that allocating functions in central government in the British system is one of the chief prerogatives of the Executive and involves vital political concerns such as the 'pecking-order' of different members of the party leadership.

Another example of managerial changes in the Civil Service is the way in which public expenditure is determined and monitored. In addition, the procedures based on the Public Expenditure Survey Committee and the introduction of longer-term expenditure programmes brought important changes in the way the public sector of the economy was treated by government itself. They recognised more explicitly that Parliament no longer in practice exercises the power to approve public expenditure in the traditional framework of the annual estimates. They were, in fact, the beginnings of progressive attempts by a succession of governments to introduce what were seen as more rational and systematic methods in public policy making, often with the help of outside experts, and drawing on techniques developed in academic studies of management and in the private sector. One of the chief aims of the new approach is to recognise that decisions about the size and content of expenditure in the public sector not only need to be taken in a longer term perspective than the annual budget, but also need to be seen in relation to their effects on the economy as a whole (Heclo and Wildavsky, 1974; Else and Marshall, 1979).

In fact, public expenditure came to be seen increasingly as the provision of goods and services, accounting for a substantial part of the nation's economic activity, and not simply as a matter of internal housekeeping requiring a balanced budget. For some time the new approach was welcomed by the Treasury as a means of strengthening and improving its own functions of co-ordination and control. But, in the face of increasing alarm at the growth of public expenditure in relation to that of the gross national product, and against the background of severe inflationary pressures, the new approach lost support during the 1970s. The use of more refined techniques to assess the value of particular activities and policies and to find more efficient methods of carrying them out, has continued. But stress on the need to contain public expenditure has brought a new emphasis on cash limits on an annual basis and re-asserted more traditional methods of Treasury control, in which the political weight of the Chancellor of the Exchequer in Cabinet remains, as always, the ultimate test (Wright, 1977; Clarke, 1978).

Technocracy as an alternative to politics

The changes which were taking place in the Civil Service were among the many developments in public administration in the postwar period. Especially in the early 1960s in the heyday of indicative planning, the view was that the new economic responsibilities of government called for a new kind of public official. Various attempts were made to supplement the traditional bureaucracy and in economic affairs to some extent supplant it, by means of specially recruited 'technicians' – meaning not only economists, statisticians, accountants of the professional Civil Service, but also special advisers of different kinds recruited on a short-term contract.

The idea of technocracy – a system of rule by such technicians – has been influential in much political theorising about the role of government in advanced, industrialised societies. As a general view of state and society, it has been traced to the Saint-Simonian view that mankind should move from 'the government of men to the administration of things' (Ionescu, 1973; Bell, 1976; Kumar, 1978). It also evokes a kind of 'anti-politics', in which rational principles of organisation are supposed to replace the division, disruption and inconsistency of political forms of leadership (Smith, 1972). It is not difficult to understand the appeal of such an approach when applied to the government of an advanced, industrialised society, especially in view of the limitations associated with the practice of representative democracy.

The authority of the 'technocrat' is supposed to come from his competence rather than from any political ideas he may be associated with, or from his election or appointment to political office. In this respect, the idea of technocracy comes up in most earlier proposals for economic planning in Britain, dating back well before the last war, and it greatly influenced approaches to the mixed economy during the first twenty years after the war (Smith, 1979).

Indeed, some form of technocracy seems to be an inevitable counterpart to the impact of economic science on government that we discussed in Chapter 2. Keynes, Beveridge and other influential figures from the world of academic social science were probably, in their individual contribution to the general direction of public policy, the real forbears of technocracy in postwar Britain. These were exceptional cases of personal influence, but the notion that government should make direct use of experts specially recruited for limited periods from universities, industry and elsewhere was by no means new in the 1960s. As we saw in Chapter 2, the war economy was managed between 1940 and 1945 with the help of numbers of professional economists and other specialists recruited into the public service on a temporary basis. The numbers fell after the war, but the role of professional economic advisers was retained to some extent in the Economic Section to the Cabinet Office which later moved to the Treasury. Since that time, and particularly during the 1960s, many government departments have recruited economists as well as statisticians and other 'professionals'.

The intense interest in technocratic forms of administration in the early 1960s came to this country, however, mainly by way of experience with economic planning in France, particularly the role there of the *Commissariat du Plan* and its associated specialised *commissions de modernisation* set up after the liberation (Hayward and Watson, 1975; Denton et al, 1968). In the first place, attention was drawn to the potential value in indicative planning of the influence of officials technical competence:

'The plan is made to work because the quality of the analysis done by the planners convinces the men wielding economic power, in the private and public sectors alike, that the conclusions offered to them provide good advice'. (Shonfield, 1965, p.231).

To wield such influence it seemed that the planner needed to be detached from established departmental structures with their direct executive responsibilities (Crozier, 1970). The idea of experts acting outside the normal official hierarchy and free from executive functions has come to have even wider application in policy making:

'The planner may be described as a back-room boy who, freed from the requirement of immediate decisions, is able to elaborate and analyse the factors relevant to some policy choice.' (Self, 1972, p. 32).

Secondly, however, the planner's independence was also seen as giving him something akin to a political role. This aspect was developed particularly in Shonfield's characterisation of the 'independent official', which he saw as a key element in the 'contemporary political method' that seemed so important to successful economic policy-making on the continent of Europe:

'The head of a national planning organisation has the obligation to engage in a certain type of politics. His job as a public servant is to lead a lobby for long-term economic growth inside the government; this may conflict with the party politician's short-range imperatives.

Like the governor of the central bank he is ultimately subject to the
order of the government of the day, but it is expected of both
governor and head planner that they will urge the policies which
they judge to be right, in their fields of expertise, on the country at
large as well as on the government, and do so with clarity.'
(Shonfield, 1965, pp. 404–08).

Finally, notice was taken of the representative function of expert officials engaged in French planning. Such officials could be seen, in one
sense, as themselves being able to speak for the 'real world' of economic activity and as by-passing the traditional, but, it was thought,
inappropriate, intermediary role of the elected politician. They also
played a key role in *concertation:* the direct involvement under the aegis
of public agencies manned by 'technocrats' of representatives of
business and labour in the preparation and implementation of the plan
(Crozier, 1970; Hayward and Watson, 1975; Griffiths, 1977).

In practice, it was the involvement of representatives of industry that
had most influence on British attempts at indicative planning. Even so,
concertation was especially adapted for what were thought to be peculiar
British needs, mostly the political requirement of giving the Trades
Union Congress and 'peak' employers' organisations a direct share in
responsibility for the body entrusted with preparing the plan. This
body was, of course, the National Economic Development Council
(NEDC). We will consider the role of NEDC in the next chapter but
for the moment will look at the position of the officials serving NEDC,
namely the staff of the National Economic Development Office.

The National Economic Development Office
The National Economic Development Office (NEDO) comes under its
own Director-General, who is himself a full member of the Council.
NEDO's independence of Whitehall has always been jealously guarded
and it is answerable to NEDC alone, though the Council is chaired by
a minister and the whole apparatus depends on funds subject to Treasury approval. It was created in the teeth of substantial Treasury
opposition and one of its main functions, at least in the early years, was
seen as offering an alternative source of economic expertise to that
provided by the Treasury; in this way, it was intended to strengthen
support for policies designed for economic growth (Leruez, 1975;
Shanks, 1977). Its original staff of 75 in 1961 soon grew to 100 in 1964,
drawn mostly from industry and to a lesser extent from universities
and the Civil Service itself (Leruez, 1975). In those years 'it included
the highest concentration of economists and statisticians ever seen in
British government' (Smith, 1979). Since its creation, Directors-
General have mostly been recruited from outside Whitehall on long-
term contracts, though some have been former civil servants. The.

Office originally had two divisions, one responsible mainly for preparing economic forecasts and drawing up economic plans and the other for relations with industry and the production of micro-economic sector programmes (Phelps-Brown, 1963). The first of these divisions, however, lost most of its members following the advent of the Labour Government in 1964 when they were largely transferred, along with responsibility for forecasting and planning into the Department of Economic Affairs (DEA). Subsequently, the influence of NEDO in these matters declined and was never restored. The industrial side of the Office contributed to planning under the Labour Government but both NEDC and NEDO have had a somewhat variable influence following the demise of indicative planning after 1966.

Prior to the general election of 1964, NEDO was arguably a significant source of advice alternative to that of the Treasury, and its influence can be seen especially in the Conservative Government's acceptance of a four per cent growth target (Leruez, 1975). Subsequently, however, ministerial departments, and especially after 1966, the Treasury, prevailed again in economic policy. It cannot be said that NEDO provides a genuine example of independent technocratic influence, in the sense of being able to challenge either the access to information or the impact on policy of Whitehall (Shanks, 1977). Not counting for the moment its role in the context of 'tripartism', its output has consisted primarily of reports on specialised longer-term aspects of economic and industrial policy.[1]

'Irregulars' and special advisers

The employment of experts from outside Whitehall on a temporary basis has, however, become a standard practice in British central government, though normally to give advice within Whitehall, and not as part of any special emphasis on indicative planning. Special advisers or 'irregulars' have been attached to individual ministerial departments, and ministers themselves (especially Prime Ministers) have adopted the practice of appointing their own special advisers whose role has been seen as partly countering the advice of departments. The scale is nothing like as great as what was seen between 1964 and 1966, and even so neither practice can be regarded as fulfilling the aim of replacing politically-based authority with that of 'technocrats'.

Departmental 'irregulars' simply supplement the existing internal channels. Special advisers to ministers must be regarded as reinforcing rather than counteracting the influence of party political leadership.

[1] It did, however, make a major contribution to the planning document, *The Task Ahead*, produced by the DEA in 1969 and itself produced a long-term programme for industrial policy in the early 1970s (Leruez, 1975; Shanks, 1977).

For the most part, they have tended to be chosen for that very purpose as policy specialists (often recruited from party research staffs and often later themselves becoming MPs) to strengthen the minister's hand against any possible Whitehall inertia in implementing the terms of the party manifesto.

In addition, however, special groups of temporary outsiders and individuals have been attached to the Cabinet or the Prime Minister with the function of supplementing, or substituting for, departmental advice in a different way. The Conservative Government elected in June 1970 appointed a group of 14 businessmen seconded from industry with the general task of questioning the *raison d'etre* of existing activities of government and pointing out examples of overlapping and duplication. It also set up the Central Policy Review Staff (CPRS) in the Cabinet Office under a leading professional scientist (who was in fact a former Labour Party supporter) to carry out mostly, it seemed, some of the 'back-room' functions of planning described above. The industrialists and CPRS were part of the Heath Government's intended 'managerial revolution' and it is not easy to disentangle their contribution from that of established civil servants in departments such as the Treasury. Whatever it was, it did not prevent the government being swept off course in the notorious 'U' turn of 1972 (Bruce-Gardyne, 1974). The CPRS has been retained by later governments and has conducted numerous inquiries into particular aspects of policy and administrative organisation across the whole range of government activities often with high political sensitivity (Pollitt, 1974). The team of industrialists had dispersed back to private industry by 1972 but Sir Derek Rayner, one of the industrialists recruited in 1970, was again appointed by Mrs Thatcher in 1979 to report directly to her on means of cutting waste in the central administration and improving the machinery of government. The main purpose of these types of specialist advice has been in many respects to assist ministers in implementing party policy; both Conservative Governments concerned began their term of office with a public commitment to 'disengagement' and retrenchment. The chief function of such groups seems to be to make up deficiencies in the Whitehall machinery by strengthening central co-ordination and control. It is difficult to find evidence that in doing so they have done much to weaken the ultimately decisive influence of political considerations, even if they have enjoyed unusual access to ministers and reduced to some extent the latters' dependence on their departmental civil servants.

Politics and the public interest
We are, therefore, drawn to the conclusion that the organisation and management of the government machine, and to a large extent of the

public sector as a whole, cannot be detached from the political considerations that affect the decisions and attitudes of ministers. If anything, it has itself tended to become one of the instruments by which one or other party seeks to govern. The main result seems to have been to confuse and derange the recipients of public intervention in industry with a bewildering flux in the personnel, structures, rules and attitudes of the public administration. On the other hand, demands for giving a more positive and independent role to particular groups or bodies with specialised competences and functions, more aligned to the needs of industry or to particular purposes of economic intervention, tend to be contradicted by the fear of political leaders that the power to command the course of events will slip from their grasp.

We have concentrated here on the shortcomings, but do any lessons emerge for a more constructive approach to the role of the public sector? One might be that the question of public accountability and that of wider relations with the public are not merely secondary concerns, to be settled once the functions of different agencies or departments have been adequately defined in a technical sense. The nature of political leadership and the way its own priorities and expectations are formed have a crucial impact on attempts to interpret and apply any view of the public interest. Attempts to place the public interest beyond political competition may simply encourage the evasion of political responsibility for uncertain or unpopular decisions. Politicians in office or approaching office have found it difficult to resist claiming the power to influence industrial performance in all sorts of ways, but when faced with the real limitations on their power they have been ready both individually and collectively to place the blame elsewhere. Finding more effective methods of recruitment and training of public officials and of organising ministerial departments is, therefore, only part of the problem. The central question is how to restore confidence in political responsibility in a way that is compatible with the needs of economic performance. Before returning to that question, we must first take account of another and related attempt to find consensus in spite of politics.

8 The Tripartite Approach

Since the first world war British governments have used different procedures for consulting representatives of those in industry directly affected by public policy and its implementation. It has long been recognised that public administration, particularly when applying social and economic measures such as those which have a direct impact on industry, would simply not be possible without the help of the specialised knowledge and the acquiescence of those directly concerned at the operating level in both private and public sectors.

At the same time, governments have felt the need to impose greater order on their relationships with industrial spokesmen. They have encouraged the growth of inclusive organisations to represent particular industries and sectors, and also to represent major economic interests at the national level.

In some other European countries similar bodies have been used much more extensively in public administration and have often been given special legal status and functions as public authorities. In Britain there has been a different tradition of leaving them primarily as private associations, but the role of government has still been vital in giving them authority by recognising them officially as correspondents in any attempt to inform or consult, and even negotiate with, their collective memberships. That has been so both in relation to particular industries, sectors or regions, when more specialised organisations have been involved, and in relation to economic policy at national level, when 'peak associations', usually those of employers and labour, have enjoyed special access to government – both at ministerial and official levels.

One particular form of the relationship, however, has become especially important. All governments in the 1960s and 1970s sought during some period to make and apply economic policy on the basis of a consensus including national representatives of organisations of employers and business, on the one hand, and trade unions, on the other. This approach has been given the popular name of 'tripartism' and as such it has usually been intended to imply something more than the customary consultative relationship between government and industrial representatives. At times during the last twenty years, governments seem to have been attempting what would constitute, if fully effective, a new approach to government, in which responsibility would be shared with the acknowledged representatives of major organised economic interests. What has resulted, however, has always fallen short of any genuine sharing of responsibility, either intentionally or because the attempt has failed. As we shall see, there are good reasons why the tripartite approach should be limited and why, given the workings of the British political system, it has even had very mixed results in achieving consensus.

In practice, British governments have not gone to the lengths of giving tripartite arrangements any formal, constitutional status; their approach has been essentially pragmatic and has always sought to avoid any hint of change in the status of Parliament or the unique answerability of ministers to it. Tripartism has been presented as if it were no more than an extension of normal consultative arrangements, based on the Executive and, therefore, conducted by ministers responsible to Parliament. But the practice has been extended into a 'grey area', in which what are, in effect, new forms of policy making and administration mingle uncertainly with traditional conventions. Three rather different approaches need to be considered:

- the use of an established forum for the regular tripartite consideration at national level of proposals dealing with longer term economic objectives and the means of attaining them (in other words, the NEDC);
- attempts to bring national representatives of employers and unions into some form of 'partnership' or compact with the government of the day for current management of the economy;
- the use of specialised working groups (based on NEDC) or public agencies designed to enable employers' and union representatives to participate in the formulation and the operation of particular aspects of industrial policy.

We shall leave consideration of the third approach, through specialised bodies and agencies, to the next chapter, because it has been developed largely as a special way of improving or supplementing the other approaches. However, while none of these three approaches has been intended so far to alter the conventions associated with party government, they have all been justified, and widely encouraged, as essential means of achieving a wider consensus than electoral and Parliamentary politics are thought to offer.

The National Economic Development Council
One of the major results of the conversion of the Conservative Government of 1959–64 to a form of indicative economic planning was the setting up of the National Economic Development Council (NEDC) serviced by its own expert staff in the National Economic

Development Office (NEDO). The role of NEDC and the structures connected with it, however, survived the demise of planning, at least in name, after 1966 and have had a much wider, though varying, significance. In fact, it is impossible to define NEDC's status or functions with much clarity or fixity. It is widely felt that this in itself helps to explain its power of survival (in contrast to most other agencies of economic policy) and its unique contribution.

NEDC was set up in the first place as part of the then government's attempt to obtain the support of industry for policies designed to promote national economic growth. At the same time, the enthusiasm of national representatives of industry for the aim of economic growth, and for some kind of planning as a means of achieving it, was itself a factor in the choice of a tripartite approach. The conversion of employers' organisations to planning influenced the government's own attitude. What happened has been somewhat baldly described as follows:

> 'The FBI held a conference at Brighton in November 1960 at which a group of industrialists called for the setting of national growth targets as a guide and stimulus to decision makers in industry. The government was interested and began consulting with industry.' (Bray, 1970, p. 133)

The trade unions, however, were suspicious of the government's motives, fearing that any tripartite machinery would be used to interfere with collective bargaining and commit the unions nationally to policies that their members could not support. The moderate leadership of the TUC's Secretary-General at the time, George Woodcock, was an important factor in gaining union agreement to participate in the NEDC. But assurances had to be given, which have influenced the role of NEDC ever since, that its remit would not extend to the procedures or results of collective bargaining or to national policies for wages (Shanks, 1977; Smith, 1979).

The new body was, in fact, given no statutory basis and was endowed with no executive or adjudicative powers. Parliament was informed of its creation, and its purposes were outlined in rather vague terms, in speeches by the Chancellor of the Exchequer. It eventually adopted its own terms of reference, largely on lines suggested by the Chancellor, and these have not subsequently been altered (Leruez, 1975):

(a) To examine the economic performance of the nation with particular concern for plans for the future in both the private and public sectors of industry.

(b) To consider together what are the obstacles to quicker growth, what can be done to improve efficiency, and whether the best use is being made of our resources.

(c) To seek agreement upon ways of improving economic perform-
ance, competitive power and efficiency, in other words, to increase the rate of sound growth.

The Council began with a membership of twenty, including four *ex officio members*: the Chancellor of the Exchequer as chairman, the President of the Board of Trade, the Minister of Labour and the Director-General of NEDO. The other members were appointed by the Chancellor to comprise six representatives of private industry, six representatives nominated by the TUC, who regarded themselves as answerable to the TUC General Council, two chairmen of Boards of nationalised industries and two independent experts. There have been some subsequent variations. Since the mid-1960s the Prime Minister has chaired the Council from time to time and the ministerial participation has changed to reflect re-allocations of functions and has been enlarged with additional ministers exercising economic functions. (In January 1979 there were seven ministers out of total membership of 26.) The main employers' organisations grouped to form the Confederation of British Industry (CBI) in 1965, and that body now nominates the six representatives of private industry, who include a spokesman for the City of London financial interests. These representatives have continued to serve on a personal basis, though the CBI normally prepares a common stance for Council business. The last Labour Government added to the membership the chairmen of two new public agencies, the National Enterprise Board (NEB) and the Manpower Services Commission (MSC), and included the Chairman of the National Consumer Council as one of the two independent experts. The total membership has usually fluctuated, therefore, around the mid-twenties and has never been, strictly speaking, simply tripartite. 'Independent' members and those from the nationalised industries are generally considered by those with direct experience of NEDC to have played a vital role by filling what might be called the 'interstices' between the corporate interests of employers and organised labour. Their contributions to the Council's monthly meetings have usually been more spontaneous, constructive and, as might be expected, disinterested than those of CBI and TUC representatives. The latter have usually spoken to a prepared brief which, especially when wider issues of economic policy are discussed, tends to reflect fixed attitudes already familiar from public statements. Participation has, however, usually been treated earnestly by both CBI and TUC and their representation has nearly always been as high-
powered as possible including, on the union side, the TUC's

Secretary-General and chief economic spokesman.

After the transfer of most economic planning functions to the Department of Economic Affairs (DEA) by 1965, and especially after the abandonment of the National Plan in 1966, NEDC cannot be said to have operated much more than on the margins of central economic decision making in government, though there have been certain exceptional periods. Since 1964, its major continuing contribution has been through the industrial work of NEDO and through the economic development committees, of which there were about twenty by 1966, chaired by an industrial representative and with a tripartite membership, and reporting to the Council on means of improving efficiency and performance in particular groups of industries (Fraser, 1967; Leruez, 1975; Shanks, 1977). Since 1975 this work has been greatly supplemented and extended with sector working parties composed in a similar way. This 'substructure' of NEDC has largely kept out of political controversy and, though subject to review and pruning with changes of government, has carried on its own relatively unspectacular existence.

As already suggested, two of NEDC's essential characteristics have been its pragmatism, and its continuity. These qualities have meant not being too closely identified with a particular government's policies, and not being used as part of any attempt to commit its members to support politically controversial measures that would be unacceptable to those they represent. NEDC has thus made a unique contribution in enabling the CBI and TUC, in spite of any differences between them and in their attitudes to a particular government, to maintain regular contact and communication and to build up general confidence in NEDC as a common meeting ground.[1]

It might be said that, though it has had long fallow periods, if NEDC or something much like it did not exist, then it would have to be invented. Hence, it did not disappear in 1970 along with other bodies and procedures that had played a part in the previous Labour Government's attempts at planning and selective intervention. It has twice proved its value for the opportunity it provided to Conservative Governments to maintain some dialogue with the TUC in spite of sharp differences in public, and even frosty distance in private, without an impression of submission on either side (Elliott, 1978; Taylor, 1978). In this respect, NEDC was brought into the centre of the stage by the Heath Government in 1972, and seems to be performing a similar function for the Thatcher Government at the time of writing. While Labour Governments have not had the same need, having more

---

[1] The TUC and CBI began in the mid-1960s to hold regular meetings between themselves outside the framework of NEDC (Elliott, 1978).

direct contacts with the unions, of course, they have always found in NEDC a valuable instrument for giving legitimacy to their economic, and particularly their industrial, policies. Moreover, the TUC itself seems to place great stress on NEDC's potential and actual authority as a source of economic advice and criticism and, at least since 1975, has seen it as having a major part to play in industrial policy, though mainly through its sub-structure of economic development committees and sector working parties (TUC, 1977). The present Director-General has described in suitably measured terms the contribution the Council makes to tripartite relationships, short of changing the public attitudes of the parties concerned:

> 'One monthly meeting of Neddy, viewed in isolation, may often be no more meaningful than one month's trade figures, although impressive in its moderation and constructiveness of discussion. But regular monthly discussions constitute a cumulative learning process which has led to perceptible positive changes in tone, language and attitude and a gradual extension of the agenda.' (Mr Geoffrey Chandler in *The Times*, 2 February, 1981).

However, NEDC's lack of formal or real powers also helps to explain its ability to survive. NEDC's essential dependence on the Executive is reflected in its non-statutory basis and the inclusion of ministers as full members and of the Chancellor of the Exchequer or Prime Minister as chairman.

The Director-General of NEDO and NEDO itself provide an important measure of autonomy, though they are dependent on the Treasury for funds and, therefore, for the extent of their official activities. Individual Directors-General have viewed their role differently, some seeing the independent status of the post as reflecting essentially the tripartite nature of the Council, others seeing it as implying a responsibility to take important initiatives of their own and on behalf of NEDO, even at the risk of getting into conflict with ministers.

The agenda is established by a co-ordinating committee chaired by the Director-General and including official representatives of the Treasury, other relevant departments and the CBI and TUC. A special meeting of the Director-General, the Director-General of the CBI, the Secretary-General of the TUC and the Permanent Secretary of the Treasury, with the last named in the chair, will be called to iron out any major disputes or problems. The agenda normally includes submissions and papers from NEDO itself, from the CBI and TUC (or from both jointly) and sometimes from the other ordinary members.

What ultimately matters, however, is that among Council members only ministers are able to 'deliver the goods' in terms of enacted measures, enforceable decisions or public funds. Ministers do not negotiate with economic interests in NEDC, nor is it even a deliberative body like Parliament, in the sense of disputation leading to a vote. Differences among ministers have from time to time spilled over to proceedings of the Council (especially under the 1974–79 Labour Government), but ministerial statements are subject to Cabinet approval and ministers are present essentially to defend and explain a collective government view. The scope of the agenda, the outcome of discussions, and the range of activities undertaken by NEDO depend on unanimous agreement among Council members. Issues of particular concern to one or other of the industrial interests will get taken up, though they will probably be treated in a rather different way from what was originally intended.[2] Clearly, however, the main initiative rests with the government of the day, for which NEDC is a useful, but by no means exclusive, sounding board – a sort of permanent royal commission. As with royal commissions, it will sometimes be used as a means of delaying or defusing decisions on awkward problems.[3] Meetings are held in private and, unless there are 'leaks' by the ordinary members, all the public learns of the results are what can be obtained from the Director-General's press conferences held after the monthly meetings, though the Council publishes numerous reports and papers (about half the total considered) and, since 1979, a brief annual report (NEDO, 1979, 1980).

The Council itself is probably best described, therefore, as a special kind of advisory committee, with vital and unique characteristics all the same. But the nature of its composition and its ultimate dependence on the Executive impose limitations. First, NEDC cannot in any real sense be a medium through which representatives of industrial interests are regularly consulted on legislative or budgetary proposals or on the way governments make use of their discretionary powers. It has considered from time to time matters submitted to it by ministers that could lead to legislation (for example, when it made what is considered to have been a useful examination of the last Labour Government's Green Paper on competition policy (Cmnd. 7198)). However, ministers and their officials still place the emphasis on dealing directly with the specialised interests affected. Ministers only let NEDC see what papers they want, and it has never made any

[2] As when the trade unions' request for a paper showing the inadequacies of the City of London as a source of domestic investment led to the appointment of a special committee on finance for industry that has tended to stress the importance of profitability in attracting investment (NEDO, 1975).

[3] For example, when Mr Wilson, as Prime Minister, was faced with explaining an embarrassing change of policy toward pricing in nationalised industries, he persuaded NEDO to undertake a major study of relations between ministers and the industries – one of many such studies undertaken by various individuals and bodies, the main recommendations of which have never been acted on.

impression on the conventional secrecy and seclusion of economic and financial policy making in Whitehall. Secondly, NEDC's survival has depended to some extent on its avoidance of 'the difficult issues'. The Council's proceedings are mainly concerned with macroeconomic questions, but it has not been the venue for working out or negotiating specific agreements on a tripartite basis. Not only has it tended to skirt round such questions as pay policy, central as these have been to most government's attempts to manage the economy, but it has not served to prevent relations between ministers and industrial interests breaking down in critical ways.

Thirdly, there are limits to what a compact national forum like NEDC can achieve with regard to longer term and more specialised aspects of public policy, even with the assistance of NEDO and with the additional dimension to its role provided by the substructure of tripartite committees. We shall consider the role of this substructure in the next chapter, where there will be an attempt to do more justice to the way NEDC has always sought to include a more specialised and 'disaggregated' approach to economic development. However, although the Council itself, usually on the basis of NEDO papers, gives consideration to a wide range of specific and longer-term questions, in fields such as competition policy, vocational training, international trade, energy policy and research and development, it is often maintained that its treatment of such matters is too discursive and superficial, and lacks influence in terms of the fulfilment of common needs and objectives. It has been described in this respect by a former participant as 'dilettante'.[4]

Two general questions are raised by this approach to 'tripartism'. First, there is the question whether the preponderant role given to leading figures of the CBI and TUC does, in fact, ensure that representation of industry and of wider economic interests is 'authentic'. In one sense, there is a need to get closer to the operating level of industry (or where, as is so often remarked, the real action is) for the sake of being better informed as well as to get more direct results. Attempts to improve this aspect will be considered in the next chapter. In another sense, the question of 'authenticity' raises the whole issue of the role of intermediary organisations representing business and labour, an issue we shall treat at length in Part Three.

The second general question is how effective such machinery as NEDC can be without a positive interest on the part of government, and even a firm commitment to involve it in policy making and application. Clearly, such machinery can have only a very marginal result in the search for consensus if the government of the day for what-

---

[4] In a contribution to a private seminar.

ever reason is pursuing policies or taking measures that make such consensus impossible. Moreover, it is highly doubtful whether, even in the realm of relatively non-controversial matters, co-operation among organised economic interests can achieve a great deal in practice without the positive support of government. This means not only introducing legal and financial measures where necessary to follow up initiatives, but also some commitment that undertakings made on the part of sectional organisations in the public interest will be matched by the government with policies and actions that do not run deliberately counter to what these undertakings are trying to achieve. But, as we see repeatedly, governments have other factors to consider.

Partnership: beer and sandwiches or tea and sympathy

In their direct dealings with representatives of industry in times of crisis, or whenever support has been required for particular policies and measures, governments may have been grateful for NEDC as a possible medium of communication, and sometimes NEDO and its Director-General as useful intermediaries, but they have relied essentially on contacts outside any permanent framework. In this respect, the national leaders in the CBI, and especially the TUC, came to play in the 1960s and 1970s a role in relation to government far beyond the wildest expectations of any non-ministerial Member of Parliament. Since most of this period was regarded as a time of crisis, at least in the economic sense, the central stage of British policies was usually occupied by a dialogue of one kind or another between leading ministers, including the Prime Minister, and leading industrial spokesmen. Prices and incomes policies were usually developed in such a setting, as were particular attempts by governments to settle major industrial disputes. Under the Labour Government of 1966–70 the style of 'beer and sandwiches' at Number Ten was developed as the chief means of obtaining the support of union leaders especially during major official or unofficial strikes, as were *ad hoc* methods of rallying the support of industry in general like the two National Productivity Conferences held at Lancaster House in 1968.

A far more ambitious attempt at tripartism, aiming, it seemed, at fully shared responsibility in economic affairs, came with Mr Heath's 'U' turn in 1972. At a conference at Chequers in the autumn of 1972 (in the preparation of which NEDO played an important part) the policy of 'partnership' with employers and labour was launched. The aims were later expressed by the then Secretary of State for Employment in a way that captures well the idea of 'tripartism' in this sense:

'At the highest level in our national life we are seeking to complement power with responsibility by offering the TUC and

CBI, as representative bodies, a say in the management of the economy, no less' (Maurice MacMillan quoted in Elliott, 1978, p. 20).

Various explanations have been offered for the failure of the Heath Government's stragegy, which ended of course with statutory control of incomes and confrontation with the miners, leading to the general election of February 1974. It was widely supposed at the time of the change of government in June 1970 that the TUC leadership was going to have to adjust to a much more distant relationship with ministers. However, union representatives continued to participate in the normal consultative channels. Although the atmosphere was, no doubt, less convivial (and any hospitality of a possibly different style), Mr Heath as Prime Minister is said to have met the TUC leaders eight times during 1971, when relations were publicly at their most hostile (Bruce-Gardyne, 1974). A major bone of contention was, of course, the Industrial Relations Act passed in 1971, which went further than any previous attempt to regulate union activities and, in particular, collective bargaining. The trade union movement bitterly opposed the Act and carried their opposition to the lengths of nullifying in practice many of its provisions with the encouragement of the TUC. The subsequent replacement of 'confrontation' with 'partnership', therefore, hardly had good foundations to build on. The way the government sought to manage the coal-miners' strike and the fuel crisis of the winter of 1973–74 can also, of course, be criticised. The CBI had itself responded far more positively to the offer of 'partnership' and had already acted earlier in concert with the government to promote voluntary price restraint with considerable success. However, even the CBI seems to have had doubts about the government's ultimate approach to industrial relations, as was indicated by its Director-General's widely quoted critical speech during the election campaign in February 1974 (Shanks, 1977; Stewart, 1977; Elliott, 1978; Barnes and Reid, 1980).

Whatever its strategic and tactical shortcomings, the Heath Government's experience has been interpreted as giving final proof of the essential weakness of representative government in the face of the trade unions' economic power. Advocates of 'tripartism' have tended to see the main salutary lesson in the government's failure to recognise the unions' power and establish an effective 'partnership' at a much earlier stage.

However, the limitations of the government/union relationship had been shown already by the Wilson Government's inability even with the support of national union leaders to find a lasting solution for repeated industrial unrest, and also by successful official union resistance to that government's own attempt to legislate for industrial relations in its abortive Industrial Relations Bill. Then, too, in 1969, the trade union movement could be said to have contributed largely to the collapse of a government's general self-confidence and authority. A later Labour Government was to learn from that experience, and to take advantage of the Heath Government's misfortunes, to adopt its own far more developed form of relationship with representatives of economic power.

The 'social contract'

In fact, the result of the February 1974 election was indecisive, showing chiefly a growth in support for the Liberals and for nationalist parties in Scotland and Wales. However, the conventions of the electoral mandate and party government remained intact, and a Labour Government, though with only 31 per cent of the votes of the total electorate (and with 29 per cent in the ensuing October 1974 election) proceeded to put into practice the agreement it had reached with the TUC in opposition.

This kind of agreement, which has become known as the 'social contract' and which the Labour Party is still committed to renewing if returned to power, sought to share responsibility far more extensively than any previous tripartite approach. It was not, however, tripartite, since it was an arrangement between government and only one major economic organisation, the TUC. Nor was it in any meaningful sense a contract. It was based essentially on status, and was devised in recognition of the economic power of organised labour, which in its political effects, at least, had proved itself far more important than that of capital or any other conceivable industrial or economic interest, to the extent, it seemed, of being able to bring down governments and survive any appeal to wider electoral support.

The notion of contract was also misleading because in strictly legal and constitutional terms no government could commit itself in an agreement with a private party to enact legislative and financial measures without the support of Parliament. However, since in practice the conventions of party government have overridden those of Parliamentary sovereignty, such an arrangement could be presented as both legitimate and credible. The 'social contract' was treated by the government, which presented it as the basis of its programme in two 1974 election campaigns, as part of its electoral mandate. Only in a regime placing such authority in a single party leadership by means of a simple majority electoral system, could such a conception of representative government be found at all admissible.

The essential instrument of the 'social contract' was a body called the Liaison Committee, representing, at the highest level, the TUC, the Labour Party's executive committee and its Parliamentary leadership, and formed originally in 1971 mainly to combat the Conservatives' Industrial Relations Bill. This body formulated the terms of the agreement between the Party and the trade unions which eventually, from the February 1974 election for at least two years, determined the main course of government in Britain. During this time the Committee met monthly, without the attendance of civil servants, to settle the main lines of the Labour Government's implementation of its programme. The latter included a series of legislative measures, including repeal of the Industrial Relations Act, abolition of the Pay Board, new legislative protection for trade unions and a substantial extension of public intervention in industry. Key decisions on fiscal policy and public expenditure were also affected. The 'Neddy Six', representing the TUC's economic committee, met regularly with the Chancellor of the Exchequer and other TUC members and officials enjoyed unprecedented access to Whitehall (Elliott, 1978).

A lasting, constructive outcome of the 'social contract' was a series of new measures and arrangements set up as part of the government's 'industrial strategy' and these will be considered in the next chapter. For the most part, however, both the Labour Party and the TUC had entered into a bargain that neither ultimately had the status to keep. While the government could summon a sufficiently stable majority in Parliament, it carried out its side of the bargain, but the economic advantages in terms of self-restraint in pay negotiations largely failed to appear.

> 'Until mid-1975 (the social contract) was a political rallying cry for the labour movement which committed the politicians in government to specific measures while the trade union response exacerbated the inflation which was the central economic and social problem facing the government' (Barnes and Reid, 1980, p. 195).

Confronted with severe economic difficulties from 1975 on, the Wilson Government gradually found itself obliged to seek other kinds of agreement in recognition of other realities of economic power. It came to rely on international borrowings arranged through the International Monetary Fund, and sought both employers' and trade union cooperation for a new prices and incomes policy. The new Callaghan Government, which took over in the Spring of 1976, soon lost its working majority in the House of Commons, partly as a result of by-election defeats. It came to rely for its survival, between the spring of 1977 and the summer of 1978, on a pact with the Liberal Party and, after that, on the support of Ulster Unionists. As it turned out, for the last two years of its life that government was largely pre-occupied with wider constitutional issues that had little or no part in any special agreement with the unions.[5]

The CBI's influence on the government was probably far greater than might have been expected from the terms of the 'social contract' and was shown in modifications to the 'industrial strategy' and in the Industry Act 1975, as well as later in the government's agreement to temper the effects of its price code after 1976. Largely through the personal influence of certain individual union leaders, in particular that of Mr Jack Jones, the unions were, however, successfully persuaded to co-operate with a series of temporary incomes policies between 1975 and 1978. These policies were settled in meetings between Cabinet ministers and the 'Neddy Six' (Stewart, 1977; Elliott, 1978; Barnes and Reid, 1980). Eventually, however, vital changes in union leadership (including the retirement of Mr Jones), and the eruption in the winter of 1978–79 of what had long been suspected as widespread rank-and-file dissatisfaction with the TUC's previous role in supporting pay policy, presented Mr Callaghan's Government with a new crisis of industrial relations in which union co-operation was not forthcoming. By the time 'moderate' union leaders had intervened to restore something of the TUC's intermediary role, and the government had agreed to moderate its five per cent pay norm and consider special exceptions in the public sector, this particular 'winter of discontent' had, like its forerunners, already weakened the government's fragile authority too far. Perhaps significantly, however, the government fell in the Commons on the first motion of confidence to have been lost by a government for over a hundred years.

The politics of tripartism

The search for consensus by both tripartite approaches considered in this chapter has confronted problems of a political nature similar to those met by attempts at devolution and technocracy considered in previous chapters. Survival of any tripartite arrangement has meant not being too closely identified with controversial policies or too much implicated in major policy decisions. At the same time, no government has found it possible to manage the economy without some sort of broad agreement with representatives of industry.

Tripartite arrangements short of an actual sharing of responsibility for management of the economy have proved difficult to develop, not only because the relationship between public responsibility and private participation is hard to work, but also because suspicions on all sides make it impossible to detach particular measures from party-political

[5] These were direct elections to the European Parliament and devolution to Scotland and Wales.

conflict. We have yet to see whether, even if these problems could be overcome, tripartite arrangements of any kind would go far towards a solution on their own.

Tripartism, as an attempt to give the CBI and TUC a share in the responsibility of government has become discredited. It has played no part since the election of 1979 in the government's actual or intended approaches to economic policy. Although vastly reduced in their influence on all aspects of government, meetings with CBI and even TUC representatives continue, in NEDC and on the usual, more informal, direct basis. Whether the present government is right in its approach, and can sustain it, there are certainly fundamental limitations to the tripartite approach. The main reasons can be briefly summarised.

Economic interests are not so easily aggregated and organised as the assumptions of tripartism seem to require. Industry is, for one thing, in reality highly diversified. There are quite natural differences of perspectives and interest, not only between employers and labour, but also among other groups. There are differences among sectors, industries and firms as well. The existence of formal organisations claiming to speak for whole categories of industrial interests is not in itself an indication of true uniformity, or even identity of interest. It is, of course, true that there are vital matters of general concern, where differences may be apparent rather than real, and where not to emphasise the common ground can be economically damaging. But divergent needs have also to be recognised and it may be illusory to think that they can be satisfied simply by summing them together in a formal structure of leadership blessed by government acceptance.

On the side of organisations representing industry, shared responsibility too often means a sacrifice of objectives that are vital to the organisation's own relationship with its members. There are always contrary tendencies at work in such intermediary organisations, and we shall discuss these at greater length in Part Three. While industrial partners to tripartism certainly see advantages to be gained from public intervention at their own behest, nevertheless, as essentially private bodies, with special interests to protect, they are fundamentally suspicious of state interference. That is as true for the trade union movement, with its general preference for 'free' collective bargaining, as it is for organisations representing employers, with their general preference for free enterprise. The national leaderships will always tend to be looking over their shoulders to see whether their members do genuinely want them to enter so far into the government's embrace.

However, on the side of government, sharing responsibility is worthwhile only if the industrial organisations involved are sufficiently integrated and 'authentic' to deliver their side of any agreement. The emergence of almost corporate structures like the CBI and TUC was an essential condition of attempting tripartite approaches and, as we have seen, owed a good deal to deliberate encouragement by government itself. But the problem is that the public interest as conceived by CBI and TUC leaders may still not be inclusive enough. The centralisation of such bodies may even be a disadvantage. Already there are signs that 'tripartism' can be actually schismatic, by creating greater distance between national representatives (who get more involved in government) and their respective 'constituencies', as may be suggested by the various 'rebellions' in the CBI during the 1970s (Grant and Marsh, 1977; Smith, 1979; Middlemas, 1979) and by the survival of a highly independent shop-stewards' movement in the trade unions (Crouch, 1978; Fox, 1978; Taylor, 1978). Tripartism may also be too exclusive, by weakening the voice of what are increasingly claimed as other interests no less vital to industry such as professional management, consumers and financial interests.

A crucial problem in Britain, however, has been the patent imbalance in favour of the political and economic influence of one organised industrial interest, the trade unions. The chief aim of consensus-building, over the last twenty years at least, has been that of obtaining the consent of the trade union movement to wage restraint and its discipline in preserving industrial peace. Whether or not that emphasis has been the right one, and self-restraint does seem to have worked for certain periods in bringing down the rate of inflation – sometimes substantially as after 1975 – the fact is that three recent governments (in 1969, 1974 and 1979) are widely regarded as having fallen mainly as a result of industrial anarchy.

The problem is compounded by the differing political relationships of organised labour and business. The trade unions exercise political influence directly not only upon Labour governments, but also of course *within* the Labour Party, while their relations with the Conservative Party have been increasingly antipathetic. Private employers continue, on the whole, to be suspicious of the intentions of the Labour Party but their relationship to the Conservatives has never been as close as that of the unions with the Labour Party and seems even to have declined (Grant, 1980). The only real experience of shared responsibility has been the short-lived 'social contract' between the Labour Government and the TUC.

As practiced in Britain, tripartism in the form of shared responsibility has been attempted largely as a means of responding to the economic power of industrial organisations. The result has made only a limited contribution to achieving genuine consensus. The instability of such arrangements lies partly in the excessive expectations that are bred on all sides.

The responsibilities of government are so broad and complex that, in spite of the apparent licence granted to a party in office, they are not available for sharing with some private interest, however numerous its membership might be and whatever its potential economic power. It is significant that what tied the hands of the Labour Government after 1975 was not only the need to respect undertakings to the IMF, but also its lack of a stable majority in the House of Commons. But even when, as is normal, a government has such a majority, it cannot usually continue to satisfy the demands of a particular interest while respecting also the more general needs of economic policy. On the other hand, confrontation, however sturdy, is no alternative. The Heath Government's failure went deep into the consciousness of the Conservative Party, so that, at the time of writing, another Conservative Government cannot risk the wholesale opposition of powerful groups of workers like the coalminers.

One conclusion is that the problem is not the vulnerability of governments, but the illusion that an electoral mandate by itself gives them some special strength, whether to concede or resist group demands. The essence of politics in a collectivist age is that 'if a "strong" party can in this way more effectively resist group demands, so also it can more effectively yield to them' (Beer, 1965, p. 351).

In Part Three we shall reflect on the possibility that, if no such illusions attached to the Executive – if governments were less confident about their ability or authority to implement party programmes – then the temptation for economically powerful groups, and the threat they present, might be far less.

9 Industrial Strategy and Participation

Two requisites of governing by consensus in economic affairs seem to be, first, that the consultative relationship between government and industry should be given a framework of reasonably clear objectives to which government itself is willing and able to conform, and, secondly, that it should include an adequately authentic representation of those engaged in industry.

The first requisite might be subsumed under the general notion of planning, though we have seen how there is no stable definition of planning in British government. After 1966 the term 'strategy' became the more accepted way of referring to governments' efforts to take a longer-term, more systematic approach to managing the economy for general ends, whether the emphasis was on management of the public sector or more widely on economic activity in the private sector as well (Smith 1979). In this chapter we shall look more closely at such efforts and the limitations they have encountered.

The second requisite has been recognised in efforts to design both industrial representation and public intervention so that they come nearer to the point of operational decisions in industry. These efforts have led to the third form of tripartite participation mentioned in the previous chapter, that of industrial representatives in the more specialised work carried on under the aegis of NEDC. There is also a much wider question of participation that has been typical in the 1970s, including different approaches to the idea of 'industrial democracy'. We shall not, however, digress very far into that question, but will continue to focus on the problems of consensus at the level of central government.

The vicissitudes of planning
We saw in Part One how economic planning has been in and out of fashion as a feature of the government/industry relationship and may anyway have a whole variety of meanings ranging from extensive physical regulation and control of the economy (as attempted during the war years) to a mere technique of administration. While political factors have invariably disrupted any particular approach to planning, planning itself has reflected particular kinds of political outlook and intention (Smith, 1979). There is now a substantial literature on the history of different approaches to planning in Britain (Denton et al,

1968; Brittan, 1971; Leruez, 1975; Shanks, 1977; Budd, 1978; Smith, 1979). Few would disagree with the conclusion of one foreign student of planning in Britain that it 'has never been more that a succession of isolated efforts which have led to nothing and which have been temporary expedients rather that thoroughgoing reforms' (Leruez 1975 p. 279).

The apparent demise of planning during roughly the last fifteen years follows a quite remarkable revival of interest in the early 1960s. The particular approach to indicative planning adopted then, however, was largely discredited by the collapse of the Labour Government's National Plan after 1966. The immediate cause was the government's decision in July 1966 to take a series of short-term measures to protect the balance of payments and the pound sterling; this decision spelt defeat for those in the Cabinet and elsewhere associated with the commitment to growth 'targets'. In one sense, however, the government had never been fully committed and had relied on a relationship of 'creative tension' between the Treasury and the Department of Economic Affairs. Economic policy still had to respond to contingencies and was a result of both internal and external tensions; indeed, the policy of supporting the value of the pound sterling was itself abandoned by the devaluation of November 1967.

In any event the approach to planning for growth that had been adopted in 1964 was subject to criticism both for being too narrow in conception and too naive and ambitious in execution. In both senses too much reliance was placed on a quantitative 'target' of national economic growth. Even had the target chosen proved more realistic, it would still have been necessary for the government to do more in the way of public intervention and the 'concertation' of industry to make the exercise worthwhile. On the other hand, the adventure illustrated the dangers of such 'target-setting' by public authorities. The real meaning and value of forecasts of growth was never clear to industry. Many feel that the main effect of 'targetry' was simply to encourage over-investment, especially in the public sector. The last act of the DEA was to publish not a revised plan but a 'planning document' in 1969, setting out alternative projections of growth based on different assumptions and indicating not some official forecast or objective, but rather a framework for government/industry consultation through the procedures of NEDC.

Of the new agencies and procedures of economic policy introduced at the time of the 'conversion to planning', those which played the most important role in the Labour Government's approach were the ones associated with prices and incomes policy. Indeed, central guidance on general increases in money incomes has subsequently come to be seen as a far more vital form of planning that the setting of growth 'targets' for the economy as a whole. It has been widely supported on two main grounds: the need to contain inflation and the need to restrain the monopoly power of organised groups to claim increases in rewards at the expense of the less privileged.

Differences about the causes of inflation, however, have continued to make general agreement on the appropriate measures to control inflation, elusive. Different technical diagnoses have been turned into prescriptions mainly thanks to special influences at the time. If anything, there has been a tendency for political attitudes, based to a greater or less extent on scientific judgement, to diverge. A range of approaches to central regulation of prices and incomes has been tried over the last twenty years by the same and by different governments and invariably as a response to some economic contingency rather that as a planned approach. Between 1970 and 1972, and since 1979, Conservative Governments abandoned any attempt at such policies for the economy as a whole, preferring to rely on direct restraint of the public sector (at the expense of the special political and administrative problems thereby raised), accompanied since 1979 by deflationary monetary measures. In practice, incomes policies have suffered from some of the limitations of public 'target-setting' in general, in that officially established 'norms' or 'guidelines', whatever their true intent, tend to be misinterpreted: 'pay norms' being regarded as a minimum in actual pay bargaining in the country. Moreover, short-term policies have tended to result in 'wages explosions' when for political or other reasons they have been terminated. The trade union movement itself, while at periods it has proved willing and able to achieve 'self-restraint', has come to be suspicious of incomes policies and extremely reluctant to forego its general commitment to 'free' collective bargaining, (Leruez, 1975; Stewart, 1977; Budd, 1978; Elliott, 1978).

Effective planning in this respect, therefore, seems to have required a more lasting consensus than has been available in British experience (Caves and Krause, 1980). There are also, of course, instrumental difficulties, not least the problem that generalised guidance fails to take account of the different patterns of demand and supply in particular industries and sectors and, even if followed, may therefore contribute to economic inefficiency. There is, moreover, the wider problem of differential rewards to which no satisfactory solution by means of centralised decision-making seems to be available.

On the other hand, whatever the status of planning in nominal or real terms, all governments have retained the elements of an industrial policy, in the sense of measures of direct intervention that may or may not be treated as part of any concerted or systematic approach. The prominence and the expectations attached to such policy have varied a great deal, and traditional concerns such as protection of domestic industry or social policy have been mixed with more highly wrought intentions to do with technological change and economic efficiency. It is difficult to discern any consistent pattern, unless it be that of successive and cumulative attempts to rescue failing business undertakings or to support prestige projects like Concorde. The influence of political pressures and of sustained lobbying by organised groups, as well as the inability of the departments concerned to fashion any longer term approach, seem to have been the main determinants in practice (Dell, 1973; Young, 1974; Hayward and Watson, 1975). On the whole, financial assistance to industry seems to have been directed mainly at 'sectional income maintenance' rather than at other protectionist ends such as defence of 'infant industries' or deliberate compensation for unfavourable terms of trade (Corden and Fels, 1976).

The approach to selective intervention has also been criticised for excessive reliance on financial kinds of support and inadequate concern with the real needs and problems of adaptation in the industries and firms affected. 'The injection of public funds into a private company', in other words, 'solves nothing by itself' (Young, 1974, p. 201). Nor, it might be added, does public ownership necessarily make past problems easier to resolve or set new managers and the public service itself tasks that they are equipped to exercise. One complaint about intervention during the 1960s and early 1970s was that the confusion of motives and the consequent inability to measure results were made worse by difficulties of holding ministers accountable for decisions and a lack of openness both about reasons for intervention and the performance of undertakings affected. Another was that technical or other non-commercial bases of judgement were insufficient on their own, while the transfer of responsibility to public boards, civil servants or special experts might actually be counter-productive if it devalued, and detracted from, the vital contribution of industrial managers themselves. Complaints such as these generally implied a failure of planning: they suggested that government was not questioning rigorously enough its own motives and methods, while it was also not taking sufficient account of the view from the operating level. However, to suggest that an answer lay in an improvement of planning would have been considered tendentious in the early 1970s.

'Industrial strategy', 1975

During its years of opposition from 1970 to 1974, however, the Labour Party worked on a re-appraisal of planning, an exercise in which the trade unions were closely involved. A new body of doctrine and set of proposals on this subject formed part of the 'social contract' to which the Labour Governments returned in 1974 were publicly committed. The new approach was, however, essentially party-political in its initial conception and aims. Except for trade unionists, representatives of industry were not consulted (deliberately so, it seems) while the influence of 'technocratic' policy advisers within the Party's own channels was strongly evident (Hatfield, 1978). Labour's traditional preoccupation with public ownership played a central part and at one stage it had seemed that the party would go to the electorate with an explicit commitment to nationalise 100 named firms. It was also intended to give trade union representatives a preponderant role in planning.

Earlier attempts at planning were regarded as inadequate. A new concept of 'mesoeconomic planning' was suggested, which would require government to formulate and establish strategies for different sectors and industries. The strategies would be implemented by means of 'planning agreements' reached with all individual firms in the private sector above a certain size in terms of turnover, as well as by means of control of the existing public sector supplemented by a substantial extension of public ownership. Planning agreements themselves would be backed up by the possibility of public ownership and would form the basis of any public assistance to the undertaking concerned. Agreements would be reached after consultation with management, but government would have compulsory powers to obtain information from private firms. What seems to have been envisaged in theory was a wholesale transfer to government of responsibility for strategic decisions in industry, both public and private, leaving to management itself discretion over only tactical matters (Holland, 1975).

What finally emerged as the government's own approach was nothing so egregious. What was presented, after consultation with the CBI and other industrial interests was described as an 'industrial strategy'. Like most government initiatives in economic policy during the last twenty years the name was different from what was proposed. The proposals were set out in two White Papers the second of which explained that:

> 'It is not a strategy but a programme for developing a strategy which will place responsibility on Government, on unions and on management for improving our industrial performance' (Cmnd 6315).

References to new public ownership were absent from this second White Paper, though some limited extension of public ownership was already under way. The second White Paper had originally been produced, in fact, as a goverment paper before NEDC and was intended to reflect the result of initial discussions of industrial policy in that body. The emphasis by this stage was firmly on the search for consensus:

> 'Above all, we must get away from policies of confrontation, and work together in the national interest towards agreed objectives' (Cmnd 6315).

The government declared an overall priority of growth, to be achieved mainly by a re-structuring of industry and improvements in efficiency, but placed responsibility on itself for adequately co-ordinating its own economic and social policies to that end, and on employers and unions for taking advantage, with the help of government initiative, of opportunities for increased productivity.

The 'strategy' was to be developed with the help of three sets of instruments that the Labour Government inherited from previous governments and two that it created by the Industry Act of 1975. The primary instrument for involving management and unions at different levels was to be the NEDC, supplemented by extensions to its substructure of tripartite committees. Manpower policy would be developed with the help of the Manpower Services Commission and its agencies. That same government's Industry Act 1972 provided most of the means of financial assistance that were to be used. New measures were the institution of planning agreements and the creation of the National Enterprise Board.

Planning agreements: the role of the Department of Industry

Any notion of compulsory planning agreements with private companies was rejected, but the aim was to give an agreement 'sufficient recognition by statute to enable the company concerned to rely on assistance promised under it' (Cmnd 5710). The Industry Act 1975 provided the Secretary of State for Industry with reserve powers to require companies to produce information considered necessary for formulating or maintaining a planning agreement. Trade unions were not to be formal parties to a planning agreement, but companies would be expected to ensure 'close consultation' between management and unions. In fact, the private sector, represented through the CBI, was generally unfavourable to the idea of planning agreements and only one was ever formally reached, with the then Chrysler motor manufacturing company in 1977, which was in receipt of substantial public financial assistance (Budd, 1978).

One consequence of the Labour government's approach, however, was a direct relationship between the Department of Industry and private firms, both in terms of financial assistance of various kinds and of largely informal, but increasingly regular consultations. Two continuing problems of the government/industry relationship remained; first, that of ensuring adequate accountability for decisions to intervene and second, that of following up the results of intervention.

By the fall of the Callaghan Government in 1979 more that 100 firms were estimated to be holding informal 'planning discussions' with the Department. But it remains unclear exactly how the role of public administrators in such a relationship is expected to help undertakings take better advantage of competitive opportunities at home or abroad, or to adapt to technological change. Meanwhile, in spite of the return of a Conservative Government with a pronounced 'philosophy' sceptical of this kind of public intervention, the growth of unemployment and other effects of the recession have meant that government aid has to a large extent continued, though seemingly still mainly on an *ad hoc* basis.

The National Enterprise Board: new approaches to public enterprise
Although its contribution may not have been particularly large in relation to public intervention as a whole, the National Enterprise Board did offer a means of managing selective intervention in a way less closely identified with the political elements in industrial policy and more influenced by commercial experience and attitudes. By 1979, it held investments in 55 companies accounting for a total turnover of £4 billion and 250,000 employees. These included, as we have seen, some of the legacy of previous rescue operations undertaken by government departments, and in terms of size such undertakings accounted for the bulk of the NEB's interests. However, the Board set out with commercial objectives, seeking to earn a rate of return on its assets and to limit its participation in individual concerns, as far as possible. New asquisitions were made only after consultation, and with the consent, of the undertakings concerned. The Board detached itself from the whole issue of planning agreements. By these means it succeeded in dispelling (as the IRC had done before it) much suspicion in the CBI and the City of London, while not falling foul of the government that had created it. It also retained its tripartite membership – four of the eleven part-time members of the Board were trade union representatives.

The NEB undoubtedly did much to prove the value of a state holding company as an alternative to direct ministerial responsibility for managing industrial holdings. It could claim much of the credit for improving British Leyland's commercial prospects and for the successful appointment of Sir Michael Edwardes as that company's chairman. The existing Board were, therefore, not suprisingly disturbed by the intervention of the new Secretary of State, Sir Keith

Joseph, in 1979 who requested the NEB to dispose of certain of its assets and to transfer responsibility for Rolls Royce to the Department of Industry. Following the resignation of that Board, trade union members have not been replaced. The change of approach was indicated in the new Board's annual report in 1980:

'The NEB is to have the function of disposing of assets in order to increase private sector involvement wherever possible. The notion that the NEB can be a major instrument of industrial re-organisation and rationalisation has gone.'

Although the new government increased the NEB's borrowing powers for 1980–81, having reduced them for the previous year, it would seem that yet again the problem of adequately assessing the contribution of such an agency is confounded by a strange combination of political dogma and inconsistency.

The notion that an industrial public corporation should be able to take a more flexible approach to its role by, for example, acquiring, and disposing of, assets in response to particular market circumstances as well as in the light of its public obligations, and mixing public with private sources of capital, would seem to offer some way to a more decentralised and possibly more efficient form of public intervention. Ironically, however, it is Conservative Governments that have been more inclined, if at all, to consider changes in such a direction for established nationalised industries, as may be suggested in recent steps since 1979 towards re-organisation, 'privatisation' and wider borrowing powers. Such measures have been obstructed, however, by the present government's concern to restrict the financial activities of the public corporations in the interests of monetary policy. And they tend to be deeply suspected and opposed by the Labour Party and the TUC as doctrinaire attempts to restore private enterprise and undermine the public sector.

Tripartite agencies

Less vulnerable to political allusions and to political fashion are various specialised public agencies recently created for administering, and advising on, aspects of manpower and employment policy and intervention in industrial disputes. These agencies have resulted from attempts to devolve functions from the Department of Employment, but have been regarded as a significant new experiment with the use of tripartite methods. Although staffed by civil servants, the agencies are placed under commissions on which employers' organisations and trade unions are directly represented.

The Manpower Services Commission (MSC) resulted from the Conservative Government's Employment and Training Act 1973 and took charge of a range of services, some of which were detached from the Department of Employment by the same Act and others set up subsequently, most notably the Job Creation Programme introduced by the Labour Government in October 1975. The Commission is appointed by the Secretary of State for Employment to include three nominees each from the CBI and the TUC, two representatives of local authorities and one of the education profession, with a chairman, who in April 1976 was appointed from the sphere of business. The Commission is given wide statutory discretion in the field of manpower policy but required to obtain the Secretary of State's approval for its plans and made subject to directions from the Secretary of State; it is financed from the Department's own vote, but is given substantial discretion in disposing of the funds available to it. The services for which it is responsible are administered by a network of largely decentralised regional bodies, with the help of local businessmen, trade unionists, local authority representatives and educationalists; it draws widely on advice from outside bodies.

The MSC has greatly expanded the services available for improving labour mobility and industrial training, and its expenditure rose from £125·4 million in 1974–75 to £643 million in 1978–79. It is also credited with successful modernisation of some traditional services as in the transformation of labour exchanges into 'jobcentres' (Ridley, 1980). Political interest in its work has been considerable, but has been largely positive, given the popularity throughout its life of measures to deal with unemployment. In this particular respect, devolution of responsibility for the services concerned has probably made no difference to the concern of ministers.

'One important factor in the expansion of MSC's activities has been its position as a favoured child of ministers, comparable perhaps to education in the 1960s. The MSC was exempted almost entirely from successive rounds of expenditure cuts between 1975 and 1979. In these circumstances the Treasury has been unable to exercise its customary role of restraint' (Howells, 1980, p. 319).

The gains in terms of administrative efficiency and professionalism are more difficult to assess. It is suggested that the Commission itself and other tripartite bodies at regional levels have only limited control over the administration of services in practice (Howells, 1980). The Department of Employment's own continuing task of assessing the value of services and deciding how resources should be allocated to this sector has, on the other hand, become more complicated. Similar problems arise as with devolution to agencies in general, and political pressure from individual MPs and others and the demands of interest groups still have to be weighed against a wider view of the public interest.

Often pressure for expanding services has come from ministers, while the MSC itself has tended actually to underspend the resources available to it. It is also difficult to tell what real difference the tripartite approach makes. Local industrialists do not have much time to devote to the work of regionalised services (Ridley, 1980). It may be that the main effect has been simply to give greater scope to the public officials concerned. Moreover, the effects of political change cannot be entirely removed: the Conservative Government after 1979 has cut MSC's funding, while the TUC has taken a less co-operative attitude in protest at that government's general economic policies.

The Labour Government created in 1974–75 as part of the 'social contract' the Health and Safety Commission, the Equal Opportunities Commission and the Advisory, Conciliation and Arbitration Service (ACAS) on a similar devolved, tripartite basis. ACAS has taken over and extended some of the Department of Employment's former responsibilities for improving industrial relations. It has become increasingly difficult for the Department to exercise these responsibilities, inherited from the Ministry of Labour, as it has become identified with government policies for wage restraint. ACAS was seen, therefore, as a means not only of devolving functions, but also of restoring the voluntary element that had previously been so important in the conduct of industrial relations in Britain (Elliott, 1978). It is accordingly more independent of the Secretary of State than is the MSC and its enabling statute expressly excludes ministerial directions (though it is still ultimately answerable through the Secretary of State to Parliament and is financed from the Exchequer).

The Council responsible for ACAS has considerably expanded the conciliation services practised earlier by the Department, and has had a good deal of success in this function. It soon found itself in some difficulties when the Labour Government resorted to incomes policies and expected its own pay norms to take precedence in settlement of industrial disputes. But the Council (made up of three trade unionists, three employers, three academics and an independent chairman) has stalwartly defended its autonomy (Tyrrell, 1980).

Although representative of employers and labour on its governing body are simply nominees rather than delegates, and are balanced by government representatives and independent experts, the TUC has had considerable influence on the role of ACAS. This has led to controversy, particularly over the latter's functions in settling recognition disputes between unions, and also to complaints by employers about the approach to conciliation and arbitration of industrial disputes. Doubts have also been expressed about the body's answerability to Parliament. The support of the Labour ministers concerned was very important to ACAS and it tended to be identified with that government's policies. However, it has survived the change of government in 1979.

Industrial participation through tripartite committees

The Labour Government's industrial policies also led to a significant extension of the functions and the machinery of NEDC and NEDO. The general aim was to extend the tripartite approach further towards the operating level in industry and, at the same time, to increase the direct participation of industrial representatives.

In fact, the 'industrial strategy' injected new life into NEDC's existing network of Economic Development Committees (EDCs). The EDCs, as described in Chapter 6, were first set up in the early 1960s and were used at the time of the preparation of the National Plan for the refinement of industrial forecasts and information for the purpose of the general plan (Fraser, 1967). About 25 of them continued to operate after the demise of the Plan, in spite of the lack of any real planning initiatives from government, often taking their own initiative in discussing proposals for re-organisations or rationalisation of productive activity in the sector or sectors within their remit and producing in some instances voluntary agreement on action by the industries concerned; 19 EDCs survived to 1974 (Shanks, 1977). Although departmental officials participated (mostly from the DEA or the Ministry of Technology and later from the Department of Trade and Industry), they operated for the most part independently of government, relying largely not only on NEDO but also on the support of trade associations (Leruez, 1975).

After discussion in NEDC of the Labour Government's 'industrial strategy' proposals it was decided to supplement the remaining EDCs with a series of 'sector working parties' for manufacturing industry, of which 39 were eventually set up by the end of 1978. At the same time, the government undertook to show a much more positive attitude than its predecessors by helping to create and maintain a framework for this kind of tripartite activity and by establishing a set of priorities for industrial development that it would respect itself and support where necessary with direct intervention. A fixed timetable was laid down for reviewing the results of the new EDC and working party inquiries. However, as we have already seen, the term 'strategy' was a misnomer at the time it was first officially used:

> 'The initiative did not consist in proposing a strategy to the NEDC but rather in suggesting the adoption of a process from which the elements of an agreed strategy could emerge' (Lord, 1976, pp. 10–11).

The tripartite machinery was now expected to work essentially upwards rather than downwards and to provide more authentic intelligence about the operating problems of industry. It was hoped particularly to facilitate the participation of trade unionists, and also to respond to the criticisms of 'the apparent lack of any real link between the development of sector policies and the conduct of overall economic policy', (TUC, 1977), on the one hand, and the failure to relate sector policies to the decisions of individual undertakings, on the other.

The disaggregated work of analysis sector-by-sector was to be given overall direction and coherence mainly by means of NEDC and NEDO. Although originally intended by the government to be the means of reaching voluntary planning agreements, the new machinery in practice successfully detached itself from the wider, and politically controversial, aspects of the government's policies. By 1979, about 1,000 people were involved in tripartite committees of one kind or another and they covered about 40 per cent of manufacturing output and 45 per cent of employment. In fact, the machinery largely survived the return of the Conservative Government in 1979, only nine former sector working parties being discontinued following a further review of their activity. Both the NEDC and NEDO collectively, and the CBI and TUC individually, are committed to the enterprise and to its continuation. In other words, this form of industrial participation through tripartism, in terms of survival at least, seems to have proved highly successful. Although we cannot offer here any assessment of its real contribution to economic performance, certain features of this kind of tripartite approach are clearly of longer-term institutional significance.

First, although they have no executive powers, these voluntary bodies represent in some ways a form of industrial 'self-government'. Most of their members are nominated, mainly by trade unions and trade associations, from the industries concerned and the chairman is a businessman or trade unionist from outside the sector under review.

The aim is as far as possible to get 'grass-roots' participation, so that those actively engaged in industry can view the decisions of individual undertakings against a wider background of the problems and prospects of the sector concerned and of the possibilities for growth. Recommendations are expected to be made directly to firms as well as to government departments, so that an emphasis is placed on the 'self-referring' results of inquiries. The main subjects treated in this way have been prospects for domestic and international market shares, problems in the relations between suppliers and consumers, special 'bottlenecks' or shortages such as problems of adaptation in labour markets, the reasons for particular failures in profitability and means of making more productive use of resources (Metcalf and McQuillan, 1979).

Secondly, although it does not replace the normal relationships based on sponsoring departments, the machinery helps to decentralise the government/industry relationship. Departments through their representatives on tripartite committees, have better access to information about the attitudes and circumstances of those directly engaged in industry, thereby supplementing, or perhaps even circuiting, intermediary organisations with their tendency to take up fixed attitudes at national level, often with political overtones. The aim is also to bring a greater element of 'shopfloor reality' into decisions at the level of industries and sectors. The impression is that trade union participation has been increased compared with the earlier experience of EDCs.

A third contribution that follows from the second is that this tripartite approach helps to relieve the participants and their discussions of posturing and dissension of a more or less political kind. The participants are there not to bargain or negotiate either with each other or with government. Above all, they are not seen essentially as the spokesmen of particular economic and social interests, as is often the case even in NEDC. It may also be said that their work can to a large extent be considered relevant whatever the personalities, policies and predilections of the government of the day. The role of NEDO in servicing the committees, and that of the NEDO official representing the Director-General in each committee, is clearly of vital importance in this respect, as is the related fact that the committees depend on NEDC and not directly on a government department.

It is to be hoped that before long a comprehensive study will be made of precisely how the machinery of tripartite committees has functioned especially since 1975. Without such a study it is impossible to assess not only its effects on economic performance, if these can be measured at all, but also its contribution in the three ways we have just considered. Meanwhile, we are left with a number of largely unanswered questions about the true nature of this kind of tripartite approach.

First of all, there is the question whether 'self-government' is the means most likely to produce any necessary changes, especially when these are uncomfortable for the interests directly concerned. What guarantees are there that agreements reached through tripartite committees will not simply turn out to be aimed at avoiding competitive influences and at protecting restrictive practices and inefficiency? One answer clearly is to point to the participation of NEDO and of departmental representatives. Moreover, the companies and other undertakings involved still have to operate within the terms of public legislation and policy on competition. The committees themselves lack any formal powers, but they can act as broadly-based pressure groups, especially in relation to government departments and probably derive much of their significance for their industrial participants from this role. For the most part, it is claimed that the kind of voluntary agreements they reach are designed to anticipate market forces, rather than to obstruct them, and to unblock restrictions to more efficient and productive methods. At the end of the day, however, 'self-government' must presumably be conditional on some form of centralised and public initiative and control, however remote for much of the time.

There also seem to be pronounced limits to the extent of decentralisation that is considered possible or desirable. There is a strong temptation to make direct recommendations to government, especially in view of the latter's functions as a source of financial support for industry. When resorting to subsidy of one kind or another public intervention may hamper as much as help an industrial undertaking's attempts to re-adapt or re-organise itself. Moreover, it is difficult to imagine the proceedings of tripartite committees not leading quite often to arguments in favour of special tax concessions or even tariff and other forms of protection from international competition. Not only is there the risk of reverting to such solutions as an alternative to some form of self-regulation, but there is also the need for government to be satisfied that claims for special help are justified and to weigh them against other policy needs and objectives. In fact, elaborate arrangements for co-ordination do exist, not only through NEDO itself, which is responsible for reviewing the work of tripartite committees and deciding whether to propose the discontinuation of some bodies or the setting up of new ones, but also through a steering committee based on the Treasury. The role of the NEDC itself, however, seems to be problematical. Although the work of the tripartite committees is regularly brought to its attention, the Council is usually interested in wider questions of economic policy and tends to lack the specialised competence and knowledge to deal very effectively with the issues raised by tripartite committees.

Finally, while such tripartite discussions may be sufficiently detached to concentrate on issues of business rather than politics, it could well be at the expense of restricting the agenda. A number of questions dealing with productivity, with labour relations and with management practices might be considered highly relevant to economic development in the sectors concerned, but they are excluded either by the reluctance of one of the parties to discuss them or by a general fear of entering too controversial ground.

The TUC showed a very positive attitude to the new framework and its extended machinery (which came partly, after all, from the 'social contract'). It has provided substantial supporting services in the form of special conferences, publications and a central machinery of its own for co-ordinating the work of trade unionists on different committees.

But trade unionists have continued to complain about the lack of sufficient impact on government policy and the irrelevance of much of the work for the interests of their members at industry and plant level. Both they and other participants question how far such activity can be worthwhile without positive government intervention and without changes that depend in the last resort on decisions taken by businessmen and industrial managers. Even the amount of support available for the work of committees itself, especially in terms of finance, depends ultimately on the policies of the government of the day.

Perhaps, however, the most significant question of all, which detailed research into the results of tripartite committees could illuminate but not altogether answer, is how far any real difference has been made to the way governments make policy affecting industry or to the effect of social and political divisions on the way industry seeks to resolve its own problems. The usual defence of the system of tripartite co-operation under NEDC is to stress its serious and on the whole, productive approach to an essentially modest set of objectives. However, there are those who will find its contribution inadequate without a far more positive and comprehensive commitment on the part of government to industrial development. And there are those who will say that it does not on its own do much to resolve the problems of economic power as an obstacle to achieving a wider consensus on the crucial questions of economic policy affecting industry. Such reactions as these bring us back to the issues that emerge from the central theme of this present study.

Industrial democracy
The extension of tripartite activities in 1975 was encouraged out of a general concern to widen industrial participation. The aim has not been only to disburden government departments or provide them with better advice for what they wish to do, but also deliberately to respond to demands for greater 'industrial democracy' in a broader sense, especially in order to interest trade unionists in something other than collective bargaining and to do so below the level of 'tripartism' among the TUC, CBI and central government.

In fact, 'industrial democracy' was one of the general aims of the 'social contract' between the Labour Party and the TUC and, among other things, this led to the appointment of the Bullock Committee, which made a series of recommendations in 1977 for legislation to require greater employee participation in the management of firms (Cmnd 6706). The Labour Government's own approach was finally rather lukewarm and very modest proposals were made in a White Paper on *Industrial Democracy* (Cmnd. 7231) in 1978.

But disillusionment with the results of both public intervention and of 'tripartism' at national level has turned the attention of a number of people to the possibilities of improving industrial relations by requiring changes directly at the level of the individual undertaking. In other words, the essential problems of Britain's economic performance can be seen as demanding an approach that works from the shopfloor rather than downwards from government (Jay, 1976; Fox, 1978; Radice, 1979). Such a perspective may be recommended both to highlight the need for reforms in management and in industrial relations, and to shift attention from the divisive posturing of national organisations and their spokesmen. In other words, 'industrial democracy' can be seen as a kind of response to the central problems identified in this book and as another approach to consensus. There are, however, many different varieties of proposal. The term 'industrial democracy' itself can be misleading and deserves much closer analysis. It could be argued that it takes an essentially political concept (democracy) entirely out of context by applying it to activities that are essentially concerned with profitability and productiveness, or at best an efficient allocation of resources (and in this way it may be no less confusing than the term 'social justice') (Plamenatz, 1973). On the other hand, as this study has tended to show, relationships in industry do seem to have inescapably political associations, not only because of the interdependence between government and industry, but also becausee of the power of industrial organisations.

Indeed, it could be argued that this book has approached its subject entirely the wrong way around. Instead of assuming a government/industry relationship and then examining the challenge it offers to representative institutions, perhaps we should have started from the relationships that already exist within industry, and then traced the influence they have on economic decisions and ultimately on economic activity as a whole, which is certainly one way of recognising the political significance of economic power. The search for consensus that we have been examining here may be said to have been doomed to failure because it took the wrong point of departure and may, therefore, have itself created the problems it set out to solve.

We shall leave examination of the merits of such procedures as employee participation and co-ownership, and of such structures as workers' co-operatives to studies directly concerned with management and industrial relations. Whatever the merits may be (from the point of view of economic efficiency, social welfare or even that of representative democracy) we shall stick to our approach of treating the problem of democracy in relation to industry as one of political representation in relation to government. That such an approach is justified (whatever the separate contribution of studies of 'industrial democracy') is suggested by the fact that different approaches to 'industrial democracy' seem themselves unable to avoid major problems of the government/industry relationship that we have been examining here. A few examples will serve illustrate that point.

One approach to the whole question of industrial strategy favoured recently on the left of the Labour Party has tended to see some form of 'industrial democracy' as a way round the problem of increasing state intervention. A continuing problem for socialists when proposing greater functions for government is that one consequence, both in theory and practice, would be an increase in the size and strength of a central state bureaucracy. Neither with experience of national planning nor with that of the running of nationalised industries has it been easy to show what improvement is made, if any, in the influence or status of consumers, workers and so on. Much recent policy making in the Labour Party has sought to deal with this problem by proposing to involve the trade unions much more closely both in planning and in the operation of individual enterprises – whether public or private – than in earlier Labour policies or measures. The various proposals for giving trade unionists greater influence by means of planning agreements, by representation on the NEB and other public agencies and through NEDC tripartite committees all represent hybrid results of the same line of thinking. It sometimes seems, indeed, in the literature of Labour polemicists that what is envisaged is a general shift of power, designed not only to reduce the influence of capital but also that of bureaucracy. And the recipients of that power are seen as the trade unions (Holland, 1975, 1978). In other words, the aim is to benefit a particular sectional group, albeit one with close political connections. But, while that helps to simplify the argument (which becomes a claim on behalf of a private interest, the trade unions) it does not contribute much to, even if it recognises, the problem of economic power and its political consequences with which we have been concerned here. (It would simply shift the power, to use its own terms, from one organised interest or 'class' to another.)

An example of a very different approach, concerned to get away altogether from reliance on collective bargaining and the power, not only of a state bureaucracy, but also of intermediary organisations like trade unions, favours a kind of workers' co-operative as a model of industrial organisation. In such an approach, both market forces and representative democracy are meant to be restored, mainly by the effects of removing the grounds for, and thereby the power of, organisations established to defend the contrary interests of employers and labour. (Indeed, there is a much wider view that tripartism places far too much emphasis on such divisions, which in effect make little sense in terms of the real interests of the members supposedly represented, let alone in terms of economic efficiency or social welfare. We shall return to this wider question in Part Three.)

However, what we might call the co-operative approach could be effective only under certain limited conditions, which may be briefly stated here. First, it would work only if undertakings could be organised on a small scale, partly because a labour-controlled monopoly would present at least similar, if not worse, problems for competition policy (and, therefore, for economic efficiency) and partly because large-scale operation would create the need for a new distinction between managers and other kinds of worker. In fact, most arguments for such an approach are based on a belief in smaller-scale operation, but, as we have seen, in this respect they have to answer satisfactorily the criticism that for technological as well as economic reasons, large scale has been the dominant tendency at least in manufacturing industry. Secondly, there is a related condition that the activities concerned should not be too capital-intensive (which again, much of manufacturing industry in modern circumstances seems to be). Otherwise, for one thing, the workers in an undertaking would be subjecting themselves to an unreasonable degree of risk, unlike the capitalist investor who would not normally put 'all his eggs in one basket'. Finally, unless conditions made it easy for new undertakings to enter the market concerned, co-operatives would tend to become unduly protectionist thus forcing prices up and creating unemployment. In fact, there is a danger that co-operatives would see it as being in their interest to restrict the entry of potential competitors, by operating a kind of extended 'closed shop' (Lipsey and Leonard, 1981).

The same limitations apply *mutatis mutandum* to various proposals for workers' control that have become popular on the Left in something of a revival of syndicalist ideas, bearing some relation to those of the celebrated British socialist thinker, G. D. H. Cole. At the same time, such proposals are often based, following the syndicalist tradition, on what is either by implication or by design a rejection of the priciples of representative government as these have mostly been understood in Britain and other liberal democracies (Pateman, 1970). They are linked to a theory that, in terms at least of Cole's presentation, sees true democracy as lying not in representative institutions of a political kind but in a system of occupational guilds based on the place of work. To the extent that it was necessary at all (and the whole concept of sovereignty is challenged in such theories), representation at the national level would not be through an elected Parliament but a 'national guild' consisting of delegates from specialised guilds at lower levels (Cole, 1917, 1920; Glass, 1966). In other words, a system of functional representation is envisaged as an alternative to parliamentary representation. We shall consider the wider implications of such an approach, both as an alternative and as a supplement to representative democracy in the liberal sense, in Part Three.

But it is necessary to distinguish what we might call broadly a syndicalist approach from those which see 'industrial democracy' as a means of strengthening the role of trade unions. In theory and in practice, it shares the concern of those who suspect the authenticity and fear the power of a corporate organisation, which the TUC in many minds has been tending to become in the context of tripartism. Indeed, as we shall discuss further in Part Three, one of the checks to that tendency has been the survival, if not the growth, of rank and file resistance to national leadership and of the alternative within the trade union movement of a shop-stewards' movement (Fox, 1978; Middlemas, 1979). In fact, trade union leadership has been divided in its approach to 'industrial democracy' and usually opposed to anything smacking of syndicalism (Elliot, 1978). However, in arguing for the transfer of power to organised labour, albeit of a different kind, the syndicalist approach still runs into certain seemingly intractable problems that are of general concern to the present study: the problem of how to avoid simply recreating monopoly economic power of a new, and in some ways more difficult, nature; that of defining the role of management – a question that is sorely neglected in every approach that narrows the issue of one of simply labour versus capital; and that of what seems to be the essentially protective nature of any organised economic interest.

In addition to the problems that have already been mentioned, there is also the pervading one of how to deal with the reality of interdependence, not so much of government and industry, as of those whose social and economic relationships provoke the intervention of government in the first place: consumers and suppliers; managers and other workers; investors and managers; and, above all perhaps, industrial decision makers, whoever they may be, and those only indirectly affected by the secondary consequences of economic activity on employment, the environment and even social status.

Nevertheless, the main conclusions suggested in this Part of the present study do little to discourage scepticism about what governments can achieve and about the political role of intermediary organisations based on collective economic power. Most procedures, methods and structures that have been tried in the search for consensus in British economic policy making during the past twenty years, and have been found in one way or another wanting in practice, have been the product of dependence on public authority as a last, and increasingly a first, resort. Above all, they and their difficulties have been associated with the peculiar stress placed in this country's government on the performance in executive office of one of two competing party leaderships based, however tenuously, on the assumption of mass electoral support.

Part Three
Pluralism and Political Renewal
10 Alternatives to Parliament

By the end of the 1970s the way the government/industry relationship was working was a source of discontent for many spokesmen of both management and labour in industry and many politicians of all main parties. It is not the purpose of the present study to deal with all the criticisms or to assess the economic arguments involved. Dissatisfaction with the government/industry relationship, however, has often been expressed as a loss of confidence in parliamentary politics and has led to demands for political reform. It has not been reduced by the change of government which took place in May 1979: on the contrary, only the short memory of political debate makes the feeling of estrangement on both sides of industry towards the present Conservative Government seem unusual.

Two things at least seem clear from the repetitious nature of industry's complaints about government. The first is that they apply to governments of both major parties, and, therefore, do not flow only from some partisan attachment or prejudice. The second is that it is something more than particular short-term policies or technical solutions that is at stake. Indeed, disillusionment with the workings of parliamentary politics has gone deeper even than was assumed by those who sought to counter the disillusionment with the devolution of responsibility to technical and other types of impartial agency or with tripartism in its various forms. At the time of writing (in the winter of 1980/81) interest in some kind of radical political re-alignment has been stirred perhaps more than ever before since the second world war by the defection of Labour MPs and proposals for a new political party of the centre. It is far too soon to discuss, in the context of this study, the full significance of those developments. But what we shall consider here is the possibility that institutional or other forms of political change could help to reconcile the use of economic power with representative government.

This part of the book will assess, in turn, proposals for improving the direct representation of industry at the level of central government and those for reforming political representation itself through Parliament.

First, this chapter will review the nature of the complaints that are now usually made of the British system of adversarial politics and briefly assess the major alternatives that have been proposed.

Politics as a nuisance

A recurring theme has been that there is a 'mismatch' between industry and politics. A number of leading figures with experience combining politics and industry have talked of an 'incompatibility between the industrial and the political approach' (Watkinson, 1976 p. 126). Both industrialists and politicians have been found at fault, but the behaviour of governments of both main parties, virtually since the war, is most often seen as the major cause. Thus, a committee sponsored by the Hansard Society concluded that:

> 'The overall result of government's apparent failure to accept the realities of industrial life is the growth of distrust and annoyance on each side' (Hansard Society, 1979).

Whatever the means of consultation that have been employed, it seems that the ultimate decisions in government have rarely paid due regard to the needs of industry. There seems, in fact to have been a feeling on both sides that communication has been inadequate. Government has been criticised for failing to provide a stable economic framework within which industrialists can plan and invest in the long term. Industry has found it increasingly difficult to understand the motives and the justification for government measures. In addition, there seems to be a general resentment of the sheer quantity of legislation of which those working in industry have to take account. More particularly, it is the frequency of legislative and fiscal changes directly affecting industrial decisions that gives cause for concern, and above all the way such changes are made. One major consequence is a divergence between industrial and political time-scales that has often made it impossible for the original intentions of either side to be realised.[1]

It has become fashionable to see a major underlying cause of the problem as 'adversary politics'. The effects of the British two-party

---

[1] Among other illustrations, a Hansard Society report points out that there were, between 1945 and 1972, five major changes in the form of investment incentives and a change in regional policy as it affected industry every 32 months; that between 1958 and 1977 the domestic appliance industry had to cope with 12 fiscal changes affecting the rates of tax levied on its products; that the rate of purchase tax varied between $2\frac{1}{2}$ and 7 per cent from 1959 to 1973, while VAT has been changed four times since its introduction seven years ago and corporation tax was altered on average every two years between 1958 and 1974; and that between 1965 and 1975 there was a change in government policy for prices and incomes at least once every thirteen months (Hansard Society, 1979).

system used to be a source of complaint only for a small minority of intellectuals and fringe political activists. They came to attract much wider attention during the 1970s as part of a general questioning of various aspects of the British system of government, and not only its consequences for industry. People of different parties and none, have joined in the criticism, and the presentation of the case against 'adversary politics' is not always the same. However, the main feature is what has been called the 'ratchet effect' of electoral competition between two mass party organisations (Hailsham, 1978), one of which eventually becomes able to command the discipline of a clear majority in the House of Commons – the oligarchical politics of the collectivist era, which we described in Chapter 5.

Four consequences of direct relevance to the government/industry relationship have been: (a) an increased tendency for repeated extreme alternations in government policy; (b) manipulation of economic policy for short-term electoral advantage; (c) premature abandonment of measures that call for a non-partisan, long-term approach; (d) and reluctance by particular economic groups to accept sacrifices in the longer-term general interest.

As we have seen in Part Two, what has tended to happen is that each governing party has adopted a distinctive approach before entering office but has then reversed it later in the face of real circumstances of government. Indeed, the notorious 'U turns' that have characterised British government in the 1960s and 1970s might be better described as a pattern of linked 'W's' (Rose, 1981). There have been periods when government policy has been the result of divergence (as after the elections of 1970, 1974 and 1979), but also periods when it has been the product of convergence (as in 1966–69, 1972–73 and 1977–79). What convergence there has been, however, has come from governments modifying their declared original intentions. And it has been punctuated by periods of great uncertainty, when one or other major party has sought to break into a new ideological departure. The way this influences a government's approach to legislation has been described as follows:

'The election manifesto, conceived in an aggressively partisan spirit, has come to be seen as committing parties more and more to legislation early in a term of office almost regardless of the possibility that views might be changed by contact with the reality of adminis- tration and the experience of civil servants. The tendency of legislate in a hurry, accentuated by understandable desires to avoid the perils of an election period, all too often produces laws which, because they are evidently in need of amendment, readily fall victim to the root and branch repealing instinct of a triumphant opposition: and so the cycle is perpetuated, to the detriment of long-term thinking and planning' (Hansard Society, 1979).

The reaction of businessmen and trade unionists has been to become exasperated with constant reversals in the impact of government on industry and with what seems a mere game of political musical chairs.

The pressures for convergence, on the other hand, sometimes appear as nothing better than a cynical attempt to employ techniques of economic management for electoral advantage.

'As a broad rule it could be said that a government with a life expectancy of four years spends the first two years of its tenure in seeking to master the inflation generated by its predecessor and the next two years in generating its own. The political cycle dominates and causes the economic' (Jones, 1973, p. 120).

The result has been aptly described as a form of government resembling the split personality of a Jekyll and Hyde (Stewart, 1977).

Moreover, although governments eventually come up against the same realities and invariably adopt similar measures to deal with them, they are unable or unwilling to sustain those measures for long enough to allow them to work. This, as we saw in Part Two, has been particularly true in relation to policies for the control of prices and incomes, and to selective intervention to promote improvements in productivity in particular industrial sectors (Finer, S. E. ed., 1975). The history of government attempts in both these respects is littered with different short-lived experiments with institutions and powers that proved abortive through the lack of sufficiently consistent and bipartisan support.

Finally, given the trends towards a corporate economy, described in Chapter 4, the effect of party competition has also been to produce an irresistible temptation for particular organised economic interests to play one party against another in a sort of blackmail that has made repeated attempts to achieve consensus impossible. A particular organised group can assume that it need not deal with a government whose policies it dislikes, while there is still an opportunity to discredit that government by whatever means, while helping to get the other major party back to power.

Party oligarchy

However, it can be misleading to trace these effects simply to adversarial politics. On closer examination, it seems that the Conservative and Labour Parties have still tended at election time to seek a middle ground and, as we have seen, their behaviour in government reveals as many trends of convergence as of divergence. The behaviour of both major parties is still best understood as the result of a pull between more moderate, pragmatic influences and those of a purist, sometimes extreme nature.

In fact, criticism of the workings of the parliamentary system has come not only from those who regret what they see as a growing divergence between the major parties, but also from those who complain of the pressures for conformity and of the way party programmes become diluted, if not altogether drowned, thanks to the apparent weakness of party leaders in office. Party leaders are seen as being deflected not only by economic realities and international obligations or contingencies, but also by the moderating effects of the Civil Service and as a result of a general obsession with the need for consensus.

We saw in Part Two, however, that the search for consensus has failed to provide either stability or coherence in economic policy, even though there have been repeated and varied attempts to limit the effects of party competition and to increase the participation of representatives of industry. What has been consistent, in fact, is the tendency of both public and politicians to have exaggerated expectations of what a party leadership can achieve when in government. The so-called 'U' turns result, less from a conscious desire to drop controversial measures, than from the need to react to contingencies of various kinds, not only those of internal and external economic trends but also the necessity to accept the views of industrial organisations on whose members the economic welfare of the nation ultimately depends (Rose, 1981). The parties were, in the 1970s, able and willing as governments to seek some broadly acceptable view of the public interest and to encompass the interest of different groups whose compliance and co-operation were seen as essential to effective administration. It was not that all wisdom rested in the Civil Service or in those with technical knowledge, or that only the representatives of the major economic interests were conscious of the need for agreement on the broad lines of economic policy. It was rather that no party, group or consultant body has a unique access to wisdom or the authority to speak for all the diverse elements of an advanced industrialised society. There is some truth in the assertion that representative democracy as practiced in Britain has hampered the exercise of effective government in the economic sphere. But it has done so chiefly by developing illusions about the significance of the electoral process and its capacity for endowing governments with the authority or the aptitude to manage the economy.

This conclusion helps to explain the seeming paradox that, while both major parties have found it necessary to join the search for consensus in government, in each of them purist or doctrinaire tendencies seem to have been strengthened in ways that would have been regarded unlikely in the 1950s. There have been times, as in 1970 and 1974, when one of the two main parties has used the prerogative of office to carry out substantial changes, and the present government still professes the aim of reversing what it regards as the whole trend of government for the previous two decades in spite of widespread criticism and economic hardship. The conventions of party government have, in fact, proved remarkably durable. It is still widely believed that the only democratic and efficient form of government is one in which a political party is expected to devise some programme for managing the country's affairs and then to be enabled to implement it over a number of years on the basis of electoral endorsement. If anything, that assumption has come to be more firmly held by the governing parties themselves, which have become increasingly conscious of a duty to detect a 'one best way' and, having found it, to ensure that they are not deflected by faint heartedness, ill luck, or adverse counsel.

On the other hand, all the evidence is that important differences of interest and view do exist, both in politics and industry, and need to be taken into account in economic as in other affairs of government. In Britain, however, it is seen to be the almost unique function of party to overcome these differences by producing a formula that will either prove them irrelevant or, by its success in application, repair them. Party government itself, therefore, has been caught up in the search for consensus. Most of the attempts considered in Part Two were undertaken as part of one or other major party's avowed performance of a consensus-seeking function. In no other European country could political, let alone economic, issues be reduced to such simple terms as to expect party to play such a role effectively. It should not be surprising, indeed, that such emphasis on the role of political parties has produced in Britain alarming differences between intention and reality. As a result, party politicians begin to suspect some sinister conspiracy against themselves and so seek to purify their intentions even more, while both the general and specialised publics start to question the grasp that any government can expect to have on events.

Indeed, there is some evidence of popular recognition that the two governing parties have failed in their responsibility. The share of the vote of the total electorate going to the Conservative and Labour Parties was 80 per cent in 1951, but had fallen to 56 per cent in 1974. The vote for minor parties, mainly the Liberals in England and nationalist parties elsewhere, rose dramatically from 1970 to 1974. Even the 1979 election, which brought the 'hung Parliament' to an end and returned a Conservative Government with a clear majority in the Commons, produced only 61 per cent support of the whole electorate for the two main parties.

Nevertheless, the conventions of party government still seem to be widely supported and allowed the Labour Government, elected with only 29 per cent of the vote in October 1974, to proceed with implementing a programme on the basis of an electoral mandate. The volatility of the electorate during the 1970s might be seen as an exception, especially in view of the result of May 1979. Since the attitudes of party politicians themselves have not changed, the mass of the electorate may well be persuaded, if not of the merits of the existing system, then at least of the lack of available alternatives. The fact that party government survived the experience of 1974 itself suggests that its conventions run very deep and that voting in general elections is not a sufficient means of challenging the oligarchical trends it represents.

It is, indeed, the oligarchical nature of party government that is important for our central theme rather than its apparently adversarial methods. What is meant by oligarchical here is the ability of two centrally organised parties, claiming a membership that (even if trade union affiliations to the Labour Party are included) accounts for a small proportion of the whole active population, to determine the range of choice available to the electorate and to so manage the House of Commons as to negate effective political obstruction to their own intentions when in office.

Such features of the British system have been defended, and even lauded, on the grounds that they clarify choice, lessen the conflicts of opinion and interest, prevent immobility and ensure continuity. In practice, at least in economic affairs in recent years, they have more often, as we have seen, had the opposite effects. The main reason is less likely to be found in temporary or fortuitous changes in electoral behaviour, than in the complexities, especially as seen in economic affairs, both of government and of society itself. In these circumstances, British politics has tended to over-simplify the problem of consensus, while at the same time exaggerating the need for conformity as a condition of effective government.

In general terms, trends of both divergence and convergence are relevant and have co-existed in British politics during the last two decades, if not earlier. Centrifugal pressures have manifested themselves in the increasing tendency of people to identify with sectional groups and to assert on that basis sectional claims (even by direct, sometimes illegal, means) and in the re-emergence of regionalism, separatism, even sectarianism as forces in social and political life. Most established institutions have been criticised and re-examined and a whole host of new procedures for increasing participation in government and in private administration have been tried. On the other hand, neither of the governing parties has abandoned its claim to rule in the interests of all, though in the 1970s both came for a time to admit their dependence on organised economic interests and from 1976 to 1979 all sorts of concessions had to be made by the party in power to parliamentary minorities in the aftermath of the unusual election results in 1974. For some time, in fact, the trend in the machinery of government itself has been to strengthen the resources of co-ordination and control available to the party leadership in office, and more particularly the Prime Minister. We shall consider the record of parliamentary reform in a later chapter, but in that respect, too, concessions to backbenchers have been justified mainly in terms of a rationalisation of procedure and a clearer recognition that in central issues of policy, electoral endorsement of a party's programme must take precedence over the views of MPs (Crossman, 1976; Walkland and Ryle, eds., 1981). While in reality it has been becoming increasingly evident that there are limits to what any party can achieve when in office and while the differences that have to be reconciled have become even more daunting and complex, the parties have become all the more anxious, in what they see as the interests of democracy, to improve their unique capacity to overcome difficulties and to mend divisions. But it is precisely in these circumstances that the search for consensus becomes counter-productive and what the parties regard as strong government is in effect invariably weak.

The dislocation between politics and society that has thus become evident in Britain, extending beyond the government/industry relationship, has prompted a whole series of suggestions for more or less radical reform of the system of government. To the extent that the problems of the government/industry relationship can be traced to the political system, these suggestions are relevant to our theme, though they also raise complex issues beyond our present scope. We shall consider in the next two chapters proposals for meeting the shortcomings of electoral and parliamentary politics by increasing the direct representation of industry. Before that, however, we should briefly review some of the main proposals for introducing new conventions of government, which also seek to temper the effects of party oligarchy, but do so from a variety of motives, not many of which fit with the analysis given here.

Party democracy
One reaction to party oligarchy is to seek greater participation by the party membership outside Parliament. Theoretically, party democracy in this sense has been most evident in the constitution of the Labour Party, though, as is well known, it has not prevented the parliamentary leadership of the party being normally dominant in practice. But the idea of party democracy has recently been revived as a central part of the general prospectus of the left-wing of the Labour Party. It has

featured among proposals intended to resist the growth in power of the parliamentary leadership and especially the Prime Minister, and also to counter what is seen as the excessive influence of the Civil Service as well as that of economic interests of business. Three main internal constitutional changes have consequently been adopted by the Labour Party: compulsory re-selection of MPs as candidates by constituency parties; greater power for the party conference in deciding the election manifesto; and participation by all elements in the party in the election of its leader.

The chief weakness of party democracy as an approach to representative government is that the 'rank and file' of political parties (the people who are prepared to join party organisations and work for them) are by no means representative of the electorate as a whole. On the contrary, not only do they form a small percentage of the whole electorate, but they tend to show altogether different characteristics from the vast majority of people, above all in the fanaticism of their interest in political ideas.

As a theory of representation, however, party democracy rests ultimately on the theory of the mandate:

> 'Voters organise or join a political party and by means of its conference agree on a programme; they then nominate candidates who advocate this programme before the electorate at large. Candidates elected on this programme must stand by it. This is precisely how they fulfil their responsibility to the electorate' (Beer, 1965, p. 90).

In other words, party unity and purity are as important to party democracy as to party oligarchy. The process of arriving at party policy and of choosing party representatives may be different from what has been normal practice in British politics, but the end result is still the preponderance of a party organisation at the expense of individual MPs and of other demands and interests that might be brought to bear on government. Party democracy would seem to have little or nothing to offer, therefore, as a way of helping to resolve the problems considered in the present study, and may even intensify them by placing even more stress on party government.

It cannot even be supposed that enhancing the influence of extra-parliamentary organs in the Labour Party would bring greater industrial experience to bear by strengthening the voice of rank and file trade unionists. Trade unions have always had the power to wield much greater influence through the party, but, in spite of recent tensions, have normally chosen rather to depend on a direct relationship with the parliamentary leadership, while retaining sufficient independence as an economic interest to be available for consultation and compromise with governments of either party. Moreover, it is unlikely that the casting of block votes by union delegates at Labour Party conferences or leadership elections, or for that matter the role of union representatives on the party's national executive committee, could be regarded as expressing the conscious views of a large number of union members, who by no means all vote for the Labour Party in general elections. For a variety of reasons, therefore, party democracy is a most unpromising way of trying to re-align politics and society in Britain, whether seen predominantly from the point of view of industry or from a wider perspective.

The referendum

Use of the referendum to enable the electorate to vote on particular issues has been increasingly seen as a way of overcoming some of the limitations of the parliamentary system in two main circumstances, when one or both major parties in the Commons are internally divided on an issue, and when an issue is regarded as being essentially non-partisan, either because neither party takes a strong view of it or because it is a fundamental constitutional or moral question. In other words, the device tends to be seen as a substitute for the electoral mandate, when this is seen, even by the party leaders themselves, as giving no clear authority. The referendum on membership of the European Community in June 1975 showed how a substantial majority of the electorate could be assembled to support a government proposal across party lines. It has sometimes been suggested that a similar device might be used to help pass legislation to regulate the activities of trade unions or to impose an incomes policy.

In the sense that it assumes that voters are able to come to informed and rational choices, and by implication that choices can be presented to voters in a clear-cut way, widespread use of the referendum suffers from some of the same limitations as the theory of the mandate. To some extent it supposes that positive consent of a majority of the mass electorate is both necessary and sufficient grounds for governments to act. In this respect, it is an intensified form of the plebiscitary approach to representation which has itself, through the mandate theory, contributed to party oligarchy.

To the extent that the referendum allows voters to express an opinion on single issues on which one or both parties is divided or undecided, then it can help to overcome limitations of the electoral mandate. Moreover, many of those who have come to favour its use in British government see it as a potential safeguard against party oligarchy or 'elective dictatorship'. Used sparingly, not as a means of submitting questions for mandatory decision by the electorate, but rather as an instrument available to Parliament for testing public opinion, especially when a Party in office seems to be abusing its status, it can be a valuable safeguard. But it may become dangerous, since success in a referendum, any more than gaining a majority in a general election, does not always guarantee consensus.

Constitutional checks and balances

Wider use of the referendum has been recommended as part of a general reform of the Constitution, designed to strengthen checks and balances against a wilful majority in the House of Commons and to increase the safeguards available to private citizens. Two particular steps that have been suggested are: a strengthening of the powers of delay of the House of Lords, most of whose voting members would at the same time come to be elected by proportional representation; and a comprehensive Bill of Rights. One way of taking such proposals further would be to adopt a written constitution. Proposals that have been made for establishing a federal system in the United Kingdom, as a method of providing regional and national devolution, also imply more entrenched constitutional provisions than could be said to exist up to now.

All such approaches, by implication at least, accept the need for limitations on the authority of the House of Commons and on the power of an organised majority within it. In this sense, they are clearly in tune with any remedy that treats party oligarchy as the main source of the problems of the government/industry relationship. Obviously we cannot do justice to such proposals in the context of the present study, but they would seem to be relevant, if in a less immediate sense. We shall have to leave for other studies such questions as the role of the courts in any moves towards greater entrenchment of constitutional checks and balances. But it is worth recalling from Part Two of this study that industry has not always preferred adjudicative procedures to direct dealings with ministers, nor have such procedures proved particularly effective in taking economic issues out of politics. The future of the House of Lords is also a major issue in its own right, and must depend largely on the way it is to be composed, a question to which we shall return in another context. The main problem however, as we shall see in connection with reform of the Commons, is that the political attitudes and mores that are still preponderant are bound to resist any inroads on the concentration of power in the governing parties.

Coalition government

The reaction against adversary politics has led to increasing support, especially among those not directly engaged in parliamentary politics, for government by a coalition of parties. What is precisely meant by this support is rarely clear, and a variety of attitudes and motives lie behind it. The 1930s and war-time experience of a virtual suspension of normal party competition seems to be the main influence for some; the postwar experience of certain other European countries, particularly that of the Federal Republic of Germany, for others. Sometimes, therefore, what is envisaged is a 'government of national unity', formed of leading members of at least both major parties; sometimes it is a system of what political scientists have come to describe as one of '2½ parties', in which one of the major parties can form a government only with the support and moderating influence of a minor party (Butler, 1975; Finer, S. E. ed., 1975; Johnson, 1977).

In either case, coalition government is not a simple, straightforward alternative to other arrangements. Whether it is considered feasible or desirable must depend on the political circumstances of time and place. Foreign comparisons can be misleading, as can historical comparisons with other periods in British politics. Coalitions can take a number of different forms. As proposed in recent public debate in Britain, the aim may be to reinforce rather than to undermine the main characteristics of party oligarchy. Indeed, without a clear diagnosis of what the problems are, it is impossible to be for or against coalition for its own sake.

There are circumstances in which coalition government in Britain would be no remedy at all for the problems of consensus. When proposals are made for a 'government of national unity' what is in effect envisaged might be described as a form of *monopolistic coalition*. Both major parties participate in forming the government and probably also one or more minor parties, so that, at most, a very truncated form of opposition survives in the House of Commons. While it can last, such an arrangement might well be seen as an alternative to adversary politics. It may even give backbench MPs increased freedom from partisanship and greater opportunity to use means of criticising the executive. It has sometimes been said that parliamentary democracy functions more effectively in such circumstances, as the late R. H. S. Crossman once reflected on the basis of war-time experience:

> 'Inter-action of the two-party machines through the usual channels was working permanently and perfectly so that the House of Commons was merely criticising a permanent central government. I now can't help wondering whether the House of Commons may not be better when there's an all-party government and a kind of consensus of criticism as a background' (Crossman, 1976, p. 627).

The outcome of such a 'grand coalition' is not likely to be to the electoral advantage of the parties participating, however, so that it cannot survive for long. Moreover, outside the obviously extreme conditions of a world war, such an arrangement assumes a large degree of common thinking, not so much between, as *within* parties, which is, as unrealistic as the assumption that government by a single, major party can encompass all wisdom or all interests.

An alternative type of arrangement might be called *competitive coalition*, which is common in multi-party systems and to some extent in '2½ party' systems. Not all major parties are included and there remains a parliamentary opposition of one or more major groupings outside the government. The coalition arrangement is based on a deal between certain parties regarding particular policies and measures and, in this way, the authority of the Executive is restricted. However, to the extent that the government depends on parliamentary support for its existence, and where there are strong pressures for party cohesion (as there often is in continental European countries where this type of coalition is common), the effect on supporters of the parties in the coalition tends to be stultifying, since they, and the members of the government, live in fear of the arrangement breaking down. All attention and interest come to be focused on the process of forming a government by entering into fixed commitments, which, whether or not related to an electoral mandate, nevertheless have a similar effect in encouraging inflexibility and unrealistic expectations. If the composition of the coalition can be altered from time to time between elections, then the parliamentary assembly can use its elective power to influence policy. But what is important then is less the existence of a coalition than the recognition that the assembly should have a positive role in the formation, as well as the content, of government.

Coalition government in whatever form may simply lead to a further concentration of power in the Executive. There are dangers in seeing it as a panacea for the effects of divisions and differences in society, even though it is true that existing political alignments exaggerate these and make them more difficult to overcome. The problems of the government/industry relationship, for example, may lie less in the differences among political and industrial groups, than in the approach taken to resolve them. There may be even worse instability if particular groups are forced into permanent opposition inside or outside the parliamentary system. Moreover, coalitions can become exceptionally vulnerable to the influence of some conventional wisdom, while limiting the opportunities for open debate of alternative views (Brittan, 1978). Monopolistic coalition, concentrating power even more than in a one-party government, and especially if based on an arranged consensus that serves only the purpose of defending executive power, may actually enhance the impact of economic sanctions available to particular organised interests.

What is most important is that no party, or alliance of parties, should expect tenure of executive office on its own to endow it with some infallibility or unique legitimacy. If the need for parties to enter into arrangements with each other before being able to form a government had the effect of removing that expectation, then it would be salutary. But to do so, it would need to be based on more, not less, competition between parties and a greater concern to take different views into account.

Meanwhile, the bias in parliamentary representation against industry would remain. Both Parliament and the direct representation of industry have in their separate ways become increasingly 'professional', in the sense that the commitment and attitudes demanded must to a large extent drive out other interests and lead to a growing detachment from the experience of other occupations and pursuits. Parliament itself appears, therefore, no longer representative of the nation, either in terms of its composition or in those of its contribution to government. It is this gap above all which has presented the problem of consensus, for it is the central function of a parliamentary assembly to bring the realities of power to the attention of those responsible for government. Chapter 13 will try to explain why the role of Parliament and the method of its election are, in the end, the crucial factors. Before coming to that, we shall, in the next two chapters, give a thorough examination of the possibilities of the direct representation of industry, whether as an alternative, or as a supplement, to Parliament.

11 The Direct Representation of Industry

We saw in Part One of this study how the growth in the interdependence between government and industry had been matched in the course of this century by a decline in industrial representation through Parliament. Not only are leading figures from trade unions and business today most unlikely to seek any kind of parliamentary career, but, even if they did, they would not find membership of the House of Commons on its own an especially fruitful means of access or influence. Leading representatives of industry in all its various aspects have their own direct access to ministers and their departments. For both government and industry the main and most convenient medium of industrial representation is the intermediary organisation, which has been so developed that now both business and employers, on the one hand, and labour, on the other, are seen as having their own central organs or representation at national level in, respectively, the CBI and the TUC. Both the numerous organisations collected under these two 'peak associations' and other organised social and economic groups are more than mere interest groups, set up on the basis of some common trade, occupational, vocational or other productive activity to serve common needs and promote common objectives. They have become part of the process of representative government itself, not only taking over from political parties much of the function of aggregating interests and reconciling private, sectional demands with some broader view of the public interest, but also assisting in the administration of public policy and helping to ensure compliance and co-operation.

In fact, it is a major shortcoming of government by political parties in Britain that the latter are not themselves adequately informed of the problems of industry or sufficiently sensitive to the time-scales or other requirements of effective industrial management. Neither the traditional links between the Labour Party and the trade unions nor those, less organic, ones between the Conservative Party and business have served to overcome these shortcomings. If anything, the trend of party oligarchy has been to make party organisation and policy making all the more professional in its own right, while the role of political activists seems to have been enhanced. Meanwhile, what relationships do exist, and especially the peculiar organic ties between the Labour

Party and the TUC, which have had a special impact in the shape of the 'social contract', have hardly been designed to create confidence in the relationship between representative government and economic power. While trade unionists may well have cause to question the lasting value of the commitments made by Labour Governments, they may also regret their relative lack of direct influence on the Conservative Party. Employers and businessmen, on the other hand, have been given good reason to mistrust the policy counsels of the Labour Party, while suspicions that the Conservative Party may be intrinsically unsympathetic to manufacturing industry have not been assuaged. In general, there is some ground for believing that the traditional ties of the major parties have done much to worsen divisions on class lines and to frustrate industry's own inclination to approach social and economic issues in a more pragmatic way.

Some alternative to parliamentary representation, therefore, seems to be inevitable, while detaching industrial organisations from close identification with the governing parties seems positively desirable. In fact, theories of representative government have come to embrace the direct representation of economic interests as an integral and necessary part of democracy. In Britain the dislocation between politics and industry has, in the pressing economic circumstances of today, greatly strengthened interest in the possibility of entrenching industrial representation alongside or as an alternative to that by means of political parties. The full implications of what is proposed are not always clear, nor is some alternative to political representation necessarily envisaged. But the idea of representation on the basis of people's social and economic status – or 'functional representation' – has received growing attention in recent years.

Functional representation
The principle of functional representation must be regarded as having an established and widely accepted place in both British political culture and the practice of British government. We have referred repeatedly in this book to the way representatives of industry have been brought into a regular, consultative relationship with government, most notably since the extension of public responsibility for industry during the first world war. It is but one aspect of the tendency of modern British government in all areas of policy to want the direct advice, support and, even at times, participation of individuals selected for their knowledge and experience, or for their repute, in some private capacity. The preceding account has dealt with procedures of consultation mainly in the economic sphere, and more specifically with relations between government and industrial representatives, paying particular attention to tripartite approaches during the last twenty or so

years. But we should not overlook the much wider, continuing process of consultation by means such as royal commissions, advisory committees attached to departments or set up to make individual inquiries, and personal, informal contacts between ministers and their officials, on the one hand, and selected representatives of different trades, professions, occupations and pursuits, on the other (Eckstein, 1960; Self and Storing, 1962; Finer, S. E., 1965; Woolton, 1966, 1978).

What has been especially important about the government/industry relationship, however, is the way the participation of industrial representatives, especially through intermediary organisations such as trade unions and employers' organisations, has reflected major developments in both the economy and the political system, so that functional representation in one form or another has come to be a vital part of the process of government, replacing in some respects the role formerly attributed to Parliament.

Even so, dependence on functional representation was prefigured in earlier periods of British history. Tory and Whig attitudes to government in the eighteenth century assumed that political representation should be based to a large extent on social and economic functions (Birch, 1964; Beer, 1965). Then and previously Parliament was the main channel of functional representation. Under the influence of liberal ideas in the nineteenth century, and with the growth of modern political parties, the basis of representation through Parliament shifted, and today, as we have seen, the House of Commons consists far more of what are in effect party nominees than the spokesmen of particular social and economic interests, let alone those who might be regarded as qualified by their own experience to speak for industry (PEP, 1974; Mackintosh, 1978).

There is, in fact, a substantial history of proposals in this century for deliberately providing an element of direct industrial representation through Parliament. Such proposals have often been made as part of a more or less collectivist approach to the role of government in economic affairs, though they have also been made in their own right, seemingly with the chief aim of breathing new life into representative government.

Perhaps the most famous and often-quoted of the latter type is Churchill's proposal for an 'economic sub-parliament' made in his 1930 Romanes Lecture (Churchill, 1930). This proposal itself may have drawn on a much more detailed, academic presentation of the case for an 'economic council', based on an institution then existing in the Weimar Republic of Germany, by Herman Finer in a study commissioned by the Fabian Society and published in 1923 (Finer, H., 1923). It has since been taken up from time to time, especially by Conservative politicians, though the implications and the precise methods of adding a special element of functional representation to Parliament have never been worked out (Smith, 1979). Many of the points with which such proposals have been intended to deal, however, are remarkably similar to those often made today. For example, in 1947 the Conservative MP, L. S. Amery, in a general study of the Constitution proposed a 'House of Industry', which would be essentially subordinate to the Commons and Lords and purely advisory, but would provide a chamber:

> 'In which the great economic problems of the day could secure practical and responsible discussion, free from abstract party catchwords and programmes as well as from purely partisan manoeuvring for power'.

Amery also argued that such a body would:

> 'soon attract the best elements on both sides of industry, which would be willing to find the time for practical and congenial business which they will not give to the House of Commons under present conditions.' (Amery, 1964, p.64)

Some arrangement for the direct representation of economic interests can usually be found as part of the case set out by those individuals of different political persuasion in the inter-war years who sought to extend the economic responsibilities of government. It was an especially important part of the programmes of leading socialist thinkers in the 1920s. In their elaborate scheme for constitutional revision designed to implement socialist policies, the Webbs proposed to transfer the legislative and other powers of Parliament in social and economic affairs to a separate 'social parliament', directly elected but organised on specialised functional lines, to provide the representative element in a centralised system of state planning (Webb and Webb, 1920). In a very different way, G. D. H. Cole developed at length, as an alternative to liberal, parliamentary democracy, his system of decentralised guild socialism, which we met briefly in Chapter 9. In this system Parliament would have been replaced by a 'congress of industrial guilds' (Cole, 1920). Obviously, when included in this and other conceptions of an entirely new form of government, the principle of functional representation is taken much further than in normal British practice and raises questions altogether beyond the scope of the present study. The Webbs had actually rejected functional representation for their own constitutional revision, but their idea of a directly-elected, but functionally specialised, parliamentary assembly also belonged to a wider set of ideas regarding the form of government (Finer, H., 1923; Laski, 1951; Smith, 1979).

However, it is not necessary to take a view about functional representation as a fully fledged theory of government in order to accept some element of it in practice or propose some new form of it as part of the British system of representative government. Taken the whole way, a theory of functional representation

> 'finds the community divided into various strata, regards each of these as having a certain corporate unity, and holds that they ought to be represented in government.' (Beer, 1965, p. 71)

Older text-books on comparative government usually made some reference to this approach and distinguished it from political representation, including that by means of a parliamentary assembly elected by universal suffrage on ths basis of equal citizenship (Laski, 1926; Finer, H., 1949; Friedrich, 1950). Academic discussion of the relative merits of functional representation has recently been revived as part of a renewed interest in political theories of 'corporatism'. This new debate has been sparked off largely by the problems of governing advanced, industrialised societies like Britain, especially in view of the economic responsibilities of government: in other words, it is directly relevant to the theme of the present study. Without going into the wider and more arcane academic aspects, we shall consider briefly in the next chapter how relevant such theories of 'corporatism' might be to the problems with which we are immediately concerned here. It is clear, however, that many practical proposals for improving the direct representation of industry in the British system have been made, and may be considered seriously, without necessarily implying any wider, theoretical or practical view.

An element of functional representation is, in other words, quite compatible with territorial or any other kind of political representation, including the parliamentary system or modified versions of it. It is now generally accepted that, especially through the activities of interest groups or intermediary organisations, it provides a vital supplement to political representation through parliamentary elections. The question is how far functional representation should go and how it should relate to Parliament. Moreover, there is also the question of how government based on political representation can best ensure that it is able to take the measure of different economic interests, responding to them while managing to arbitrate among them and to maintain a view of the public interest.

Functional representation may not be the same thing as the representation of interests: essentially the constituency on which it is based is a productive unit (Beer, 1965). What qualifies those represented is not some abstract notion of citizenship, but, on the one hand, their economic power when organised collectively, and, on the other, their peculiar skills and knowledge. Advocates of functional representation argue that participation on this sort of basis is more feasible and meaningful then by means of political representation based, say, on a territorial constituency or on voting for a political party. Voters in parliamentary elections rarely know, or care much about, the issues so that parliamentary democracy is vulnerable to the criticism of being a mere 'sham' (as we have seen, this may well be the case with respect to notions such as the theory of the electoral mandate). In theory at least, people are far more knowledgeable and responsible when asked to express an opinion about something that affects them directly and materially, such as their own occupation, than they are in the generalities of politics. Be that as it may, we should be aware that there are risks in basing representation on people's place in the economy or on their skills and qualifications; it could lead to serious inequalities and may at the same time make the problems of economic power all the more intractable.

Without getting on to such wider questions, to which we shall return in the next chapter, we shall now consider a number of possibilities for improving the direct representation of industry at the level of central government. These involve in different ways some development of the existing arrangements for functional representation in Britain, but they do not seek to alter the system of parliamentary representation, only to supplement it. All, in some sense, aim at overcoming the limitations of the parliamentary system as it has been seen to affect the government/industry relationship during the last two decades. As we shall see, however, like the past search for consensus during the same period, they run up against limitations of their own, chiefly because of general reluctance to take functional representation too far.

Reform of the National Economic Development Council
It makes every sense to start from machinery that already exists and has the general sanction of the main political partites and the main organisations representing industry. The chief formal and, to all intents and purposes, permanent organ for the direct representation of industry, which fits these criteria, is, as we have seen, the National Economic Development Council (NEDC). Indeed, most proponents of reform do seek in one way or another to build from the achievements of that body, while recognising its existing limitations.

The most important proposals for reforming NEDC itself concern its composition and these proposals are of two kinds, not necessarily exclusive of one another. The most widely supported at the present time and favoured by a number of those with direct experience of NEDC, is the suggestion once made by Mrs. Shirley Williams as a minister that the front-bench economic spokesmen of the official Opposition should be included as members of the Council. The other proposal, which is less widely supported and appeals naturally enough mainly to organisations not so far directly represented in the Council, is that NEDC's membership should be extended to include nominees of a much wider range of industrial interests than those represented by the CBI and TUC.

The reason for wanting to include Opposition spokesmen is to broaden the consensus-forming work of NEDC in longer-term, but nevertheless crucial, aspects of economic policy, so that it covers probable ministers of some future government. In other words, it is to counter the more damaging effects of 'adversary politics' and reduce the chances of a government coming to power that does not adquately appreciate the real prospects and problems of economic management and lacks a sufficient mutual understanding with industry. The proposal may be seen, therefore, if not as a complete alternative to political re-alignment or parliamentary reform, then at least as a stopgap or some form of relief for those consequences of the British system of party government that have led to complaints of intolerable inconsistency and lack of communication in economic policy making and application.

The main difficulty with the proposal is that it might break down the rather delicate understanding that has been developed in NEDC, which makes it possible for ministers of the time to enter into a frank and productive exchange with leaders of the main industrial organisations, given especially that the latter will usually have their own, often politically flavoured, differences with the party in power. Could ministers be even as open as they are if Opposition spokesmen were present, albeit that the proceedings would still be formally in private? How would the attitudes of TUC nominees be affected under a Conservative Government, if the discussion were to include statements by Labour spokesmen? Under a Labour Government, especially if something like a 'social contract' were being operated would they regard themselves along with CBI representatives as holding an essentially industrial rather than political brief. In other words, there would be a new danger of replicating in NEDC, the partisan confrontation that is considered so futile, and even misleading, when practiced in the House of Commons. And the real opportunities for co-operation between TUC and CBI on certain matters, together with the salutary influence of independent members of the Council, might be lost.

On the other hand, the more they were effectively involved in a consensus on economic policy, the more Opposition leaders might find themselves in difficulties with their party supporters. The proposal is clearly not a very satisfactory alternative to political reform designed to overcome undesirable effects of 'adversary politics'. And as a measure of partial relief it runs the risk of spoiling the modest achievements of

NEDC up to now. Indeed, NEDC could do with much more openness on the part of ministers, especially in their willingness to share information with industrial representatives. The proposal has what is perhaps a surprising measure of support, but this may reflect rather the degree of dissatisfaction with the present parliamentary system than a feeling that NEDC is inadequate in performing its present functions without Opposition spokesmen. The nettle to grasp here is surely that of Parliament itself.

The other proposal would in effect entail enlarging the membership of the Council to include, alongside CBI and TUC nominees and the other ordinary members, nominees of organisations such as the British Institute of Management and the Retail Consortium, and those representing financial institutions (such as the Governor of the Bank of England), small businesses and specialised trades and professions. It is certainly true, as we have already remarked and shall see further that the authenticity of the TUC and CBI as exclusive spokesmen of industry can be questioned. That fact is one of the major problems with the tripartite approach, another being the tendency to increase the sense of confrontation on political or class lines by stressing a bi-polar relationship between employers and labour. At the same time, as we have also seen, NEDC pays a cost for its intimacy in a lack of specialised knowledge and experience. It has been a continuing assumption of this study that industry in Britain, while meaning preponderantly manufacturing industry, also has a much wider denotation, including not only services and financial interests, but also categories of interest that are blurred or altogether ignored by the simple distinction between employers and labour. In particular, there is the role of industrial managers, who may not identify themselves as employers, and there is also the more problematical question of a consumers' interest.

However, a wider representation on NEDC may not be the best way to take account of those needs. As we have seen, the Council has always included a number of 'independents' including now not only chairmen of nationalised industries and professional economists, but also representatives of financial institutions, public agencies and consumers' organisations. It is strongly argued by those familiar with its workings that the present size of just above or below 25 members has hit something of a magic number. Not only does it enable meetings to be held around a table in conversable circumstances, but it allows relative informality among the participants at Millbank Tower, extending to the buffet lunch normally held after meetings. Such an atmosphere can prove vital at times of sharp public antagonism between the parties concerned. Above all, not only is NEDC more properly regarded as a kind of 'summit meeting', but it is important to eschew at least in principle the idea of its members serving as delegates of particular organisations or of defined constituencies, like the members of a parliamentary assembly or of a negotiating committee. None of this excludes the possibility of varying the membership so as to limit dependence on TUC and CBI representation and this has been the normal practice. But, if taken too literally, the proposal for a more widely representative membership becomes in effect a proposal for a different kind of body altogether.

Another kind of reform might be to enhance NEDC's independence of government, so giving it possibly greater scope, an even greater prospect of avoiding short-term, partisan concerns and greater authenticity as industry's own voice. One means to this end could be to appoint an independent chairman, as is the rule with some other official consultative bodies (including the Economic Council for Northern Ireland). Ministers could still be ex officio members or they could attend at the invitation of the independent chairman. There is a good deal to be said for this proposal, if the aim is essentially to produce a body that focuses on industry's own needs, however these may be defined, and is less concerned with providing a regular dialogue with the government of the day. The Economic Council of Northern Ireland has succeeded in steering clear of partisan or other politically divisive influences, remarkably so in view of the political system in which it operates (and in the absence of a Northern Ireland political assembly). It has also produced a number of searching reports, (most of them published), on its own initiative directed at the Northern Ireland Office. It has also commented on matters, including delegated legislation, that the Office has submitted to it. On the other hand, the bulk of its work has been of a longer term, more specialised nature, based on elaborate research, rather than that of a forum in which general questions of national economic policy are discussed with ministers. The reason, one suspects, is not only that it has been concerned since 1972 with the economic affairs of a directly governed province but also that its very independence gives it in other respects an essentially different function from NEDC. If the latter were itself made more independent of central government, then there would come a point at which its own functions would probably change so that its longer-term, researching role came to be preponderant over its unique status as a forum in which the main protagonists in government and industrial organisations meet regularly, with the opportunity from time to time of actively getting back to speaking terms. Indeed, there is an alternative view that NEDC should concern itself more with this latter function, especially by doing more to restore its former emphasis on macroeconomic issues.

Most of the major issues surrounding the possible reform of NEDC come back to the question of what its functions really are. As we have seen, there is a certain ambivalence at the very root of that question, but, to the extent that the lack of definition has actually served to give NEDC some kind of continuing purpose that all participants have found indispensable, whatever their other doubts and discontents, there might be a case for not pursuing the question too far, at least in practical terms. NEDC's status as a consultative body dependent on the Executive clearly limits the extent to which it could, say, consider legislative proposals on any regular basis. Its relatively restricted composition might also be seen as a limitation in that respect. We have already seen that a tripartite approach can be used for certain, specialised executive functions (as in MSC and ACAS) and for the management of public enterprises (as in NEB), but it is difficult to see how a body composed like NEDC could be given any executive responsibilities, unless it was as part of a much more dramatic and fundamental departure from parliamentary government than has been envisaged seriously up to now. There are other ways, however, in which the representation of industry could be developed without necessarily affecting the way NEDC plays its existing role.

A new 'economic forum'

A number of suggestions have been made in recent years for setting up what is rather vaguely called a new 'economic forum' with the primary purpose of improving communication and understanding between government and industry on the main issues of economic policy, but intended especially to reach some voluntary agreement about the control of inflation. In many ways, the idea seems to be to provide a more fixed and a more open arrangement for conducting a tripartite arrangement in economic policy.

The aim would not be, however, to attempt any sharing of responsibility as was sought in 1972 or in 1974, nor would either government or industry enter into any firm commitments as in a 'social contract', let alone a statutory prices and incomes policy. Although this idea was canvassed both by the CBI and by members of the TUC General Council before 1979, (Allen, et al., 1979; CBI, 1979) it has been ventilated more particularly since the general election of May 1979 and since, in other words, the return of a Conservative Government that is sceptical of tripartism and seeks to be non-interventionist (CBI, 1980; British Institute of Management, 1979). The main purpose now seems to be both to compensate for the new government's 'arm's length' attitude, especially towards the TUC, and to provide the means for representatives of industry themselves to work out some voluntary agreement.

The CBI has proposed the setting up of such a forum, to be backed by an independent secretariat and to consist of representatives of employers and unions, which would be presented with different projections of the main economic variables, such as prices, incomes, employment, investment and consumption. The representatives of industrial interests could thus see for themselves what the possible range of choice was, for example, in making pay claims or pay awards, and what the consequences of different decisions would be likely to be.

This idea has been presented in different forms, none of them precise about the methods or, for that matter, about any new body's relationship with the existing NEDC (Jones, 1973; Watkinson, 1976; Gilmour, 1978). Indeed, from some statements it would almost seem as if the existence of NEDC as an economic forum for discussing macroeconomic issues had been altogether forgotten including its role in 1972 in attempts to devise a formula for pay guidelines.

In the summer of 1979, however, the government was widely reported as showing a positive interest in creating such a new economic forum, though not with the intention of adopting a prices and incomes policy or of interfering with collective bargaining at company and plant level. It was also considered likely that its membership would be wider than that of NEDC. However, no initiatives have subsequently been taken and the government seems to have confined its direct contacts with representatives of industrial organisations to personal meetings (including eventually in the autumn of 1980 visits by TUC leaders to 10 Downing Street) and to the normal proceedings of NEDC, to which in the winter of 1980/81 special attention seems to have been paid. However, some members of the Cabinet (including the Secretary of State for Employment) were thought to favour the general idea of extending tripartite discussions of economic policy to include such issues as pay, prices and even taxation.

It seems, therefore, that this particular approach to industrial representation is closely tied to the whole question of whether a national incomes policy of some kind is necessary or desirable, and whether, for that matter, it would be feasible. But what is relevant to the present study is the belief that it is part of the responsibilities of government to bring together leaders of intermediary organisations representing different social and economic interests with a view to reaching an agreement – voluntary or otherwise – to exercise self-restraint in the public interest.

In other words, such a belief reflects the general view that in a modern, industrialised democracy effective government demands some sort of compact reached directly with representatives of employers, trade unionists and others engaged in industry. The electoral process, whether or not it gives the party in power a clear majority of votes or parliamentary seats or both, is not enough on its own. It does not guarantee, among other things, that people understand the economic realities faced by the government or accept the consequences for themselves or the nation of their own actions. The implication is that, however they may be arrived at, some general rules are necessary to guide the way decisions about economic rewards are made. As the Chairman of the former NBPI has put it:

> 'Rules on prices and incomes are required, because, if those groups in the best position to extract high increases in pay and profits pursue their self-interest to the limit, both the resulting inflation and the attempt to conquer it will go to nullify their efforts; besides hurting the weaker, therefore, they also do little to benefit themselves. The purpose of the rules is to remind them of the bounds beyond which, in their own interests, as well as those of society, they should not go.' (Jones, 1973, p.179)

Intermediary organisations of industry are not only themselves a reason for establishing such rules (in view of their own influence on economic decisions, often with monopoly power), but also offer a means of formulating and applying them.

Certain refinements have been offered as part of the continuing debate on incomes policy. First, it is suggested that a forum would need to be supplemented by a public agency, respected for its impartiality and technical competence, which would make recommendations about future rates of income, including questions of relativities and differentials. Secondly, both to get away from confrontation and to ensure a more authentic representation, a forum should be appointed to represent, not so much the TUC and CBI, but those actually engaged in pay bargaining as well as a wider range of economic interests. Thirdly, however, it has also been suggested that a forum should not concern itself only with guidelines for future pay settlements but with the whole range of economic issues that in the end provide the essential framework within which pay decisions have to operate and on the basis of which a fuller understanding may be reached (Blackaby, 1980; Lipsey and Leonard, 1981).

We seem, in other words, to be back at the fundamental issues of the responsibility of government in the economic sphere and of the role of intermediary organisations in politics. Economists and others are very fond of falling back on proposals for independent, 'expert' agencies to get round the difficulty of determining the distribution of economic rewards by some centralised, technical process. As the experience of earlier attempts shows, however, it cannot adequately compensate for the effects of party government. Whenever guidelines or other projections of economic activity are called for, it is difficult to see how the responsibility of ministers can fail to be involved, if only because it is they who must provide the necessary information. There is also the recurring question of the status and credibility of the organisations regarded as representing economic interests. What criteria are to be used for deciding whether they are genuinely representative, whatever that means? What weight can be attached to the commitments made in their name? These can be vital questions, because, if subjects such as pay are to be considered, as is appropriate, against the wider economic background, then it is difficult to see how such organisations can be prevented from exercising direct influence over a whole range of public policy decisions, including even aspects of public expenditure and other matters formerly regarded as the preserve of Parliament.

A 'House of Industry'

Nevertheless, it can be argued, the role of intermediary organisations is such an essential part of government today that one way or another their direct influence is going to be felt. Without them, indeed, it is difficult to see how any advanced, industrialised democracy could possibly achieve sufficient cohesion and compliance to make not only management of the economy possible but also social and political order. The main problem is to meet three particular requirements: first, that government should keep sufficient distance to make the public interest inviolable (in order, among other things, to be able to arbitrate among the demands of different interests); secondly, that representative organisations should be as authentic as possible and should not be allowed to use their power to the unfair disadvantage of other groups; thirdly, that such organisations' influence should be exercised as far as possible in the open and within some framework of checks and balances. It may well be that for these purposes something more is needed than an economic forum composed on a tripartite basis and designed specifically to reach agreement on the level and distribution of economic rewards.

In fact, proposals for an economic forum often seem themselves to be hinting at some wider and more elaborate kind of institution for the direct representation of industry. As we have seen, there is a substantial history of proposals from various sources for the establishment of a national body on a permanent basis and with its own rules of procedure in which social and economic interests would be represented according to a pre-determined allocation of seats, including proposals for creating some kind of 'industrial parliament'. The earliest attempt to put such an idea into practice, though only on an *ad hoc* basis, was probably the National Industrial Conference held in 1919, at which it was actually proposed to set up some permanent arrangement. Similar proposals were made from time to time by academics and politicians throughout the inter-war years and have been revived subsequently, more especially in response to the problems of the government/industry relationship of the last two decades (CSSP, 1976; Parker, 1977; Richardson and Jordan, 1979; Smith 1979). Most recent proposals, including those for a wider economic forum, seem to take the existing NEDC as their starting point. Others seem to envisage a body that would be separate from NEDC or an alternative to it. In either case, a similar purpose is envisaged to the orginal one of NEDC as defined by Mr. Selwyn Lloyd at its creation, namely, to 'promote a greater sense of national purpose in the conduct of our economic policy'. And the aims of an economic forum in achieving consensus on broad questions of economic rewards would also be included. The special characteristics that are sought, which vary from one statement of the idea to another, seem to be roughly speaking the following: greater independence from government than previous bodies (and especially greater publicity and openness); a wider and more regularised basis of representation; and more flexible and comprehensive terms of reference.

A number of leading Conservative politicians have espoused the idea, most recently Sir Ian Gilmour who takes NEDC as his starting point:

> 'Its membership should be widened, and some of its proceedings should be in public and preferably televised. Both sides of industry would be subject to public scrutiny. Trade unions would be forced to argue how higher wages could be paid without adding to inflation or increasing unemployment. Industry would be forced to explain the defects of management, obsolete techniques and inadequate training.' (Gilmour, 1978, p. 246)

Certain industrialists have gone further and have been more explicit in recommending an entirely new body. Sir Peter Parker, Chairman of the British Railways Board, has proposed that alongside NEDC there should be a new 'Council of Industry' (Parker, 1977). Sir John Pile, formerly Chairman of Imperial Group Ltd, has elaborated a proposal for an 'economic and social council' referring specifically to institutions that already exist in France and in the European Community. What seems to be envisaged by these proposals bears a good deal of resemblance in their form to Herman Finer's economic council, which has already been mentioned, and would probably meet most of the objectives of the 'House of Industry' proposed in varying and usually vague terms over the past fifty or more years.

Like all forms of functional representation the idea of a 'House of Industry', as soon as it comes to be elaborated in practical terms, raises some formidable problems. It is no doubt because of these – whether consciously or not – that NEDC was set up on such a pragmatic basis as a consultative body attached to the Executive.

If the aim is to set up a body that is substantially independent of the

Executive, then a number of questions arise as to how this is to be achieved without involving far-reaching constitutional changes that would take functional representation much further than is actually intended. If a new institution were created by statute, then it would indeed be dependent on Parliament, though it could be given large discretion to settle and operate its own rules of procedure, elect its own officers and be responsible for its own staff and services (within budgetary constraints laid down also with parliamentary approval and controlled by the Treasury). However, it is not the lack of its own statutory basis that has inhibited NEDC: in the present system most governments would have the means of determining the constitution and form of any new body, whether an Act of Parliament was involved or not. We have already considered the possibility of giving NEDC an independent chairman, and there is no obstacle to that in any consultative body attached to a government department. But it would be most unusual for Parliament to create an institution for which some minister was not ultimately responsible, unless it were a select or standing committee of its own or an agent of either House (like the Comptroller and Auditor-General).

However it was set up, there would arise the vital question of how the body's members were to be selected. It is clear that the aim is to have a wider interpretation of what constitutes 'industry' than is often used in British practice, and anyway to go beyond the tripartite framework of ministers, CBI and TUC. A new body could, in fact, be of an entirely different dimension from that of NEDC, with anything up to 200 members representing specifically not only management, financial institutions, consumers, farmers and others as well as employers' organisations and trade unions, but also different sectors and industries, regions and activities, as well as including the usual 'independent' specialists. But the question remains of who is to decide what the different categories are, the allocation of seats among them and the qualifications of membership? If ministers are to appoint the members, whether or not on the nomination of organisations approved in Whitehall, then the process, though much more inclusive than before, is unlikely to be any less artificial or more significant. If the aim, as it seems usually to be, is to achieve more authentic representation than that normally provided by organisations like the CBI and TUC, and to get behind national leaderships of industrial organisations so that among other things, they are made more accountable in public before their own members, then a more discriminating procedure of selection seems to be required. But what procedure could this be? It is well known that organisations like trade unions are extremely averse to public intervention designed to regulate their own internal rules and procedures. If, on the other hand, some form of direct election is to be devised, the limitations of functional representation become all the more apparent, as the need arises to define the qualifications of voters, determine constituencies and decide the method of election. There is also the more mundane, but no less vital, question of whether practical men and women in industry would have the time required to serve in such a body. If it were to be genuinely representative in this sense, it could hardly hope to meet more than at most twice a year. Otherwise its active members will be the familiar figures – spokesmen of interest groups, paid officials and 'experts', the 'great and the good' – who already do the rounds of the government/industry relationship.

It is generally supposed that a 'House of Industry', however constituted and composed, would have no more than advisory and consultative powers. The aim in going beyond what already exists, however, is to give industrial representatives greater opportunity to feed their own proposals into the process of government and to make their views heard on the major proposals and measures of government. It is usually thought especially important for such a body to be able to comment on legislative measures affecting industry, before these are enacted, for the advice of both Parliament and ministers. Certainly, if it provided a more systematic and public means for industrial spokesmen to advise on relevant legislation, it would go far to deal with the complaints now so frequently made of the parliamentary system. On the other hand, Parliament's legislative and financial supremacy is not usually questioned. Even if it had no powers to approve or amend legislation, a new body could still exercise a kind of legislative sanction, if the need to obtain its advice raised the possibility of delaying a particular measure. What is most likely is that, ministers would retain the right to decide (even if subject to parliamentary resolution) the selection of measures for submission to the new body at some stage of their own choosing, but that, again, leaves the initiative very firmly with government, albeit subject to parliamentary criticism and pressure.

Although such a body might not provide, therefore, anything very significant in the way of a new check on party government, at least not without substantial support in Parliament itself, it might, less ambitiously but not less valuably, provide the opportunity for a much fuller, more regular and more open discussion by representatives of industry of a range of economic and industrial issues.

It would be no mean achievement to extend understanding of the central economic issues beyond national leaders of the trade unions and employers, and to give a wider span of industrial representatives the opportunity to air their own views in public. Of course, the more proceedings got on to questions of the economic strategy of the government of the day, the greater the likelihood that partisan considerations would become uppermost, especially when meeting in public. Ministers could be invited to explain their policies and measures before the new body and might welcome the opportunity. It is uncertain, however, whether they would want to be even as frank as in NEDC, which at least meets in private. Moreover, to the extent that partisan issues did come up, then trade unionists and other groups might be expected to close ranks among themselves, with the possibility of emphasising, rather than attenuating, existing divisions. On the other hand, though much useful work might be done of a non-controversial nature, it would be necessary to question the value of yet another agency for the production of papers and reports on specialised aspects of economic and industrial policy, especially if NEDC continued to serve this purpose, along with all the other public and private bodies ranging from parliamentary select committees to research institutes. However, both ministers and the major industrial organisations might be reluctant to allow the body's remit to extend in practice too far into sensitive areas not already covered by other means. And there is the question of what significance to attach to the final opinions of such a body, whether reached by some sort of majority vote (hardly productive of greater mutual understanding) or as a result of some bland consensus.

These remarks are intended, not to disparage the idea of a wider forum of direct industrial representation, but to point to its natural limitations. In fact, a number of different forms could be adopted. As has been said by many of its exponents, what matters most are the purposes of the idea rather than its precise methods of application. It is possible to envisage a sizeable assembly that was broadly representative of the main social and economic interests meeting in public annually or twice a year to discuss economic trends and policies under the aegis of NEDC and with the services of NEDO. The aim would not be to seek the sort of tripartite consensus of NEDC itself or of the proposed economic forum on pay, but rather to allow a more open and more wide-ranging expression of different views and interests. Such an arrangement would not, of course, make possible the sort of regular consideration of legislative and other measures that some have proposed, nor provide the more specialised work on economic and industrial policy on which NEDC and its sub-structure of tripartite committees are engaged. Moreover, it has to be recognised that, unless functional representation is to be built into the British system of government to a far greater extent than has so far been acceptable to proponents of any new type of body, no form of direct industrial representation can get round the conventions of ministerial responsibility of Parliament or substitute on its own for the role of intermediary organisations recognised by ministers as the true representatives of economic power.

Representation through a reformed House of Lords

Before returning in the next chapter to those central issues and more especially that of the limitations of functional representation in general, we should consider a particular version of the idea of a 'House of Industry' that has been canvassed from time to time. It has been suggested that use might be made of the existing second chamber of Parliament to extend and formalise the direct representation of industry (PEP, 1974). This might be a way to resolve the problems associated with the constitutional status of such a form of representation, by bringing it directly into Parliament, but not in such a way as to challenge the authority of the House of Commons or to confuse it with the normal party-political process. It might also fill the need of enabling industrial spokesmen to play a more regularised and openly direct part in the legislative process.

Especially since the introduction of life peerages in 1958, the House of Lords has already included leading figures with business and trade union experience. Prime Ministers have not, however, used their power of appointment to the upper House systematically to represent industrial interests. The House of Lords continues to be dominated by members with other backgrounds and is still for much of the time preoccupied with party-political issues, though far less so than the House of Commons. Life peerages are granted for the life of the incumbent and most of those given for industrial experience have gone to people after they have retired from positions of responsibility in industry. Precisely how a reformed House of Lords could include a measure of functional representation is a complicated question, especially in view of the political controversy surrounding the role and even the existence of the second chamber. We have already seen that its remaining powers have a vital constitutional importance, and an importance that some would like increased. The House performs a number of functions that many would regard as no less vital than, and possibly not entirely compatible with, the representation of social and economic interests.

The question of reform of the House of Lords is too wide for the present study and needs to be considered in its own right (Morgan, 1973). Retention, and even some extension, of its powers to delay legislation, to give additional or even prior consideration to certain types of legislation not adequately considered by the Commons, to scrutinise policy and administration (especially in relation to delegated legislation) and to deal with various less partisan matters, could be recommended in their own right as means of limiting the effects of 'adversary politics' and, more importantly, checking the oligarchical tendencies of party government (Gilmour, 1978; Hailsham, 1978). But reformers always have to confront the question of how such a revising and scrutinising chamber is to be composed. Inclusion within a reformed House of Lords of a substantial number of members appointed to represent the main social and economic interests would serve to give industrial spokesmen a much more direct and public opportunity to express their views on relevant policies and measures, on which they would have valuable specialised knowledge and experience to offer. It would be one sensible way of approaching the functions of a reformed second chamber. But is is still far from clear how such members would be selected and what organisations they would represent and on what terms. These questions would be all the more crucial and problematical if functional representation were being established within Parliament itself, especially in view of the Lords' residual functions of a constitutional nature.

Some comparison is possible with the Senate of the Republic of Ireland. The majority of the members of that body, the second chamber of the Oireachtas, are elected in different occupational and professional categories. In practice, however, party politics are usually decisive both in elections to the Senate, and, to a large extent, in its proceedings. Senators simply have to justify their candidacy within a particular occupational or other category. It may be thought, at least under the existing conventions, that party politics would also come to be preponderant in the nomination and conduct of social and economic representatives in a reformed House of Lords. Moreover, the Irish Senate operates under the terms of a written constitution.

In many ways, the delaying and other remaining powers of the House of Lords survive because of the absence of a written constitution in Britain. In these circumstances, the ultimate supremacy of the directly elected chamber can be assured only while the Prime Minister has the right in the last resort to use his or her powers of appointment to the Lords on political grounds. As we have seen, it has been proposed that the Lords itself be directly elected as a way of further checking the powers of an 'elective dictatorship' based on the Commons. But that is a different matter from composing the Lords with representatives of industry on a non-political basis. If the Lords were to become a chamber for functional representation, what would happen to its potentially vital constitutional functions? There is a danger here of confusing two separate issues: the need for the direct representation of industry and the need to maintain, if not strengthen, constitutional checks and balances against party government. Even so, it is questionable whether reformers would want to take functional representation to the extent of endowing it with the remaining legislative and other powers of the Lords even in normal day-to-day conditions.

We have remarked that the representative nature of the Commons is itself questionable under present circumstances, since it is itself largely dependent on what may be considered as outside organisations: the oligarchical parties. As a result, important sections of the nation, including especially for our purposes different industrial interests, are inadequately represented. We must soon turn directly to the possibilities of reform of Parliament as a way of dealing with this and related shortcomings in the government/industry relationship. But any attempt to meet it by giving new powers to industrial organisations themselves should be approached with extreme caution. It is high time, therefore, that we looked again at the nature of those organisations and their role in relation to government.

12 The Limits of Corporatism

Most proposals for improving the direct representation of industry would not want it to replace electoral parliamentary politics. But how useful can direct representation be unless it does effectively temper party rivalry and doctrine? Moreover, to be effective as mediators, do not bodies like trade unions and employers' organisations need to acquire their own political authority to be able to commit their members to national agreements and to be able to keep a measure of internal self-discipline? It has often been suggested that the way to overcome the political problems of the government/industry relationship is to reach some sort of compact, 'concordat' or similar arrangement, which, however voluntarily arrived at, will serve to bind both government and industrial organisations to a series of general undertakings in the public interest. There is nothing new in that idea, which was prominent in British government earlier in this century, and was applied with some success. The problems of the last two decades could be explained by an exceptional failure to apply the idea successfully. Many, in fact, would agree with those scholars who have seen fundamental changes at work in the adaptation of representative government to the conditions of an advanced, industrialised society: changes that take the form mainly of a new dependence of government on organisations based on economic power and that demand a reassessment of the role of such interest groups (Ionescu, 1975; Crouch, 1977; Middlemas, 1979; Schmitter and Lehmbruch, eds., 1979).

It has been suggested, for example, that some form of 'corporate bias' in the exercise of political authority should now be seen as inevitable, so that suitable reforms should be made on that assumption (Middlemas 1979). In this chapter we shall re-examine the grounds for such a view, mainly by re-considering what we already know of the real nature and prospects of corporatist institutions in Britain. First, we should consider some of the main examples from other European countries that are usually cited both generally to support a more or less corporatist view and more particularly to recommend an extension of functional representation in Britain.

Some foreign examples
The Scandinavian countries have, in particular, attracted the attention of political scientists as examples of industrialised, democractic states in

which functional representation has been a major source of economic and social stability and of political order. The Swedish experience has been especially important since the last war in terms of economic management by means of effective income policies. What seems to have been the key element in that kind of system are highly centralised intermediary organisations, especially those representing trade unions and employers, acting in a very close relationship with the central government. In the 1950s and 1960s in Sweden, the role of such organisations was responsible for achieving a large measure of consensus on the distribution of economic rewards and of stability in economic policy. In fact, such interest groups could be said to be more important in the Swedish political system than political parties, precisely because, it is claimed, they can be seen to represent distinct and fixed 'constituencies' of social and economic interests, which they have for much of the time been able to commit in centralised, national negotiations. The parliamentary assembly has tended to be by-passed by the main interest groups, whose influence is exercised in Sweden by means of royal commissions appointed by ministers to report on all major legislation before it is considered and voted by parliament. Agreement among the representatives of interests is usually the decisive factor (Barbash, 1972; Vernon, 1974, Griffiths, 1977; Castles, 1978).

For a long time the Netherlands also provided a good example of centralised and disciplined national bargaining on incomes and prices, even though economic interest groups are more diverse there and society subject to complex traditional divisions which are reflected in a highly stratified system of parties and groups. Shortly after the war the main governing parties were able to agree on the principles of a 'guided social market economy', in the operation of which specialised, technical bodies like the Central Planning Bureau have played a vital part. No less essential, however, has been the Social Economic Council, established by the constitution and composed of three categories of membership, each consisting of 15 members nominated respectively by employers' organisations, the trade unions and the government. The Council has to be consulted by the cabinet on all social and economic matters, in which it also exercises some executive powers of a regulatory nature. It was for a long time the forum in which binding national settlements on pay were reached. In practice, however, its influence declined in the mid-1960s and in 1969 its role in incomes policy was terminated. Its chief failure was its inability to deal with the problems of differentials and it was unable to prevent widespread industrial unrest in the early 1970s (Barbash, 1972, Griffiths, 1977, Coombes and Walkland, 1980).

In both Scandinavia and the Netherlands political life has not remained as stable as seemed likely in the 1950s. In Scandinavia, the apparent consensus on economic policy has been broken by the revival of centre and right-wing 'bourgeois' parties and the end of the era of largely uninterrupted Social Democratic or Labour Governments often based on minority support in parliament. In the Netherlands there has been a new polarisation of party politics in economic affairs and renewed differences between the main economic interest groups. Consensus-building procedures based on functional representation do not seem there or in Scandinavia to have been able to cope with the problems of inflation and recession in the 1970s. The Dutch Social Economic Council was already being widely criticised during the 1960s for the inflationary effects of its role in incomes policy. The political parties in government have found it necessary to re-assert their responsibility for economic policy, while differences among the parties have had to be resolved, if at all, by electoral and parliamentary means.

A more fully-fledged and durable system of functional representation is to be found in postwar Austria, which has been widely quoted by students of corporatism as a model of the possible transformation of representative democracy into a new kind of 'corporate state'. Austria's combination of relative economic prosperity and social order has been attributed to the elaborate system of *Sozialpartnerschaft* based, again, on centralised intermediary organisations. The major economic interest groups of business, labour and farmers, as well as a whole range of other professions and occupations, are, in fact, organised nationally in separate 'Chambers', set up as statutory public corporations in which membership is compulsory. Although prices and incomes policies, which have played a vital part in management of the economy, are decided and implemented on a voluntary basis, they and other economic questions are dealt with in Joint Commissions in which the main Chambers are represented under the chairmanship of the Federal Chancellor or Minister of the Interior and with the relevant economic ministers attending. In practice, the main decisions are settled in advance by agreement among the main interest groups themselves, which is also the way most economic legislation is determined, since the Chambers have to be consulted under the constitution before the federal parliamentary assembly votes. The corporate system has wide ramifications in Austrian society and politics and seems in many respects to have supplanted political parties as media for influencing public policy and even for regulating the economic aspects of life. In spite of its contribution to economic success, however, it may be criticised for encouraging a somewhat stagnant and materialistic form of society, for entrenching the privileges of professional and other elites and for enhancing the conservative influences of special interests (Schmitter and Lehmbruch, eds., 1977).

All the countries considered so far are small in terms of population and in their separate ways differ significantly from Britain in terms of their international commitments and status. Moreover, historically functional representation and even corporatism have had a special part to play in their political and social systems. In these, as in other continental European states, corporatist structures of economic policy-making since the war have been needed to meet special needs left by the complex divisions of parties and interest groups, and especially because historically the trade unions, divided internally on political or religous grounds, were less readily accepted than in Britain as interlocutors with government.

In many ways a more telling comparison might be made with the experience of the Federal Republic of Germany, a country often singled out for contrast with British postwar experience in terms of economic success. There, as in the other countries often used as models of corporatism, centralised business and labour organisations seem to have been an important factor in effective management of the economy. The role of intermediary organisations and their relationship with government are far more informal than in Austria, however, even though the procedures of *Konzertiert Aktion* were given a legal basis in 1967. Those precedures have included regular meetings of the Federal Minister of Economic Affairs with major economic interest groups, and on a relatively wide basis of representation involving anything up to 50 or more participants. The aims have been very similar to those envisaged by supporters of a new economic forum in Britain to promote voluntary income restraint. Public intervention in collective bargaining (though not in labour markets) is relatively limited, however, though in the national 'concertation' of economic interests the initiative and ultimate powers of decision have rested with government itself, without the devolution of authority to autonomous organisations of interests that is found in Austria. In fact, the role of the 'social partners' in economic policy making in the Federal Republic of Germany has been highly controversial. Under recent coalition governments dominated by the Social Democratic Party the relationship with employers and union representatives has been largely informal, resting on the personal influence of the Federal Chancellor, especially with the main union leaders. 'Concertation' seems to have served mainly 'as an instrument of crisis management, not of continuous economic guidance' (Vernon, 1974; Griffiths, 1977; Policy Studies Institute, 1978; Schmitter and Lehmbuch, eds., 1979). Probably more important in economic management has been the role of the central bank and the latter's legal obligations to protect the value of the currency and use control of the money supply to restrict inflation, together with a general anxiety among the major groups to avoid repetition of the disastrous inflation of the 1920s. Even so, the emphasis on consensus-building among 'social partners' has not prevented a more recent outbreak of industrial unrest or successful attempts by individual unions (like that of the metalworkers) to challenge the national leadership.

Comparisons with France, too, may often exaggerate the effects of 'social partnership' based on the direct representation of economic interests. The role of unions in the procedures of national planning was never as positive as that of employers, while:

> 'The conception of planning as a process representing an alternative avenue of democracy based on functional representation, in vogue in the early 1960s, has gone out of fashion'. (Hayward and Watson, 1975, p. 456)

Since 1968 most union representatives have deliberately withdrawn from major planning bodies. National 'peak associations' of employers and labour never became strong enough to overcome sectionalism. The authority of the Plans has always rested essentially on their acceptance as a strategy by the Executive itself, while industrial representatives have never participated on more than a consultative basis in which direct, personal contacts between public officials and industrial managers have been the vital factor, usually to the exclusion of union representatives (Dion, 1973; Hayward, 1973; Lindberg, 1975; Warnecke and Suleiman, eds., 1976; Zysman, 1978).

The *Conseil Economique et Social*, a body provided by the Constitution for functional representation, has attracted a lot of attention in Britain among proponents of a 'House of Industry' or some other kind of large national assembly for social and economic interests. However, its role is extremly limited and it does not offer a very promising model for the innovation sometimes proposed in this country. Indeed, there seems to be no recent study, even in France, of the role of the *Conseil*, and the lack of public or academic interest in it reflects its peripheral role. It may have been more important before 1958 when the new Constitution of the Fifth Republic attached it to the Executive rather than to Parliament. What importance it had probably depended most on providing an almost unique opportunity for the national representation of trade unions. However, its composition since 1958 has been such as to provide a substantial majority against these and to prompt the charge that certain larger unions (and especially the Communist CGT) were grossly under-represented. The *Conseil*'s 200 members include 141 representatives of economic interests appointed by the government to one of four Sections for trade unions, business, agriculture and other interests (mainly cooperatives, the middle classes, consumers and so on). The other 59 members are nominated by the government as 'independents', and are usually appointed in reward for political or other services, rather along the lines of life peers in the House of Lords (Hayward, 1966). Contrary to what is sometimes supposed by British observers, the *Conseil*'s influence on the planning process is usually not much greater than that of parliament itself:

> 'The Council remains outside the planning process, since unlike the (planning) commissions, it does not actually share in the preparation of the Plan and is only consulted after the government has made its choices'. (Hayward and Watson, 1975, p. 38)

Its consultative role in relation to legislative and other economic proposals has been important from time to time, though as often in showing up divisions among economic interests as in creating consensus, and it did play some part in incomes policies in the early 1960s. But the idea of functional representation has not been widely supported. As President of the Republic during the 1960s General de Gaulle wished to transform the Senate into a body composed on functional lines, thus supplanting the *Conseil Economique et Social*. Constitutional amendments to this end were rejected, however, in a referendum and proved abortive. The real object was widely seen as that of bringing the Senate under greater government control and tempering its opposition to Gaullist policies (Hayward, 1966, 1973).

Most member states of the European Community now have some kind of national body for the representation and consultation of the major economic interests and these (including Britain's NEDC) now send representatives to an annual international conference held under the auspices of the Community's own Economic and Social Committee. That Committee, however, set up on rather similar lines to the French *Conseil*, itself offers little cause for excitement about the possibilities of functional representation on the model of a special assembly or forum. Indeed, its role has tended to be peripheral and Committee. That Committee, however, set up on rather similar lines to consultation.

Nearer home and in a somewhat more familiar institutional environment, the National Economic and Social Council in Ireland is similar to the British NEDC in many vital respects, being non-statutory, appointed by the government (after consultation with the organisation entitled to representation) and including ministers. Its powers are purely advisory and most of its work consists of considering, and finally reporting on, various aspects of economic, social, industrial, agricultural and regional policy with the help of its small secretariat and outside professional consultants. It is, however, much larger than NEDC (especially when account is taken of differences in size of population), having 46 members, and its chairman is usually an independent member. Its detailed work takes place in one of three specialised committees. The Council has not served as an economic forum for national discussions on incomes, which have taken place in a special Employer-Labour Conference. Nevertheless, there has been some political controversy about the Council's very existence, and doubts about its future have tended to restrict its work (especially after the change of government in 1977).

Such bodies always seem to face the choice either of being virtually an arm of the Executive, designed for reaching consensus, or politically divided, in which case both governments and group representatives tend to prefer more direct forms of negotiation. In practice, they can work only by relying on some bland consensus or by limiting the range of subject matter to issues of a mainly technical nature. What is usually required (as with NEDC) is that they meet in private, so that the aim of greater openness and public debate of economic issues is frustrated. When the membership is more widely representative, then even in private sessions, proceedings can help to test the monopoly of corporate power, and the opinions and reports published may themselves reflect differences between leaders and followers as among different interests. But there is still the prospect of stalemate unless there is a broad base of agreement among the groups participating. The basic dilemma has been aptly explained by the Irish National Economic and Social Council in a conclusion about its own work that is worth quoting at some length:

'It could be argued that the differences of view on major issues within the Council reflect those in Irish society. But it would be too simplistic to expect that such differences might be resolved by the use of technical expertise of an economic and quantitative kind.

What such technical analysis can do, and what it has tried to do, is to inform different interest groups and attempt to help them to evaluate what the long-term consequences of particular policy measures might be, so that choices might be more rationally made between the long-term interests and the short-term gains of particular strategies. Moreover, it is not by any means clear that differences in beliefs, ideologies and interests can be resolved and consensus reached by discussion in representative bodies such as the Council. To the extent that such discussions succeed in getting to grips with the basic issues, differences and divisions are exposed, articulated and possibly re-inforced rather than reconciled. While the exposures and articulation of unreasonable viewpoints may not change them, it could detract from their support. However, in the last resort such differences may be resolved, or the action that is appropriate to the circumstances taken despite them, only by a political process or procedure'. (National Economic and Social Council, 1977, p. 23)

The 'corporate state'

Evidence from the experience of other European states about the development of functional representation is, therefore, at best patchy. Austria is the one example of a parliamentary system and a mixed economy where corporatist structures seem to have taken over effectively, and on what seems to be a lasting basis, much of the consensus-building role of political parties. Elsewhere, though they contributed to growth with stability for a time, centrally-negotiated agreements among representatives of the 'social partners' have not proved adequate to overcome the effects of inflation and recession, at least since the mid-1960s (Harrison, 1980). However much the direct involvement of organised interest groups may have led to a diminution of parliament's traditional functions, party conflict and competition have turned out to be still decisive in economic policy (Schmitter and Lehmbruch, eds., 1979). Moreover, there seem to be limits to what can be achieved by means of the direct representation of interests, unless it should be thought desirable and possible to extend the logic of Austria's longstanding corporatist traditions to other countries. Governments usually seek to retain the upper hand in any consultative process, preferring direct and informal rather than institutionalised methods; the marginal powers of economic and social councils seem to render them generally harmless enough as an alternative to political representation, but also largely ineffectual.

Nevertheless, the idea of corporatism as a distinct and alternative political mode has become increasingly attractive for many who aim to account, and sometimes also to compensate, for the decline of parliamentary forms of representative democracy. British observers are included among those who regard the economic responsibilities of modern government as making some form of 'corporate state' the most likely future political development (Winkler, 1975; Crouch, 1977; Pike and Stritch, 1977). The growing literature on the subject reflects a variety of opinions and different meanings of corporatism. Recently an international group of academics have made a valiant attempt to reach more precise definitions, though unfortunately in a language so sophisticated as to be inaccessible to practical men and even frustrating for other academics (Schmitter and Lehmbruch, eds., 1979).

In popular debate in Britain corporatism has become something of a political slogan meaning whatever the user wants it to mean. Indeed, different meanings of 'corporate state' tend to cancel each other out. Left-wing Labour politicians and trade unionists seem to see corporatism in the political power of private capital, or as an attempt to 'neutralise' the potential opposition of free trade unions (Heffer, 1973). Conservatives and businessmen are more likely to see it as a surrender of the state to the economic power of trade unions and excessive public intervention in industry (Harris, 1972; Buchanan, et al, 1978) In other words, political debate has hardly defined corporatism as an alternative to adversary politics, but rather treated it as a new football in a game played by the old rules.

There is, in fact, a fundamental ambivalence in the notion of corporatism when applied to politics, conveying as it does both the idea of greater autonomy for private groups and that of greater centralised, public intervention. In theories of the 'corporate state', the presentation of these ideas can become altogether self-contradictory. In practice, corporatism as a form of government has usually been no more that a disguise for an authoritarian regime, as in Fascist Italy, Nazi Germany, Salazar's Portugal and Franco's Spain. Indeed, it is difficult to read much meaning into the idea of a 'corporate state' except as a regime in which public and private rights have become entirely merged. Political representation based on some uniform principle of citizenship (with free elections and competing political groups) gives way to a national structure of representation based on people's occupations. Private ownership of capital remains in form, but public regulation is extended to all the major decisions of businessmen and others engaged in economic activity, so that the market system hardly survives in practice. Economic, like political, activity is organised by means of associations (or 'corporations') of different categories of producer. These associations are intended not only to represent their members but also to exercise executive functions over them. Moreover, each of the associations is organised on hierarchical principles: they are established and organised by public law; they are specialised to avoid competition; membership is virtually compulsory for those in the category concerned; and the leadership is oligarchical. There is also a hierarchy of the associations themselves, producing a structure over the whole country in the shape of a pyramid. At national level a general council contains representatives of the various national associations of different categories (employers, farmers, labour and so on). These national associations are in turn representative of sectional and other associations of local and regional, or industrial, branches. In its pure form the corporate state would exclude representative democracy, by denying the principle of equality of representation based on individual citizenship, and by rejecting the separation of state from society (Perroux, 1944; Winkler in Skidelsky, ed., 1977; Schmitter and Lehmbruch, eds., 1979).

Is it conceivable, however, that any of these elements could, suitably adapted, form part of a system of representative government, so that it might be better equipped to deal with the challenge of economic power? Many of the developments in the British government/industry relationship that we have been examining in the present study match what some have interpreted as a general trend towards 'liberal corporatism' (Lehmbruch in Schmitter and Lehmbruch, eds., 1979). Management of the economy has relied less on legislative and regulatory means and more on procedures of 'concertation' in which both the impartial, professional role of 'technocrats' and trade unions and employers' organisations brought together by government in 'tripartism' go some way to replace the functions of elected party politicians and parliamentary assemblies. The compulsory element is limited, however, in that most agreements made on the basis of 'tripartism' are still reached voluntarily, just as the trade unions and employers' organisations themselves are left for the most part to make their own rules of membership and association. Moreover, although the aim is a national consensus between different economic interests, these interests are still separately represented in their own organisations and are regarded as normally being in a competitive relationship, as in collective bargaining. Finally, however, the role of political parties tends to be seen as making the task of reconciling economic interests more difficult. And parliamentary politics is thought to be 'unreal', in contrast to the dealings of industrial organisations based on specialised functions in the economy.

Greater devolution to organisations representing industry, which at the same time are given greater official recogntion as corporate bodies, has been justified, therefore, both on grounds of efficiency and of democracy (Ionescu, 1975; Middlemas, 1979). On the other hand, it can also be seen simply as an alternative way of imposing conformity to some established view of the public interest.

Indeed, we should not be misled by appearances into thinking of 'concertation' as an alternative to government by political organisations. Attempts to set up corporatist methods of economic management at national level have invariably been politically inspired. In both Austria and West Germany, major steps to formalise procedures of 'concertation' were taken by 'grand coalitions' of the major political parties (Lehmbruch in Schmitter and Lehmbruch, eds., 1979) The more conservative of the parties have seen such methods as a way of responding to the challenge to their own role in government of the economic power of the trade unions, while the latter, along with socialist parties, have seen it as a way of redressing the balance of political influence in their own favour. In Britain, both the Heath Government's attempts at 'partnership' and the 'social contract' between Labour and the TUC might be interpreted in similar ways. In any event, political differences between parties and groups are invariably the decisive factor in placing limits on the influence of 'concertation'. That influence seems inevitably to depend on the government's own preparedness to back the results of tripartite and other consultations. We have seen in Britain how the significance of such procedures can vary with changes in economic policy.

One factor making governments reluctant to depend too much on a consensus with corporate organisations may well be that there are risks in going too far towards sanctioning authority based on economic power. On the other hand, economic groups themselves may well recoil from too close an embroilment with government, which has its own wider concerns and constituencies. In other words, corporatism may demand a degree of transformation in the role of interest groups beyond what is possible or desirable in a representative democracy. One factor is the multiplicity and diversity of economic interests, which neither interest group leaders themselves nor governments can afford to overlook, whatever the advantages of treating groups as 'governing institutions'. Another is that, given the essentially specialised and protective nature of organisations based on economic interests, their role in politics should not be confused with the responsibility of government.

The pluralism of economic interests

Even if we confine ourselves to interest groups in Britain with some direct relevance to industry, we should be wary of making generalisations about the potential role of intermediary organisations. Students of interest groups have for long wanted to know more about their internal structures and procedures, the attitudes of their membership and their relationships with each other and with government before taking too much for granted about their role in politics (Finer, S. E. 1965; Eckstein, 1966; Parry, 1969). There seem, on the surface of things, to be significant differences between employers' and business organisations, on the one hand, and trade unions, on the other. Certainly, in recent times at least, it is the latter which seem to have been making most of the running in Britain at least in terms of the political use of economic power. Even so, as we have already seen, the very notion of tripartism hardly seems realistic, when the true range and complexity of the interests associated with industry are taken into account.

No more will be offered here than a brief indication of the real multiplicity and diversity of industrial interests. That should be enough, however, to show up the main limits to the corporatist approach. We shall consider first the question of organisations intended to represent business interests in the widest sense.

In the first place, as we already saw in Part One, there is a distinction between employers' organisations and trade associations, in that the former grew essentially from bodies formed to deal collectively with labour questions, including pay, and the latter from bodies formed initially to provide common services or to manage restrictive trade agreements. The distinction is now usually considered to have lost most of its significance. The establishment of the CBI brought both types of organisation under the same umbrella of central representation, though some differences of outlook and structure remain among the organisations themselves.

There is probably a more significant distinction between representative bodies grouped centrally under the CBI, on the one hand, and chambers of commerce, on the other, concerned mainly with local or regional aspects of business and affiliating to their own national umbrella organisation, the Association of British Chambers of Commerce (ABCC). Also separate from the CBI are the Retail Consortium, including numerous associations of retail traders, as well as associations representing small businesses. These other bodies for representing business interests have sometimes been included in tripartite consultation and decision making, but their continued independence goes to show the differences that are still recognised between manufacturing industry and other forms of trade or commerce. No less important are the distinctions that survive between firms of different size, though there is considerable overlap, in that many small and medium-sized businesses affiliate directly to the CBI (Clarke, 1972; Grant and Marsh, 1977).

Given the size and importance of publicly-owned enterprise in the British economy, the representation of the boards of nationalised and other public undertakings forms in many respects a further potential category of its own. These boards are now members of the CBI, though they are represented separately on the NEDC, and also have their own organisation, the Nationalised Industries' Chairmen's Group.

Financial institutions, based mainly on the City of London, include a greater variety of types of institution than is usually acknowledged and are also difficult to fit into any simplified structure. The various financial institutions have traditionally been reluctant to be organised collectively. Different attempts to stimulate them to do so, mainly at the initiative of the Bank of England, have not proved particularly successful. Since the early 1970s, the Committee of London Clearing Banks has played its own role as a kind of trade association separately from the British Bankers' Association, while insurance and accountancy firms continue to have their own trade or professional associations (Smith, 1979; Cmnd 7937, 1980).

Professional associations also provide, in fact a distinct type of organisation in their own right. Mostly formed to protect and maintain professional standards and qualifications, they have tended to play an increasingly important role as spokesmen for their members' special interests, covering significant categories of people vital to industry. In particular, there has been the growing assertion of management as a distinct interest, not to be confused with those represented by employers' organisations and trade associations. As we have already seen, the British Institute of Management has been in the forefront of demands for government consultation of industry to include a much wider spectrum than that implied by tripartism and has called for its own representation on the NEDC.

It hardly makes sense, therefore, to treat the representation of employers and business as if it were based on a single corporate interest, especially if that is taken to imply a class interest based on the ownership of capital. Not only are there distinctions to be made among different types of business undertaking (including those between manufacturing industry and other forms of trade or commerce), but three elements in particular in the organisation of modern business need to be taken into account. First, there is the tendency in the modern business corporation for ownership and capital to be separated from management. The providers of capital include not only individual entrepreneurs, but dispersed small investors and large financial institutions (including sources such as trade union pension funds and public investment and loans). Secondly, even the distinction between employers and labour is inadequate, given the importance of professional managers and technicians of various kinds, who are themselves employees. Thirdly, account must be taken of the substantial section of industry in public ownership, which in Britain is so constituted as to be considered in some essential respects as commercial business, though with well-known and often crucial differences from the private sector. These and other elements also complicate the functional representation of business in other European countries. Special arrangements are usually made to take account of the particular interests of small businesses, of professions, of public enterprises and of agriculture. There is no ready-made or easily agreed measure available to weigh the claims of such different interests for purposes of national representation. If the criterion is simply the availability of specialised advice for Parliament and public authorities, then numbers are not so important. But, if the aim is to base political authority on functional representation, then it is difficult to conceive of any reliable method of distributing access to influence. Even when it is left to government to weigh the demands of different groups, the problems of assessing claims can be daunting (Finer, H. 1949; Friedrich, 1950; Laski, 1962).

We have seen that the CBI itself was formed, partly with government encouragement, to simplify the process of business representation. Business organisations have themselves since examined the possibilities of making representation even more rationalised and inclusive. In particular, the Devlin Committee, set up by the CBI and the ABCC, proposed the setting up of a new Confederation of British Business. The Committee's report gives an impressive and useful account, both of the existing functions of business representation in relation to government and of the view that in effect this should be organised on more corporate lines (ABCC and CBI, 1972). But the Advice Centre created after the publication of the report, to keep a record of the structure of trade associations and employers' associations, continues to discover an increasing number of specialist bodies. As for the CBI itself, the elaboration of its internal machinery for central policy making since the late 1960s does not mean that anything like a corporate view is normally established, except on the most general issues.

'It is easy enough to secure general agreement in the advocacy of measures for reducing profits tax or increasing depreciation allowances, which affect the whole of business, but it is virtually impossible to get a common commitment to measures which, for example, discriminate between different sectors of industry and commerce. Inevitably, for the most part, sectoral policy is dealt with in bilateral discussions'. (Smith in Vernon, 1974, p. 101)

Similarly,

'the survival and development of the FBI and the CBI owe as much to the provision of services to their members as to their performance as spokesmen for manufacturing industry'. (Grant and Marsh, 1977, p. 28)

Indeed, it is probably safe to assume that businessmen are more interested in representative organisations for their ability to protect special interests and to provide special services to their members, than from any belief in the value or practicability of the collective organisation of business interests in general. It is believed, for example, that large firms rely mainly in matters that affect them directly on a straight approach to government, whether departmentally or at a personal level of political leaders. Firms join representative organisations in spite of their awareness of the economic irrationality of so doing (given that the collective benefits obtained by the organisation would accrue to them in any event) (Olson, 1971; Grant and Marsh, 1977). We may assume, perhaps, that they do recognise the need for 'constant representation' at the level of central government, in addition to bilateral contact on particular issues, as was suggested by the Devlin Committee. But the real initiative for more inclusive forms of organisation tends to come from government and from the 'peak associations' themselves.

As for trade unions, these may more readily consider themselves as representing collectively some wider, even class interest. Their party-political alignment, as well as their concern with issues much wider than the wages and conditions of their own members would indicate such a general purpose. However, the collective organisation of labour has been more advanced than that of business, because organised labour has acquired a compulsory element and, must, therefore, be seen in certain essential respects as coercive (Olson, 1971). These characteristics in turn mean that trade unions are no less sectional and protective than other interest groups. Whatever their political connections and their claims to represent inclusive social interests, it is the industrial muscle of trade unions that gives them potential significance as a corporate power. The trade union movement's purpose in acting collectively on a national basis has clearly been to extend the rights and improve the particular material conditions of its members and not just to assist in furthering general ends of economic policy.

Even so, the movement's multiform, and often random, internal structure has, of course been the subject of numerous commentaries and public inquiries. Criticisms have been made by comparison with some other European countries where organised labour has adopted a far more rationalised structure, and some internal changes have been made in Britain. Sources of indiscipline, if not of industrial anarchy, have meant that periods of shared responsibility, partnership or, more often, simply co-operation, imply anything but an inevitable growth of corporatism based on centrally-organised trade unions.

The potential political influence of a collective organisation with such a mass membership cannot of course be denied. And there is the additional factor of its links with the Labour Party. But the unions' special political ties have in practice always been limited by the ultimate concern of union leaders with industrial questions (PSI, 1978). Moreover, patterns of voting behaviour indicate that the movement's political influence is partly dissipated in electoral terms by members' support for other parties. Recent opinion surveys suggest that a majority of union members do not share the leadership's views on vital questions and themselves have no desire to see the organised power of unions increased. In spite of their close relationship with Labour Governments it cannot be said that the trade unions are willing or able to present themselves as an alternative political force with uniform purpose (von Beyme, 1980).

It might be more useful, therefore, to treat unions as sharing with other economic interest groups the general characteristic of being essentially private organisations for the defence and promotion of sectional, material interests.

Government and organised interests

However, the characteristics of economic interest groups mean that in a representative democracy the government cannot be entirely passive about their activity. Students of politics are familiar with the shortcomings and side-effects of leaving interest groups unfettered. For one thing, given the already extensive involvement of public authorities with some aspect of virtually every conceivable organised economic interest, it is hardly realistic to think of the activities of groups as being unaffected by government. Some element of public regulation is usually present, whether in the form of sanctioning the rights of trade unions to practice the closed shop or to withdraw labour or in that of limitations to restrictive trade practices.

Moreover, intermediary organisations representing industry are unlikely to appear effective to their own memberships, if they are not able to claim successes in instigating, or else forestalling, public intervention, as the particular interest of the membership may require. Although selective intervention by governments may be justified in terms of a wider view of the public interest, it invariably leads in practice to particular applications of uncertain criteria, the full consequences of which public officials are only partly able to understand or control. The more the responsibilities of government require the co-operation of organisations representing special economic interests, the greater is the possibility that general and particular interests will be confused. In the British political system, with its dependence on concentrated power of the Executive, the risks of confusing the public interests with some special or partial view can be greatly enhanced. The pressures on political responsibility are probably no less great than in a system where groups participate openly and competitively through parliamentary or other political channels as they do, for example, in the USA and some continental European regimes. The difference is that in Britain co-ordination and control in the public interest have to be exercised by an essentially clandestine process within the Executive.

Interest groups themselves will usually be forthright in putting claims in terms of a wider view of policy. One vital function of such bodies, as we have seen, is to mediate between particular private demands and a larger perspective of what is possible in view of general circumstances or a longer term perspective. But, just as a group's collective outlook may not be free of ideological or even specifically partisan objectives, so the force of its claims may be, and usually is, affected by its economic power. We still need further enlightenment about the internal procedures by which individual groups reach common positions and attitudes, and about the real extent and influence of participation by the membership. Although people previously excluded, or under-organised (such as small businesses, consumers or the socially and physically handicapped) have in Britian recently themselves become better organised as interests, and although there is competition between groups and governments try to embrace a wider range of interests in consultation, who decides the agenda of consensus is still a vital and unresolved question (Parry, 1969).

There must always be doubts, therefore, about a consensus based on economic organisations sufficiently strong to be recognised by government. Government must have a unique responsibility for identifying, and seeing to, the interests of the largest groups of all, which are not only those which 'have no tendency voluntarily to act to further their common interests' but also those for whom the defence of a common interest is most important (Olson, 1971).

There seems to be no simple solution to the problem that governments need the intermediary functions of trade union, employer and other groups, yet are charged also with defining and upholding limitations to the way they use their economic power. Political responsibility may be asserted over them by appealing to the electorate against the demands of some powerful section or by means of restrictive legislation. But that approach can be self-defeating, as British experience has painfully illustrated. On the other hand, it can be equally dangerous to rely too much on such organisations to govern themselves even when they are brought within the pale of political rights and obligations by means of legal sanction or some formal process of direct economic representation. The danger is partly that the public interest will be allowed to depend too much on organisations that are still essentially private and sectional in nature and purpose. But it is also that the scope of public authority will be extended behind the cover of what seem to be autonomous private bodies and without the checks and balances that would normally be expected to apply in the public sphere. Corporatist explanations tend to imply that such different needs are irreconcilable on the basis of representative democracy.

The oligarchical trends in British government that we have repeatedly mentioned in this study have themselves been explained in terms partly of 'corporate bias', the key factor being an 'abdication' by the political parties (Middlemas, 1979). In the present study, a contrary explanation has been proposed. In fact, there has been an apotheosis of the two governing parties and it is that which explains both the concentration of executive authority and its difficulties in face of the challenge of organised economic power. Indeed, it is above all the effect of the Conservative and Labour Parties' own approach to representative government that has perpetuated and encouraged the view that industrialised society is necessarily divided and destructive confrontation on the basis of economic interest is inevitable.

The conclusion offered here, therefore, is that a more open and truly competitive political system might itself make the role of organised economic interest less intractable, without the need for corporatist explanations or solutions. In other words, the instinct of representative democracy may not be so ill-adapted as is so often nowadays supposed. That instinct is to accept the sectional and competitive nature of organised interests as ultimately compatible with a wider public interest and not to treat it as some inherently anti-social force. It is also to encourage voluntary co-operation and self-government by private bodies, if only in the interests of limiting the scope of public intervention. It is, on the other hand, to recognise that given the nature of economic power in an advanced, industrialised society, the state has to extend its sphere of concern to the behaviour of private organisations based on economic interest and in this its responsibility must be indivisible. But that does not mean that the state's role has to be incontestable or exempt from a whole range of possible influences. It may include the possibility of special national forums or a social and economic council to represent more extensive industrial and other economic interests on a consultative basis (Olson, 1971). Indeed, such a body could be a means of bringing the influence of organised interests more into the open, while subjecting it to more formal codes and procedures. It could help to recognise the importance of organised interests, while making their leaderships more answerable and their authenticity more subject to appeal.

What any kind of 'industrial parliament' could not do, however, is to compensate adequately for the shortcomings of political representation. Indeed, unless they form part of a recognised corporatist system of rule, such bodies are bound to be overshadowed or infiltrated by the political parties if they seek to pass beyond a certain point in their dealings. Although that limitation is in some respects their very strength, in other respects it may help to explain why they are so often unable to justify the value of their existence, or to bring much influence directly to bear, either towards government or towards industry. It is also why the primary and essential need in Britain is for reform of parliamentary politics.

13 The Reform of Parliament

Many of those who, at different times, have also diagnosed the problems treated in this book find a major cause in politics but look outside politics for amendment. They tend to see representative government essentially in terms of a competition between two major political parties as on the British postwar pattern, a competition, that is, conducted largely on a plebiscitary basis in 'winner-takes-all' conditions (Schumpeter, 1943; Brittan, 1978). But what if a different pattern emerged? It is by no means unrealistic to suggest that it could, given that the postwar two-party oligarchy has itself not always been with us and given that it has anyway made Britain politically unique among advanced, industrialised countries of a similar size. Moreover, there has been growing evidence recently that public opinion might welcome such a change (see pp. 119), while there are some changes in the ground rules, especially the electoral system, that would help to accommodate it.

Can we, then, imagine a change in politics that might among other things make the government/industry relationship more manageable and fruitful? We should begin with the qualifications that such a change cannot be expected overnight and should not be turned to as a panacea. The chief aim should not be to solve all the problems by a set of political reforms, but to create conditions in which solutions would be more likely to be found and applied. Even so, general issues arise from suggesting such a change that cannot be adequately treated in the scope of the present study.

As will become evident in this chapter, something more radical is meant by political change than is usually the case with proposals for adapting the procedures of Parliament. Something much more than procedural change is envisaged here. Put as simply as possible, the idea is that Parliament should develop four main functions in relation to the government/industry relationship.

First, there is its general representative function, in which it is presently deficient (see pp. 47–9). The problem is not so much the absence of a sizeable number of MPs with direct industrial experience (though it is likely that industrial managers, trade unionists, leading businessmen and others would be more prone to seek election to Parliament if the hold of the existing party machines was loosened). The Commons can restore to itself more of its rightful place as the forum where the diverse needs and interests of industry find expression, in all their different aspects, without numbers of MPs having to have an industrial background themselves. The important thing is for Parliament to be far more in touch with the people in general, and for Members to be more inclined to look outwards to the country rather than inwards to their own party and the Executive.

A second way Parliament can help is by subjecting legislative and budgetary measures to much more rigorous scrutiny and check. Industrialists and others would probably not complain if one effect were to slow the legislative process down. Parliament should not only be able to guard more effectively against ill-considered measures, but also have a greater positive role in bringing the specialised knowledge of industry to bear. The contribution of industrial advice need not be confined to direct dealings with departments and might well be enhanced by coming more into the open. But for the hold of party oligarchy, there is no reason why the Commons should not be the rightful place for that contribution to be made.

Thirdly, in a general sense, the function of Parliament should be to counter any assumption that there is some 'one best way' in economic, or for that matter any other, policy. If governments were obliged to work harder for support for their measures and to obtain it from a wider basis, there might not only be the greater stability in policy sought by industry, but also a greater prospect of genuinely radical change when the need is widely acknowledged. Such change (for example, in the tax system) nowadays tends to be excluded partly because the life expectancy of one party's government is not usually enough to bring it about. If it were no longer possible to expect every new government to undo the work of its predecessor, that obstacle would be overcome. A more independent and powerful Commons could perform such a function, however the government was formed, whether as a coalition or by a majority or minority party.

Finally, Parliament has the advantage, most notably in contrast to different types of corporatist representation, that, while it can reflect sectional and private differences, its ultimate purpose and inclination is to take some general view apart from the claims and conceptions of special interests. That function has under the prevailing conventions been largely transferred to the Executive, so that the public administration finds itself in the recurring dilemma of both responding to sectional demands and sustaining some view of the public interest. When the Executive is based so exclusively on party oligarchy, it is a function even more perilously performed. There should be nothing to lose and much to gain from letting the play of interests come more freely into the open, while relying on Parliament's traditional function once so famously expounded by Edmund Burke as:

'A *deliberative* assembly of *one* nation, with *one* interest that of the whole; where, not local purposes, not local prejudices ought to guide, but the general good, resulting from the general reason of the whole'. (Burke, 1887, p. 447)

There is an assumption that has so far blocked effective reform more than any other. It is that only by retaining the myth of Parliament's single sovereignty (which came into our system as late as the latter half of the nineteenth century) can such a function be effectively performed. The great advance would be to realise that there is no contradiction between the evocation of 'different hostile interests' and the arrival at 'unbiassed opinion', 'mature judgement' and 'enlightened conscience'. (Burke, 1887). But the link can only effectively be forged through a political assembly, and it should be the prime purpose of politics in a representative democracy to reach that consensus which has caused the yearning of so many of those who have deplored the recent past of the government/industry relationship.

From such rather lofty principles, we should now turn to examine in a more practical way the results of reform so far and the future prospects.

Parliament and legislation

The gradual advance of parliamentary reform over the last fifteen to twenty years has been restrained by the inherent reluctance of the bulk of MPs to challenge the conventions of party government. Reform has mostly flowed from a desire to 'rationalise' the procedures of the Commons, with the ultimate object of easing the Executive's task of passing its legislative and other measures and of managing the House (Walkland and Ryle, 1981). This tendency has been evident in the role of Parliament in legislation, which itself raises vital questions about the functions of legislation itself. Two general onbservations are relevant that go beyond the question of procedural reform.

First, although there is talk of a decline of Parliament's legislative functions of legislation itself. Two general observations are relevant both increasing congestion in the parliamentary timetable as well as annoyance and confusion in industry. At the same time, there has been resistance to any revision of legislative procedures that might deprive the official Opposition of its opportunities for confrontation with the government on the floor of the House (Drewry in Walkland and Ryle, eds., 1981).

Secondly, there has been a general change in the nature of legislation, which is now usually directed less at establishing general rules to constrain the conduct of individuals, than at empowering public, and even private, bodies, to take discretionary decisions affecting the status and welfare of particular groups. S. H. Beer has described this trend as 'the increasing specificity of the essential governmental decision', which does much to account for the shift of focus from Parliament itself to a direct relationship between goverment departments and private organisations (Beer, in Crick, ed., 1967; Lowi, 1969).

It may be considered all the more serious, therefore, that the framing and presentation of Public Bills, as is well known, is almost entirely a preserve of the Executive. Moreover, in conformity with the theory of the mandate, it is unusual for governments to be outvoted on their own legislation (though this does not take account of legislation that is withdrawn or not proceeded with on account of opposition in the Commons, or of that which is amended on a minister's own initiative). These prerogatives of the Executive mean that industrial interests apply pressure directly on departments at the preparatory stage. But, to the extent that legislation flows from internal party sources, such influence is a poor substitute for parliamentary proceedings leading to genuine amendment. For example, it seems that the CBI was able to secure modifications to the Industry Act of 1975 during parliamentary stages, even though that measure was originally conceived within the Labour Party with little, if any, apparent consultation with employers or management who would be affected by it (Drewry in Walkland and Ryle, eds., 1981).

It is, indeed, at committee stage that the Commons now has the greatest opportunity to influence the final shape of legislation by means of amendment, However, although numerous amendments are sometimes moved by individual MPs, these are rarely successful, while ministerial amendments are almost always agreed to (Griffith, 1974). Proceedings at this stage, which most often take place in standing committee, are considered unsatisfactory mainly because of the attitudes that Members normally adopt to the function of legislative scrutiny:

> 'Committee proceedings on Bills on important social issues partake of challenges to the government's fundamental attitudes. They are not concerned primarily to improve the Bill or even, in ordinary language, to examine it.' (Griffith, 1974, p. 233)

Inadequate information is provided by ministers on the reasons for different provisions in Bills, and the discussion of amendments invariably falls into a confrontation similar to that across the floor of the House, so that 'the examination is, in reality, of the principles that lie behind such legislation – which is why so many debates (in standing committee) resemble discussion on second reading'. Contributions to debate 'often perform no function other than that of advancing or retarding the personal reputation of the speaker' (Griffith, 1974, p. 298).

To make consideration of legislation at committee stage a more genuine attempt 'to examine and establish the factual and technical background' it has been proposed by the most recent Commons' Procedure Committee that standing committees should be enabled to hold sittings in select committee form, before proceeding to debate and vote on a Bill clause by clause (HC 588, 1977–78). At these sittings, the committee would take evidence from those responsible for drafting the Bill and also from the various interests affected. The House has agreed to adopt such a procedure on an experimental basis for certain measures considered as largely 'non-partisan'. There would clearly be some advantage for industrial representatives if such a reform were taken further and used for economic and industrial measures since it would give them an additional opportunity to be heard. The short-comings of standing committees go much deeper, however, and it is doubtful whether substantial difference can be made without a funda-mental change in MPs' attitudes towards their functions in revising Public Bills.

Another proposal is for Bills to be considered more often by commit-tees at a pre-legislative stage. In the case of taxation measures, there has been something of a revival of the practice of submitting possible legislative proposals to *ad hoc* select committees. There is opposition to pre-legislative scrutiny as a general practice, however, even from some parliamentary reformers, on the grounds that it would tend to dilute criticism of government proposals when they eventually come before the House. Such a view, however, is acceptable only in terms of the conventions of party government as they are now practiced. Nevertheless, there seems to be little support for pre-legislative scrutiny, except on 'non-partisan' proposals and at the initiative of the government of the day.

Another area where reform has been proposed is that of delegated legislation. Procedures for the scrutiny of technical aspects of delegated legislation have been elaborated over the years to provide a means of bringing to the attention of the House as a whole any use of such powers which, according to certain criteria, may be considered extra-ordinary. The main problem continues to be how Parliament should deal with the merits of delegated legislation and, in spite of new proposals by a Procedure Committee, progress on this aspect has been slow. In this, again, the House of Commons faces a typical dilemma. Members have not ceased to delegate powers and functions to ministers but they then complain of the lack of means of keeping those powers and functions under the Commons' full control. The funda-mental problem remains of trying to do too much by means of legislation and creating new detailed powers of public intervention, the use of which inevitably from time to time becomes controversial. At the same time, the House continues to be reluctant to take matters of political significance out of the arena of confrontation between the two governing parties so that ultimate control by the Executive is ensured.

Parliament and public expenditure

Much the same can be said for another vital aspect of Parliament's traditional role: the control of public expenditure. It has long been recognised that the Commons exercises no real prior control of expenditure decisions, since the relevant procedures are used either as a mere formality or for purposes other than the direct review of expenditure.

Although efforts have been made to enable Parliament to examine more usefully the Executive's longer term programmes of public expenditure, those programmes have proved to be too little related to actual expenditure for Parliament's intervention to be particularly significant. Debates on the annual public expenditure White Papers have, therefore, tended to be poorly attended and of little general significance. The main direction of reform has been to make better use of select committees, while acknowledging that voting supply is itself something of a formality. From 1971 to 1979, the Expenditure Committee's General Sub-Committee regularly considered the annual White Papers and used them as an occasion to issue reports dealing with expenditure in relation to economic policy in general, based on evidence from a wide range of experts as well as from representatives of industry (Robinson, 1978). But there were still complaints of the lack of information made available to Parliament, both the Expenditure Committee itself and a Commons Procedure Committee making proposals for improvements (Robinson in Walkland and Ryle, eds., 1981).

The Commons has also tended to rely on committee scrutiny and report where expenditure in particular sectors was concerned. Opportunities to review on the floor of the House or in standing committees the use of powers to give financial assistance to industry in various forms have not been used very often. Review after the event is, of course, still possible through the Public Accounts Committee assisted by the Comptroller and Auditor-General. But such review is still concerned primarily with the regularity of expenditure rather than the merits and does not do much to influence particular departmental decisions before they are made. The former Trade and Industry Sub-Committee of the Expenditure Committee, on the other hand, produced wide-ranging reports on such particular matters as the relationship between the government and British Leyland (HC 617, 1974–75) and on the use of funds granted to Chrysler (UK) Ltd. (HC 596, 1975–76). The former Commons' Select Committee on Science and Technology also held inquiries into particular industries where state funding had been important and, from 1956, the Select

Committee on Nationalised Industries reported from time to time on most major industrial public corporations. By such means Parliament has been able to give closer examination to the Executive's own reasoning in some major expenditure decisions affecting industry, and to the way such decisions have been implemented, usually with the help of evidence from those directly concerned on the industrial side. But these means have not ensured a regular or comprehensive review of the policy implications of expenditure decisions. It has not been thought appropriate to challenge the Executive's power to take such decisions, in effect on its own discretion, in the light of its own assessment of what the public interest requires.

In 1980, a select Committee on Procedure was appointed to re-examine procedures for control of public expenditure which, it was admitted, were 'in need of radical review'. But a fundamental problem so far is that there is an underlying contradiction in the attitudes of Members of Parliament. Although there are complaints about inadequate means of ensuring economy and efficiency in public expenditure, the Commons has continued to pass legislative measures enabling ministers to spend with discretion vast sums over which Members know they will have little or no subsequent control. Once they have voted expenditure with little, if any, real scrutiny MPs have tended to see their function as one of scrutinising in a rather piecemeal fashion, especially by means of select committees, the activities of government after the event. Parliament has thus confined its contribution to one of analysing the main choices involved, usually in a rather academic way, and recommending improvements in administrative methods for the future (Coombes et al, 1976; Robinson, 1978; Walkland and Ryle, eds., 1981).

Specialist committees

The typical response to this dilemma under the existing conventions has been to accept the shift of initiative to the Executive and the extension of the latter's reponsibilities as inevitable, while finding better means for MPs to exercise an informing and critical function. The main objects of reform from this point of view are better access to information, greater expertise in the use of it once obtained, and enough time away from more 'partisan' concerns for Members to assess the effectiveness with which the Executive seeks to achieve its own ends. Such activity is regarded as separate from the normal procedures on the floor of the House or in standing committee. It is not expected to lead to voting on the Executive's programmes or measures, but rather to report and recommendation, on which the majority in the Commons may act as it sees fit but which can also have a direct impact on public opinion, especially with the help of the mass media.

It is in this spirit that the House of Commons has now developed its use of select committees of backbenchers to conduct regular inquiries mainly by taking written and oral evidence, to deliberate in private, and to report, with a record of evidence received, to the House as a whole. The development of specialised select committees has now come to its fullest fruition so far with the present government's support for certain major proposals of the Procedure Committee that reported in 1978 (HC 588, 1977–78).

During the 1979/80 session of Parliament fourteen departmental committees were set up for the length of the Parliament, most with between nine and twelve backbench members, and given wide terms of reference enabling them 'to examine the expenditure, administration and policy of the principle government departments . . . and associated public bodies'. Each committee has the basic powers normally granted to a select committee, namely: to send for persons, papers and records; to sit notwithstanding the adjournment of the House; to adjourn from place to place; and to report form time to time. They were later given, and they have used, the right to appoint specialist advisers to supplement the assistance provided by the department of the Clerk of the House. The new system has replaced most previous select committees, including the Expenditure Committee and the Select Committee on Nationalised Industries.[1]

It is still too early to judge how far the new committees will make a practical difference to the relationship between Parliament and the Executive. Their arrival has caused considerable excitement and they are widely regarded as a major 'new deal' for the individual Member. Mr St. John Stevas, who was then Leader of the House, described the package including the new committees as 'one of the most important parliamentary reforms of the century'.

All the same, the innovation has not been made as a revolutionary change, at least if the major debates in 1979 and in 1980 on the Procedure Committee's report are anything to go by.[2] The rationale of reform is still that the extraordinary growth in scope and power of the Executive warrants improved means of parliamentary scrutiny and criticism. It is not that the balance of power in the House itself should fundamentally change. Specialist committees of this kind are still acceptable mostly because they are not seen to challenge the basic conventions of party government.

Previous select committees were far from comprehensive in their review of the public administration; indeed, each committee or sub-

---

[1] The Public Accounts Committee, the Joint Committee on Statutory Instruments and the Select Committee on the Parliamentary Commissioner for Administration remain.
[2] HC Debates, Vol. 968/9, cc 33–251, 1979; Vol. 974, cc 1020–69, 1979–80; Vol. 991, cc 716–831, 1980–81.

committee's coverage of its subject matter was at best patchy. On the other hand, extremely thorough, usually long reports were published on the particular issues selected for inquiry including masses of published verbatim evidence from ministers, departmental officials, independent experts and private bodies. (One estimate suggested that the reports and minutes of evidence from the Expenditure Committee between 1971 and 1979 covered four feet of library shelf space.) By the same token, however, the output of committees tended to be academic rather than polemical: a contribution often to the thinking of officials and experts than to other MPs or to public debate. The proceedings of select committees were conventionally non-partisan and:

> 'The outcome is often a report which is elegant in exposition, but sometimes rather loosely related to the evidence on which it is said to rest and revealing those signs of compromise which enable ministers and officials to interpret it according to their judgement of what is opportune and desirable.' (Johnson in Walkland and Ryle, eds., 1981, p. 216)

Both committee and other Members complain of the absence or delay of debates on the floor to consider committee reports, and thus of the frustration of much committee work by the lack of consequent attention.

On the whole, the new departmental specialist committees have taken a different approach. Many of the issues selected for inquiry have been more controversial and an attempt has been made to report in a much shorter time, in order to make a greater impact on public debate and on the accountability of ministers. What seems to be turning out as the senior committee, at least in terms of its high-powered and experienced composition, is that on the Treasury and the Civil Service. It had issued two short and pungent reports by the summer of 1980, both of which questioned sharply the assumptions on which two aspects of the government's economic policy were based (HC 712 and 713, 1979–80). Both reports proved embarrassing to ministers and obtained wide publicity. The Committee has now made a fuller report on the place of monetary policy in management of the economy. This criticises many of the assumptions of the present government's policy and the effectiveness with which it has been implemented (HC 163, 1980–81).

The new committees have made much more effective use than their predecessors of the practice (adopted following the 'Crossman reforms' of the mid-60s) of taking some oral evidence in public, and from ministers as well as departmental officials. The cross-examination of ministers on current issues of policy has subjected them in some ways to more rigorous public accountability than question time or debate on the floor of the House. Such an activity would normally have been considered too controversial for select committees. But the new committees have continued to behave in a relatively 'non-partisan' way, illustrating that it is possible to avoid the conventional party confrontation without being non-controversial or 'non-political'.

It has yet to be seen whether this more topical approach will replace, if only by the sheer pressure of time, that of providing more thorough analyses of longer-term problems. The other committees that have reported so far have collected a wide range of evidence, both oral and written, from the affected interests outside Parliament. In particular the Trade and Industry Committee has conducted and reported a major inquiry into import and export trade, during which, in addition to evidence from the relevant government departments and agencies, it heard representatives of the TUC and CBI, and of a number of trade associations and large companies, as well as receiving substantial written evidence from similar sources (HC 109, 1980–81). There can be no doubt that in these ways the new committees could be a valuable means of bringing representatives of industry into direct contact, in a public forum, with MPs and could provide a valuable opportunity for industry's views to be aired.

What is less clear is whether the development of specialist committees will on its own bring a significant change in the conventions of Parliament. The new reforms themselves indicate a greater spirit of independence among backbenchers and attendance in the new committees seems to have been higher than in past experience with select committees. The scope of the new committees is limited by the restrictions on their power to appoint sub-committees, and behind that limitation lies a fear that too many Members might be involved in committee work at the expense of the chamber itself.

Such work is still intended, at least by business managers in both major parties, to be an adjunct of parliamentary activity rather than part of its main focus. This fact is illustrated by the way that the new committees do not contain chairmen of party backbench committees or groups in their subject, or Opposition spokesmen. On the other hand, whereas previous select committees were appointed through the usual channels (subject to formal approval by the House as a whole), so that the parties' managers were able to keep the membership 'safe', the new committees have been appointed for the full Parliament by the Commons' Committee of Selection. Allegations about the continued influence of the whips in appointments to the new committees led to a debate on the subject in November 1979 and to a division. The independent way in which some of the committees have behaved so far may well suggest that a growing number of Members have been disabused of the conventions of an Executive-dominated Parliament (Davies, 1980; Taylor 1981).

To what extent can a Parliament, still essentially subject to the customs of party government, tolerate such a development? Unfavourable reactions by some ministers, at least according to press reports, have been heralded as a mark of the new committees' success, but there has also been concern about the effects of overload on the public administration. The burdens of responding to committee demands had already been set as a cost against the benefits of select committees before the new system was introduced. Some backbenchers would have liked to give the committees new powers to resist ministerial obstruction, above all regarding the supply of information from departments and the attendance of ministers and officials as witnesses. In fact, a memorandum 'leaked' from the Civil Service Department revealed that officials giving evidence to the new committees have been warned to avoid giving certain categories of information.[3] The liaison committee of all select committee chairmen (which has been established both to co-ordinate the work of individual committees and to see to the interests of the system as a whole) decided not to make a major issue of this aspect of the committees' relationship with the Executive. Nor were efforts to give committees new powers to obtain information successful when put to a division in November 1979 or when debated on private Members' motions in January 1981. It is assumed that, if refusal to supply information were pressed to the floor of the House, then a free vote would be allowed. But committees, as creatures of the House, depend on the ultimate support of a majority there for any powers they may have in relation to ministers.

A fundamental doubt about the role of specialist committees is whether the House of Commons can or should devote its time and energy to specialised, non-partisan activity of this kind. There are obvious advantages where economic and industrial affairs are concerned, in adopting an approach which allows the collection of evidence from a wide range of public and private sources, employs specialist advice, is withdrawn from the party confrontation typical of the chamber and permits a longer term and dispassionate assessment of complex issues.

On the other hand, the significance of specialist committee work of investigation and report must not be got out of perspective. Such specialist committees in the present British system are by their very nature limited, if only because of the ruling convention that the powers

---

[3] Excluded were advice given to ministers, interdepartmental exchanges on policy issues and interministerial consultations, the existence, terms of reference and composition of cabinet committees and the identity of their chairmen, and matters outside the department's responsibility and 'questions in the field of public controversy'. Committee inquiry is not intended by the Executive to include the role of the Cabinet Office or co-ordinating machinery within government.

of the whole House cannot be delegated to committees. The new committees, like their predecessors, do not have a legislative function, nor, in spite of their competence to deal with public expenditure by the departments assigned to them, do they have any direct control of supply. Their influence rests on access to information and publicity and on their own expert authority and spirit of critical inquiry. Ultimately they could not withstand either concerted opposition by the party managers backed by a majority of the House, nor a general transference into their own proceedings of the conventions practiced elsewhere in the Commons. The real question for us is whether parliamentary reform could be more than a device merely for making government more transparent and accessible.

Parliament and the Executive

What is of greater interest for us than the development of specialist committees itself are the signs during the last ten to fifteen years of greater independence among backbench MPs, and some loosening of the grip of the Executive over parliamentary business. The experience of the years of minority government between 1974 to 1979 may have represented an exception to the rule rather than a change of rule, but certain longer term trends may also be at work.

Recent studies of backbench voting behaviour and other attitudes during the last few Parliaments give some indication of such trends (Norton, 1980; Rose, 1981). Between 1945 and 1972 there were no examples of a government being defeated in the House of Commons because of the dissenting votes of its own supporters. In 1968, however, the Labour Government withdrew two major legislative proposals (the Industrial Relations Bill and its proposals for reform of the House of Lords) following opposition among its own supporters in the Commons. The Conservative Government of Mr. Heath suffered five defeats as a result of backbench rebellion between, 1972 and 1974. Roughly two-thirds of Conservative backbenchers voted against the government at least once during its whole term of office from 1970–74. None of these adverse votes were considered as requiring the resignation of the government concerned, and in most respects measures lost were re-introduced and carried later. Between February and October 1974, however, the Labour Government, which lacked an overall majority in the House, suffered 17 defeats, and, between October 1974 and March 1979, 35 defeats; (the Callaghan Government was in a minority after February 1977). The Callaghan Government finally resigned following defeat on a motion of confidence, the first time this had happened for over a hundred years. Even the 'comfortable majority' of the new Conservative Government elected in 1979 has proved to be more prone to backbench pressure than is usual with such a majority (for example, on MPs' pay, cuts in the external services of the BBC and again on rules for immigration).

If there were a longer term trend in parliamentary behaviour and attitudes towards restoring the power of MPs acting individually or in groups to resist even policies and measures proposed by their own party in office, then it might be possible to revise our expectations of the functions of Parliament. There have, in recent years, been a number of famous examples of backbenchers acting independently on particular issues. The most notable, perhaps, was the last Labour Government's devolution proposals. One sure way of enabling Parliament to perform the functions described at the beginning of this chapter would be for MPs to assert their independence more fully and more often in the way they vote. In other words, they would have to break the habits of party government that were formerly seen as the basis of consensus and stability in Britain.

Procedural changes could support such a shift of attitudes, though they could not be expected to bring it about themselves. With regard to public expenditure, something could be instituted far more like the annual consideration and vote of expenditure proposals, section by section, that takes place in most continental European assemblies in budgetary procedure. This might be thought to increase the risk of Parliament defending special claims against the general interests of economy and the overall objectives of economic policy, but it would bring the process of resolving such claims more into the open and cause budgetary decisions to be based on a much wider and more conscious political commitment than is now the case (Coombes, et al, 1976). Over the whole range of major legislation, including that dealing with taxation as with other economic matters, the present largely ineffectual committee stage could be replaced by consideration and amendment in specialist committees, which could as a normal practice also take the views of the affected interest, while including for the purposes of deliberation on the Bills, the relevant ministers and Opposition spokesman. In general terms, however, such changes would have to be seen as part of a wider evolution of the conventions that now place so much emphasis on a mere confrontation of the front benches (Study of Parliament Group, 1977–78; Walkland and Ryle, 1981 eds.,).

Some new clarification of those conventions is overdue. Both the experience of the 'hung' Parliaments from 1974 to 1979, and the blatant exceptions in recent years to the convention of collective responsibility have made it more difficult than ever to sustain the view that the Executive must be inviolable between elections. It ought to be possible for ministers to have to adapt their policies and measures in response to Parliament, without feeling that the government's survival, or even necessarily its reputation, were thereby always at stake. From time to time between 1977 and 1979 the relationship between ministers and Parliament did acquire something of this nature. One effect was that the Labour Government actually found itself in a stronger position towards organised economic interests, including the trade unions.

The same period also illustrated, however, to what extent the conventions need to be clarified, and would need to be adapted, if it became more difficult for governments to rely on parliamentary support. Under what conditions should the House of Commons exercise its elective functions with regard to the appointment and dismissal of governments and what checks, if any, should be applied to the prerogative of dissolution, now exercised by the Prime Minister? (The decision of the Callaghan Government to hold out during the winter of 1978/79 raised these and other controversial constitutional issues.) Clearly, the sort of changes that are envisaged here in the relationship between Parliament and the Executive raise all sorts of wider questions of this kind. What is envisaged is no less than an entirely different set of assumptions from those which have pertained in the living memory of those now active in politics. That such a change is possible is suggested by increasing disillusionment with the idea that there can be some unique and infallible capacity in the Executive to determine the public interest and govern in its name. Such disillusionment has grown with the distance between parliamentary government and those on whom its power must ultimately rest, not simply for electoral support, but for economic performance.

Parliament and the people
In the context of this study, the problem of Parliament is much wider than its relative failure to reflect, either in its composition or procedures, the needs of industry. The problem is a general and a profound one, as expressed in some reflections quoted from an ex-minister:

> 'What alarms me at the present time is that so much of the discussion that goes on is divorced from the truths and realities that exist outside. Once we realise that the House of Commons only becomes important when it reflects or strengthens outside movements, then parliamentary debate and so on become more important because it would reflect such a link-up.' (King, 1974, p. 119)

The concern of industry with the place that Parliament has come to occupy is, therefore, justified, but it leads to issues far beyond the government/industry relationship. The need for a new relationship between Parliament and the Executive arises, in other words, from the need for a new relationship between Parliament and the people.

The search for consensus has too often taken forms that are

essentially escapist, from a fear of recognising the diversity of needs and opinions that must exist in an advanced, industrialised society, a fear that in a healthy parliamentary system should be unnecessary. In effect, by accepting the notion of Parliament as the source of government, we have allowed it in Britain to become an *instrument* of government. Political parties, which were developed following the extension of the suffrage as means of popular expression, have become instead means of protecting political leaders from realities.

It can be misleading to ascribe the problems diagnosed in this study to 'adversary politics' rather than to the restrictive effects of a mould of politics based on two oligarchical parties, tied to outdated doctrines. Much of the analysis presented in this study suggests that the problem is that, in some vital senses, British political life is in effect not adversary enough. To break the mould, it seems necessary to accept the case for electoral reform which has anyway gained unusual support in recent years. The strength of the argument for proportional representation is that it would produce a House of Commons that was both more capable of weighing equitably different views and interests, but also more capable of bringing its judgement in this respect to bear on government. It would not be enough simply to engineer some form of coalition government for its own sake, or even to ensure greater fairness to certain minority parties. The over-riding need for change to some form of proportional representation is to restore confidence in representative government and bring Parliament closer to the people (the mass of whom are, after all, in Britain engaged in, or in some way dependent on, industry). In this respect, the role of political parties since the extension of the suffrage during the latter half of the nineteenth century has tended to increase the distance between Parliament and people, so that electoral reform to widen choice and make the Commons less dependent on the two governing party machines is as vital to representative democracy today as universal suffrage itself was in an earlier era.

It is true that proportional representation in some forms might not weaken, and could even increase, the importance of centralised party organisations. For British purposes, the most suitable system would seem to be one using the single transferable vote in multi-member constituencies. The system of political representation could then still be based on geographical constituencies related to local communities, while giving greater weight to each individual voter's preferences and avoiding the need for national party lists. This could lead in turn to a widespread change in voting behaviour and in the party system itself, producing altogether different conditions in which the conventional rules of parliamentary politics would have to applied. Those rules have already been strained by the general decline in electoral support for the two major parties (and most recently of defections in Parliament to the Social Democrats), so that the allocation of time and other privileges to minority parties has to be assessed by an awkward and often invidious process. But the longer term outcome need not be a multiplication of parties, permanent coalition government or even a major decline of the two existing major parties. Nor should the argument for electoral reform be seen purely in terms of these possible effects. The opportunity to vote for more than one candidate of the same party would give electors a far more effective means of influencing the composition of the House of Commons and should thereby give Members of different views from the current party hierarchy greater confidence in acting on those views. The leaderships of the major parties (whatever they were) would also have to be more responsive to the general inclinations of the electorate, both when dealing with party activists and when assessing the claims of special economic interests, and both these elements would need to show greater humility when confronted with the moderating influence of public opinion expressed in elections and sustained by Parliament.

Such an evaluation of British politics need not, in fact, be foreign to the aspirations of many of those active in the Conservative and Labour Parties nor to the traditions that those parties were themselves once much more prone to respect. But it seems, in the short term at least, that the sort of changes considered here run counter to the ingrained views of the leaderships of those parties. For that reason, (which is also why such changes have usually been considered too remote and far-reaching to be practical), an effective reform of Parliament has come to require a political renewal.

14 General Conclusions

Through the length and breadth of our nation a sense – vague and obscure as yet – of weariness with the old organisations, of desire for this transformation, works and grows. In the House of Commons the old organisations must inevitably be most enduring and strongest, the transformation must inevitably be longest in showing itself; and it may truly be averred, therefore, that at this present juncture the centre of movement is not in the House of Commons. It is in the fomenting mind of the nation; and his is for the next twenty years the real influence who can address himself to this.
(Matthew Arnold, *Culture and Anarchy*, 1869 p. 270)

This book set out to test a widely-held view that there has been a serious dislocation between industry and politics in Britain. The view is that, regardless of which major party has been in office and in spite of repeated reversals of policy, the government of Britain in recent decades has taken inadequate account of the needs and interests of industry. It is true that other aspects of British government might give equal cause for concern and also form the basis of the sort of critique that has been given here of some general features of the political system. But, given Britain's dependence on industry and her critical need to restore industrial competitiveness to correct continued economic failure, the perspective adopted here must surely be recognised as one of special significance. There have been signs of increasing awareness not only among industrialists but also among politicians and public administrators, that the impact of politics on industry has been harmful. The problem has been traced both to the methods by which policy decisions are made in government and to the way that political competition has tended to perpetuate antiquated divisions within industry and so exacerbate industry's own efforts to evolve relationships that would be more in keeping with the needs of today.

On the other hand, there is an equally important sense in which industry has itself contributed to the wider problem of governing Britain as an advanced, industrialised society. Indeed, the difficulties of the government/industry relationship need to be seen in terms of a general dislocation between government and people. The problem of industrial representation must not be reduced to one simply of dampening the effects of politics or improving the machinery of consensus among national spokesmen of industrial organisations. The challenge is essentially that of finding a much wider and more complex basis of common understanding and consent. The tendency has been, however, to seek to give even greater legitimacy to organisations representing vital social and economic interests and capable of wielding economic power, but proving inadequate in the function bestowed on them of mediating between the public interest and private, sectional demands. One effect of that tendency has been to underpin the oligarchical trends in politics, especially the authority expected of the leaderships of the two governing parties when in office, which has itself in turn been a major cause, if not *the* major cause, of the threat of corporate power in its different forms.

If the diagnosis offered here can be summed up in terms of a single fault, it is excessive expectation of government. But that should not be taken as a denial of government's vital responsibilities in the economic sphere or as a version of the view that the scope of politics should be limited. On the contrary, the preceding account has been at pains to emphasise the degree of interdependence between government and industry and the extent to which the issues at stake require political solutions. Above all, the authority of government has been seen here as all the more necessary in view of the tendency of all kinds of groups to organise themselves on the basis of economic power both for economic and political ends.

The question is rather one of how governments seek to acquire and to exercise authority. And the main conclusion here is that to cope with the interdependencies and complexities of an advanced, industrialised society, the concept of legitimacy implied by the present British system, dominated by a single-party Executive with plebiscitary authority, is altogether inadequate. In other words, the Executive needs to be subject to a far greater and more sensitive range of influences than those of the oligarchical party machine and crude electoral choice. Such a conclusion leads, however, to what many would still regard as a radical view of how government should be conducted in Britain. Before summarising the reasons for recommending such a view, a brief digression is in order.

The international perspective

It is in some ways to be regretted that this book did not set out with an international perspective. Certainly international comparisons can be highly misleading, especially when not based on an adequate understanding of the historical, social, economic and political background of the countries concerned. However, our conclusion should prompt reflection in a wider setting for two vital reasons.

The first is that, although certain aspects of the problem are peculiar to Britain, and in spite of the many unfavourable comparisons that can be made of Britain's performance with that of certain other industrialised countries, the problem of reconciling representative government and economic power is a general one. The problem of representative government that has been treated in this book demands a comparative perspective.

The second reason is that excessive expectations of government are partly fed by a failure to recognise the international constraints on any national government, at least of Britain's size and international circumstances. We are bound to wonder, though it would take us beyond the scope of the present study to pursue the question further, whether the problems of representative government diagnosed here do not owe a good deal to the incapacities of governments acting at a purely national level to handle the economic responsibilities with which they are confronted (Ionescu, 1975; Harrison, 1980). An international perspective would be likely to provide yet further arguments in favour of a more limited view of the real power of the Executive. It would, for example, show up the constraints on any British government from the effects of international monetary arrangements and fluctuations, from those of developments in international trade, as well as those of interdependence in defence and of multinational control of vital industrial undertakings. It would be especially fruitful to examine the development of the European Community in the light of the problems diagnosed here and to re-consider its wider constitutional and political implications. Again, the problems may have acute application in Britain, but they are relevant to all Member States of the Community as are the kind of international constraints just mentioned.

As it is, this book has confined itself for the most part to the British response and has tried to simplify the argument by leaving mainly to one side the influence of international factors. Since the problem has these wider applications and aspects, however, the analysis and conclusions offered here cannot be seen as ready-made solutions. What is suggested is that Britain has found herself in an especially unfavourable position to attempt an adequate response. And a major reason given for that is the failure of political institutions to adapt to the three central and related trends set out in the first chapter. Those trends, the implications of which will now be summarised in turn, are the growing responsibilities of government in the economic sphere, the effects of the use of economic power by organised social and economic interests, and the decline of Parliament.

Industry and politics

The relationship between government and industry has extensive foundations that go beneath political differences about the functions of government in the economic sphere. In many respects the responsibilities of government have grown as a reaction to public demands. What has tended to cause both dissatisfaction in industry and ineffectiveness in government, however, has been more than anything, the uncertainty surrounding the role of government bred by the pretensions of competing party oligarchies. In fact, there has been far more convergence in the practice of different governments than the more purist claims of the governing parties would suggest. But that convergence has not defrayed the costs of repeated uncertainty about the real intentions of governments in relation to fundamental aspects of the economic framework or the costs of a constant chopping and changing with measures and devices.

In this and other respects, a government that denies the need for public intervention, and practices it reluctantly, may be no better than one that makes claims for public intervention that exaggerate what it can achieve and underestimate the costs of interference for industry. By the same token, the role of government has become discredited by the confusion of motives for which both general and particular measures have tended to be taken. While there has been no shortage of arguments of a technical nature to justify different kinds of public intervention, those arguments have invariably been distorted, whether by a government's concern to realise some tenet of party doctrine or by its attachment to some special group or groups.

But these tendencies call for more, not less, ventilation in a political arena of the issues bearing on policy in the industrial and wider economic sphere. Consensus will be effective only if it is sufficiently inclusive of the differences of interest and opinion that are inevitable in a pluralistic society. Methods of conducting controversy, expressing differences and sustaining criticism are required that will range far more widely, and pierce far more deeply into specific applications, than the normal confrontation of the governing parties has provided, at least in the period since 1945. Politics has been set fruitlessly on a compulsive exchange over what the responsibilities of government should be, while there is far less vitality in questioning how those responsibilities should be exercised and by what kinds of organisation. More energy could be devoted to finding means of organising economic activity that are best suited to meet the particular needs involved, including those needs that are regarded as not purely economic.

Decisions affecting economic activity in Britain are taken by a whole variety of methods, none of them uniquely appropriate or adapted to all purposes. A full account of the methods available would have to include reference to the market system, co-operatives, voluntary or altruistic provision (what Hayek calls 'the independent sector')

(Hayek, 1979) bureaucratic and even judicial methods. In most advanced economies such different procedures and a mixture of them are employed. One advantage of a developed society and of representative government should be the opportunity to choose and to mix methods.

But that opportunity can become foreclosed when it is assumed (usually wrongly) that one particular method is infallible or preferred exclusively in some higher end of group interest or party dogma. Unfortunately, the British approach has tended to make that assumption uppermost. If, on the other hand, new measures could not be carried without a much broader base of support in Parliament and elsewhere, not only might they be more carefully prepared and less narrowly conceived, but they might also have a more adequate period in which to be tested. In this respect, a genuine politics of consensus, or procedures that subjected the more primitive notions of policy to a wider and more effective kind of criticism both before and after their implementation, far from fudging issues or confusing purposes, would help to clarify aims and keep measures more in tune with reality. Because most issues in industrial and economic policy are so complex, a political party's own channels of information and policy making are usually inadequate. But the dependence on such party channels in Britain has led to a false dichotomy in which it is maintained either that problems are resolved simply by transferring them to some public authority or, on the other hand, that some wholly private sphere is available for simplifying and automatically resolving differences about the allocation of resources and rewards. In fact, there is no particular magic to be evoked in either public or private modes of operation.

The idea of the mixed economy may be one way of recognising the need for such a wider view of the public interest. However, we have seen that as a basis for governing an advanced, industrialised society it needs much greater refinement and elaboration. The mixed economy has not overcome the mystique attaching – in both positive and negative ways – to public and private modes of operation. Its overdue re-appraisal should take the following warning as its chief guideline:

'Growth is only feasible if there are clear criteria for the distribution of resources within the public sector and incentives for it to operate well; and also if there is some clear legitimacy attached to the private sector so that it feels it is doing a useful job for the nation, that there is some point in the work load and the risks involved' (Mackintosh 1978 p. 268).

From the experience of most other West European countries it seems that this problem of reconciling the public and private modes is peculiarly acute in Britain. Given the nature of the British economy, a prime need would seem to be that of assimilating industry itself more effectively within the political system, but that in turn must be seen against the wider background of the functioning of representative government.

The use of economic power

As Chapter 1 warned, it is not always clear what is meant by the interests of industry. Like society in general, what we call industry may have certain obvious common interests, but it also comprises, for other purposes, differentiated interests of occupational and other groups. In an advanced, industrialised society an increasing range of economic activity is dependent in some way on the behaviour of organisations set up to represent such groups and especially on their role in one or other form of collective bargaining. Moreover, collective action through such organised interest groups has increasingly prevailed in the political sphere, being substituted in many respects for the more traditional role in representative government of parliamentary channels. Indeed, not only has the economic power available to different organised groups been an additional reason why the responsibilities of government have grown but governments have themselves treated the collective organisation of industrial and other interests as a vital means of exercising public authority in new ways and over new areas of concern.

The role of government in relation to decisions affecting the re-distribution of income and wealth, especially when, as in the prices and incomes policies of the past fifteen or more years, it tends to become the centre of management of the economy, is highly controversial no less among professional economists than politicians. This book has not been concerned to settle such issues. But the government/industry relationship seems to be unavoidably affected by the impact of group bargaining using the currency of economic power, whatever the general strategy of a particular government for managing the economy and whatever instruments are chosen to respond to the effects of group power. The role of such groups has become a central issue of politics, not only because it affects society's prospects of achieving economic growth without inflation, but also because of the negative effect the nature of group competition has on the particular interests of group members themselves. This is especially true as resort to collective forms of organisation has spread for both economic and political purposes.

The issue for this book has been how well political institutions have responded to the economic power of organised groups. It is another vital aspect where the public interest cannot simply be left to the free play of private organisations. Consequently, a government that sought to stand apart completely from the competition of groups would be no less irresponsible, in effect, than one that sought to give special advantages to one group or class of groups over others. It is also an aspect of government, therefore, in which a relationship with industry can be seen to be crucial to the wider interests of society. That is not because public intervention can by itself resolve the problems of re-distribution, but rather because it is vital for groups to have confidence in the utlimate impartiality and arbitrative authority of government.

Many have been tempted for this reason to see the conditions of an advanced, industrialised society as leading inevitably to some form of 'corporate state'. As we have seen in earlier chapters, however, the whole political application of the idea of corporatism is riddled with ambiguity.

On the one hand, corporatism implies the direct involvement of industry in government, with a view to transferring to industrial organisations themselves the responsibility of achieving compliance with some wider public interest. By itself, functional representation might well be seen as an essential means to governing an advanced, industrialised society since it provides government with the means of taking account of the occupational and other social and economic interests with which most people now identify so closely. But, to the extent that participation in government places constraints on industrial organisations themselves, above all in the way it requires centralisation and hierarchical patterns of authority, then the leadership of an organisation tends to become unresponsive to its membership and to find itself torn between wider political concerns and the sectional demands and properties of the group itself. It is no accident that the trend of oligarchy in political parties has been associated with a similar trend in organisations based on social and economic interests.

In the hope of making their own exclusive tenure of power more effective, the governments of both major parties have tried to strengthen the formal authority of group leadership at national level. But a vicious circle is thus set up, in which, as the parochialism and partiality of the groups assert themselves, yet further pressures for centralisation and public intervention are applied. To be caught up in such a vicious circle is against the natural instincts and purposes of the groups themselves as it is against the pluralism that representative government is designed to reflect (Smith, 1979).

Indeed, corporatism implies on the other hand, a devolution of authority to small-scale groups, which would be self-governing, usually on the basis of easily recognised common occupational interests. It is in this sense that comparisons are often made with mediaeval guild corporations. But, in view of the nature of economic groups in an advanced, industrialised society, there can be little hope that this side of corporatism might be detached from its other, centralist aspects (Kumar, 1978).

For one thing, the self-governing rights of groups are not always seen by the individual members – and quite rightly so – as the best defence either of their own personal freedoms or of their own economic welfare. Indeed, given the way the interdependence of modern society gives certain groups the power to hold the rest of the community to ransom, there must be limits to self-government by corporate groups in their own ultimate interest. While these and other aspects of the economic power of groups show why limitations on their autonomy are essential, they also explain why self-government is itself often not enough as an aim for the leaders of groups. The latter, as recent British experience has shown, cannot always resist the temptation to use monopoly power and even the power of the state itself to act on a wider stage – not always in the ultimate interests of their members.

While modern corporatism may be closely related to industrialisation, so, however, were nineteenth century liberal institutions and the principles of representative government on which they were based (Kumar, 1978). Those principles would seem to be all the more essential now, in view of the potential use of economic power by organised groups. They are principles that recognise a plurality of interest, seek to channel these through constitutional as well as purely economic means and support checks against any tendency of government to become too closely identified with the interest of one group as opposed to others.

In the circumstances of today, the application of those principles must include a substantial element of functional representation, both in recognition of the power of organised social and economic groups and in an attempt to tame that power by bringing groups within the frame of constitutional procedures. There is, therefore, a strong case for supplementing existing consultative organs based on the Executive with some kind of widely representative deliberative and consultative forum - an Economic and Social or Industrial Council – which could be seen as the interests' own venue, independent of the Executive. The constitutional and technical difficulties of devising such a new organ are important but not insuperable. The essential point is that the chief purpose of such a body would be to give diverse representatives of industry an opportunity to question in public the attitudes of both the party machines and the leaderships of employers' organisations and trade unions. The aim would not be to substitute for Parliament or to attempt some kind of corporatist form of government based on shared responsibility between ministers and national group spokesmen. Rather it would be to support a revival of pluralist forms of representation and to counter any drift into corporatism.

However, as we discussed at length in Chapters 11 and 12, there are unavoidable limitations in the role of such a forum. The problems addressed in this book call for nothing less than a re-assessment of the role envisaged for Parliament in the system of government and, therefore, of the political setting in which that role is conducted.

The neglect of representative democracy

We have dwelt in earlier chapters on the decline of Parliament, meaning by that a movement of the political order away from earlier principles of representative government in other directions.

The transformation of the British system of government into what has prevailed since the last war is familiar enough. Through the agency of two preponderant disciplined parties based on mass electoral support, the Executive is able to claim a direct relationship with the electorate. Parliament's role is thereby reduced either to what is largely a ritual of mere debate and formal voting on government measures, or to opportunities for individual Members or groups of Members to scrutinise, obtain information, criticise and protest through such procedures as questions or select committees. To the extent that the parties depend on some form of regular electoral support and that the Executive is composed of leaders of the majority party, then this order may be described as representative. But the primacy granted to the Executive during a party's term of office, and the extent of discretion it can obtain for itself (especially, it might be stressed, in economic affairs), have tended to make its real relationship with the people more of a plebiscitary than a genuinely representative nature.

Moreover, the two governing parties are organised on the assumption that tenure of office must be the over-riding means, while the purposes to be achieved may be formulated primarily through their own channels. Political success is measured in terms of a party's ability to act according to tenets and commitments adopted through its own channels and sanctioned by a simple electoral majority obtained by the crudest of methods. In practice, of course, the governing parties in Britain have found themselves adopting a far more pragmatic approach in office, mainly as a result of the necessary process of bargaining and bidding that the support of both electorate and groups requires. In practice, therefore, the promised power of office invariably turns out to be chimerical. But it is still assumed that the mediation of the governing parties, one of which will be enabled to govern entirely according to its own assessment of affairs, is uniquely capable of providing responsible government.

Such an outcome of representative democracy should not be taken as inevitable. It follows from a particular interpretation of the sovereignty of Parliament that has failed to take account of the realities of government in an advanced, industrialised society. That is broadly why the mere reform of the procedures of Parliament is not enough on its own and why it has been found necessary here to open the question of a possible political renewal.

Many will find the emphasis placed on Parliament old-fashioned or too limited in other ways. Over the past two decades a number of distinguished commentators have challenged fundamental aspects of the British system of government, and a whole range of proposals have been ventilated, from reform of the Civil Service to regional and national devolution, and including, as we have seen, those for new forms of functional representation. Proposals for greater participation are often lumped together uncomfortably with those for greater efficiency and fuller use of technical specialisation. It is argued here, however, that, whatever the merits of individual proposals, the limits to what can be done in the way of adapting government to modern needs are set by the nature of our parliamentary politics.

For example, it is not enough to appeal to political responsibility to offset the inadequacies of the public administration, without taking account of the nature of that responsibility. Many of the constraints on the Civil Service must themselves be traced to its relationship with ministers. Decentralisation must also be viewed in terms of what arrangements are made for deciding how the vital functions of central government are to be exercised. Few would want to disagree with the typical view that the work of government:

'Should be kept always as close as possible to the citizen rather than withdrawn unnecessarily to some bureaucratic stratosphere, and should be handled in ways which are as near as possible to those of commonsense reality, everyday life, and as far as possible from the mystiques and pretensions so beloved in Whitehall'. (Nicholson, 1967, p.368)

The fact is, however, as has been seen repeatedly in this account, that people have relentlessly expected government to be infallible, especially in the economic sphere, and at least in matters that affect them directly. And they have condoned a political order which has sought to rely on increasingly centralised and concentrated forms of or-ganisation.

As suggested in earlier chapters there are some signs that the attitudes of both the electorate and of MPs may be changing. It may be that the mould established by the governing parties will be broken. It may even be that with the help of electoral reform a new order will emerge, in which it would be far more difficult for a single party to sustain the primacy of the Executive and in which the authority of governments would depend on the active support of different groups of MPs, who would be prepared to use their votes far more independent-ly. In other words, it is not a simple change of personnel or of prevailing doctrines that is meant here by political renewal, nor a withdrawal from political competition altogether into some form of inclusive coalition or government by 'wise and moderate men'.

In fact, the study that has led to this book is unfinished, since what is envisaged is a change in the role of Parliament that has wide-ranging constitutional, as well as political implications. It has not been thought relevant in Britain to consider these in practical terms, at least for some time. Some of the major issues can be mentioned here.

There is, first, a series of questions affecting the management of the House of Commons and the role of the 'usual channels', such as the allocation of time, the order of business, the appointment of committees and their chairmen and the arrangements for divisions of the House; such matters may sound pedestrian but in fact would be of vital importance for the conduct of government without the existing party system. Secondly, there are the conventions of collective and individual ministerial responsibility, which affect not only the legislative process and that of the budget, but also the conduct of departments of state and thereby the role of the Civil Service. They also connect, thirdly, with the whole question of the formation of governments, the use and effects of motions of censure and confidence and the prerogative of dissolution. It is worth mentioning, finally, the role of the second chamber, especially its powers over legislation when this is not passed by disciplined government majority in the Commons.

It is enough only to list such constitutional implications to get the measure of what is involved, which is no less than turning on its head Bagehot's famous characterisation of the Constitution as 'framed on the principle of choosing a single sovereign authority and making it good' (Bagehot, 1964 edition). But it is against the setting of those implications that we should approach the kind of political renewal supported here, and increasingly recognised as the necessary preliminary to trying to resolve effectively the problems analysed in this book: a renewal made possible by measures such as electoral reform, the state financing of political parties and redressing the balance between Parliament and the Executive. These and other fundamental issues of the political order have tended to become more than academic as the primacy of the two governing parties has been challenged in recent years. They will be of increasing practical importance if the efficacy of the existing order continues to decline both in terms of popular support and ability to govern.

Bibliography

Abraham, N. *Big Business and Government: the new disorder*, London, 1974
Alderman, G. K., *British Elections: myth and reality*, London, 1978
Allen, A. et al, *A Better Way*, London, 1979
Allen, G. C., *The Structure of Industry in Britain*, London, 1970
Amery, L. S., *Thoughts on the Constitution*, (revised edition), London, 1964
Aron, R., *The Industrial Society*, London, 1967
Association of British Chambers of Commerce and the Confederation of British Industry, *Report of the Commission of Inquiry into industrial and commercial representation,* (Chairman: Lord Devlin) London, 1972
Bacon, R. and Eltis, W., *Britain's Economic Problem: Too Few Producers*, London, 1976
Bagehot, W., *The English Constitution (1867)*, London, 1963
Bannock, G., *Juggernauts, the Age of the Big Corporations*, London, 1971
Barbash, J., *Trade Unions and National Economic Policy*, London, 1972
Barber, A. and Rush, M., *The Member of Parliament and his Information*, London, 1970
Barnes, Denis and Reid, Eileen., *Governments and Trade Unions*, London, 1980
Barry, Brian, *Sociologists, Economists and Democracy*, New York, 1970
Beckerman, Wilfred, *In Defence of Economic Growth*, London, 1974
Beer, S. H., *Modern British Politics*, London, 1965
Bell, D., *The End of Ideology*, New York, 1961
Bell, D., *The Coming of Post-Industrial Society*, London, 1974
Bell, D., *The Cultural Contradictions of Capitalism*, London, 1976
Berry, D. F., Metcalfe, L. and Neddy, an organisational metamorphosis, *Journal of Management Studies*, Vol. II, 1974, pp. 1–20
Beyne, Klaus von, *Challenge to Power: trade unions and industrial relations in capitalist*
Birch, A. H., *Representative and Responsible Government*, London, 1964
Birch, A. H., *Representation*, London, 1971
Birnbaum, P., Lively, J. and Parry, G. (eds), *Democracy, Consensus and Social Contract*, London and Beverly Hills, 1978
Blackaby, F. T. (ed.), *British Economic Policy 1960–74*, Cambridge, 1978
Blackaby, F. T. (ed.), *The Future of Pay Bargaining*, London, 1980
Blake, Lord (ed.), Report of the Committee on Electoral Reform, London, 1976
Blank, Stephen, *Industry and Government in Britain*, London, 1973
Bloch-Lainé, Francois, *Pour une réforme de l' enterprise*, Paris, 1963
Bogdanor, V. and Skidelsky, R. (eds.), *The Age of Affluence 1951–1964*, London, 1970
Bray, Jeremy, *Decision in Government*, London, 1970
British Institute of Management, Letter from the Director-General to *The Times*, 14 December, 1979

Brittan, Samuel, *Steering the Economy*, London, 1971
Brittan, Samuel, *Capitalism and the Permissive Society*, London, 1973
Brittan, Samuel, *Left or Right: the Bogus Dilemma*, London, 1968
Brittan, Samuel, *The Economic Consequences of Democracy*, London, 1978
Bruce-Gardyne, Jock, *Whatever Happened to the Quiet Revolution?*, London, 1974
Buchanan, J. M., et al, *The Economics of Politics*, London, 1978
Budd, Alan, *The Politics of Economic Planning*, London, 1978
Burke, Edmund, *Works*, Vol. I, London, 1887
Burns, Tom, *Industrial Man*, London, 1969
Butler, David and Kavanagh, D., *The British General Election of October 1974*, London, 1975
Butler, David and Kavanagh, D., *The British General Election of February 1974*, London, 1975
Butler, David and Kavanagh, D., *The British General Election of 1979*, London, 1980
Butler, David and Stokes, Donald, *Political Change in Britain*, London, 1971
Butler, David (ed.), *Coalitions in British Politics*, London, 1978
Butt, Ronald, *The Power of Parliament*, London, 1967
Castles, Francis, *The Social Democratic Image of Society*, London, 1978
Caves, R. E. and Krause, L. B. (eds.), *Britain's Economic Performance*, Washington DC, 1980
Centre for Studies in Social Policy, *The Corporate State – reality or myth?*, London, 1976
Chandler, A. D., *The Visible Hand*, London, 1977
Channon, D. F., *The Strategy and Structure of British Enterprise*, London, 1973
Chester, D. N. (ed.), *Lessons of the British War Economy*, Cambridge, 1951
Chester, D. N. and Willson, F. M. E., *The Organisation of British Central Government 1914–1956*, London, 1957, 2nd edition, 1968
Chester, D. N., *The Nationalisation of British Industry 1945–51*, London, 1975
Churchill, W. L. S., *Parliamentary Government and the Economic Problem*, Romanas Lecture, Oxford, 1930
Clarke, P., *Small businesses*, London, 1972
Clarke, Sir Richard, *Public Expenditure: management and control*, London, 1978
Coates, R. D., *Teachers' Unions and Interest Politics*, London, 1972
Coats, A. W. (ed.), *The Classical Economists and Economic Policy*, London, 1971
Cole, G. D. H., *Self-government in industry*, London, 1917
Cole, G. D. H., *Guild Socialism Re-Stated*, London, 1920
Cole, G. D. H., *The Machinery for Socialist Planning*, London, 1938
Confederation of British Industry, *Pay: the choice ahead*, London, 1979
Confederation of British Industry, *Pay: Facing the Future*, London, 1980
Conservative Central Office, *The Right Approach to the Economy*, London, 1976
Coombes, David, *State Enterprise: Business or Politics*, London, 1971
Coombes, David et al, *The Power of the Purse: Budgetary Decision Making in Six European States*, London, 1976
Coombes, David and Walkland, S. A. (eds.), *Parliaments and Economic Affairs*, London, 1980
Cordon, W. M. and Fels, G. (eds.), *Public Assistance to Industry*, London, 1976
Crosland, Anthony, *The Future of Socialism*, London, 1956, revised edition, 1963

Crick, Bernard, *The Reform of Parliament*, London, 1964

Crick, Bernard (ed.), *Essays on Reform*, London, 1967

Crossman, R. H. S., *Diaries of a Cabinet Minister*, Vols. 1-3, London, 1975, 1976, 1977

Crouch, Colin, *Class conflict and the industrial relations crisis*, London, 1977

Crouch, Colin, *The Politics of Industrial Relations*, London, 1978

Crozier, Michel J., *La Société Bloquée*, Paris, 1970

Crozier, Michel J., Huntington, Samuel P., Watanuki, Josi, *The Crisis of Democracy: report on the governability of democracies to the Trilateral Commission*, New York, 1975

Dahl, Robert A., *A Preface to Democratic Theory*, Chicago, 1963

Dahrendorf, Ralf, *Class and Class Conflict in an Industrial Society*, London, 1959

Dahrendorf, Ralf, Effectiveness and Legitimacy: on the 'governability' of democracies, *Political Quarterly*, Vol. 51, No. 4, 1980 pp. 393-410

Davies, Ann, *Reformed select committees: the first year*, London, 1980

Dell, Edmund, *Political Responsibility and Industry*, London, 1973

Denton, G. et al, *Economic Planning and Policies in Britain, France and West Germany*, London, 1968

Department of Economic Affairs, *The Task Ahead: Economic Assessment to 1972*, London, 1969

Dion, L., The politics of consultation, *Government and Opposition*, Vol. 8, 1973, pp. 332-53

Eckstein, H. H., *Pressure Group Politics: the case of the British Medical Assocation*, London, 1960

Economy, The, the Government and Trade Unions: joint statement by the TUC and the Government, London, 1979

Edwards, Sir Ronald, *Nationalised Industries: a commentary*, Stamp Memorial Lecture, London, 1967

Elliott, J., *Conflict or Co-operation? The growth of industrial democracy*, London, 1978

Ellis, J. and Johnson, R. W., *Members from the Unions*, London, 1974

Else, P. K. and Marshall, G. P., *The Management of Public Expenditure*, London, 1979

Evans, G. (ed.), *Labour and the Constitution*, London, 1977

Fels, A., *The British Prices and Incomes Board*, London, 1972

Finer, Herman, *Representative Government and a Parliament for Industry*, London, 1923

Finer, Herman, *The Theory and Practice of Modern Government*, London, 1949

Finer, S. E., *Anonymous Empire*, London, 1965

Finer, S. E., The power of organised labour, *Government and Opposition*, Vol. 8, No. 4, 1973

Finer, S. E. (ed.), *Adversary Politics and Electoral Reform*, London, 1975

Foster, C. D., *Politics, Finance and the Role of Economics*, London, 1971

Fox, Alan, *Socialism and Shop Floor Power*, London, 1978

Fraser, Tom, Economic development committees - a new dimension in government-industry relations, *Journal of Management Studies*, May, 1967

Friedrich, C. J., *Constitutional Government and Democracy* Boston, Mass., 1950

Galbraith, J. K., *The New Industrial State*, London, 1967

Galbraith, J. K., *Economics and the Public Purpose*, London, 1974

Garrett, J., *Managing the Civil Service*, London, 1980

Giddens, A. (ed.), *Elites and Power in British Society*, London, 1974
Gilbert, M. (ed.), *The Modern Business Enterprise*, London, 1972
Gilmour, Sir Ian, *The Body Politic*, London, 1969
Gilmour, Sir Ian, *Inside Right: a Study of Conservatism*, London, 1978
Glass, S. T., *The Responsible Society*, London, 1966
Granada Television, *The State of the Nation: Parliament*, London, 1973
Grant, Wyn and Marsh, D., *The Confederation of British Industry*, London, 1977
Grant, Wyn, Business Interests and the British Conservative Party, *Government and Opposition*, Vol. 15, No. 2, 1980, pp. 143–161
Green, Diana M., The Seventh Plan – the demise of French planning?, *West European Politics*, Vol. 1, No. 1, 1978, pp. 60–77
Griffith, J. A. G., *Parliamentary Scrutiny of Government Bills*, London, 1974
Griffiths, R. T., *Government, Business and Labour in European Capitalism*, London, 1977
Grove, J. W., *Government and Industry in Britain*, London, 1962
Habermas, Jürgen, *Legitimation Crisis*, Boston, Mass., 1975
Hague, D. C., Mackenzie, W. J. M. and Barker, A., *Public Policy and Private Interests: the institutions of compromise*, London, 1975
Hailsham, Viscount, *The Dilemma of Democracy*, London, 1978
Haines, J., *The Politics of Power*, London, 1977
Hansard Society for
Parliamentary Government, *Politics and Industry – the great mismatch*, London, 1979
Hansard Society for
Parliamentary Government, *The British People – their voice in Europe*, London, 1977
Harris, Nigel, *Competition and the Corporate Society: British Conservatives, The State and Industry 1945–64*, London, 1972
Harrison, R., *Pluralism, Corporatism and Democracy*, London, 1980
Hatfield, M., *The House Left Built: inside Labour policy making 1970–75*, London, 1978
Hayek, F. A., *Law, Legislation and Liberty*, Vols. 1–3, London, 1973, 1976, 1979

Hayward, J. E. S., *Private Interests and Public Policy*, London, 1966
Hayward, J. E. S., *The One and Indivisible French Republic*, London, 1973
Hayward, J. E. S. and Watson, M. M. (eds.), *Planning, Politics and Public Policy: the British, French and Italian experience*, London, 1975
Heclo, H. and Wildavsky, A., *The Private Government of Public Money*, London, 1974
Heffer, E., *The Class Struggle in Parliament*, London, 1973
Hemingway, J., *Conflict and Democracy: studies in trade union government*, London, 1978
Hirsch, Fred, *Social Limits to Growth*, London, 1977
Hirsch, Fred and Goldthorpe, J. T. (eds.), *The Political Economy of Inflation*, London, 1978
Hogwood, B., Monitoring of Government involvement in Industry: the case of shipbuilding, *Public Administration*, Vol. 54, 1976, pp. 409–24
Holland, S., *The Socialist Challenge*, London, 1975
Holland, S. (ed.), *Beyond Capitalist Planning*, Oxford, 1978
Hollis, C., *Can Parliament Survive?*, London, 1949

Howells, D. J., The Manpower Services Commission: The First Five Years, *Public Administration*, Vol. 58, 1980, pp. 305–32

Ionescu, Ghiţa, *Centripetal Politics*, London, 1975

Ionescu, Ghiţa, Saint-Simon and the Politics of Industrial Societies, *Government and Opposition*, Vol. 8, No. 1, 1973, pp. 24–47

Jay, Peter, *Employment, Inflation and Politics*, London, 1976

Jenkins, D., *Job Power*, London, 1973

Johnson, Nevil, *In Search of the Constitution*, London, 1977

Jones, Aubrey, *The New Inflation*, London, 1973

King, Anthony, (ed.), *British MPs: a self-portrait*, London, 1974

King, Anthony, Overload: problems of governing in the 1970s, *Political Studies*, Vol. XXIII No. 3, 1975, pp. 284–96

Kumar, Krishan, *Prophecy and Progress: the sociology of industrial and post-industrial society*, London, 1978

Laski, H. J., *A Grammar of Politics*, London, 1926

Laski, H. J., *Reflections on the Constitution*, London, 1962

Lee, J. M., *The Churchill Coalition, 1940–45*, London, 1980

Leonard, R. (ed.), *The Backbencher*, London, 1971

Leruez, Jacques, *Economic Planning and Politics in Britain*, London, 1975

Lethbridge, D. G. (ed.), *Government and Industry Relationships:* the Lubbock Memorial Lectures 1974/75, Oxford, 1976

Lindberg, L. et al, *Stress and contradiction in modern capitalism*, Lexington, Mass, 1975

Lindblom, C. J., *Politics and Markets*, New York, 1977

Lipsey, D. and Leonard R., *The Socialist Agenda: Crosland's Legacy*, London, 1981

Lord, Alan, *A Strategy for Industry*, Sir Ellis Hunter Memorial Lectures, University of York, 1976

Lowi, T., *The End of Liberalism*, New York, 1969

MacKenzie, R. T., Parties, pressure groups and the British political process, *Political Quarterly*, Vol. 29, 1958, pp. 5–16

Mackintosh, J. P. (ed.), *People and Parliament*, London, 1978

Mackintosh, J. P., Has Social Democracy failed in Britain?, *Political Quarterly*, Vol. 44, No. 3, 1978, pp. 259–70

Margach, J., *The Abuse of Power*, London, 1978

Marris, Robin, *The Economic Theory of Managerial Capitalism*, London, 1964

Marris, Robin, (ed.), *The Corporate Society*, London, 1974

Martin, Ross M., *TUC: the growth of a pressure group 1868–1976*, Oxford, 1980

Mason, E. S., *The Corporation in Modern Society*, Cambridge, Mass., 1959

Meade, James E., *The Intelligent Radical's Guide to Economic Policy: The Mixed Economy*, London, 1975

Metcalf, L and McQuillan, W., Corporatism or industrial democracy?, *Political Studies*, Vol. XXVII, No. 2, 1979, pp. 266–82

Middlemas, R. K., *Politics in Industrial Society*, London, 1979

Mill, J. S., *Representative Government*, London, 1910

Milliband, R., *The State in Capitalist Society*, London, 1973

Milward, A. S., *War Economy and Society 1939–45*, London, 1977

Morgan, Janet, *The House of Lords and the Labour Government*, London, 1973

Moss, R., *The Collapse of Democracy*, London, 1975

National Economic Development Office, *Conditions Favourable to Faster Growth*, London, 1963

National Economic Development Office, *Growth of the United Kingdom Economy to 1966*, London, 1963

National Economic Development Office, *Finance for Investment*, London, 1975

National Economic Development Office, *A Study of Nationalised Industries in the UK*, London, 1976

National Economic Development Office, *NEDC Annual Report*, 1979, 1980

National Economic and Social Council, *The Work of the NESC, 1974-76*, NESC, Dublin, 1977

Nettl, J. P., Consensus or elite-domination: the case of business, *Political Studies*, Vol. XIII, No. 1, 1965, pp. 22-44

Nicholson, Max, *The System: the misgovernment of modern Britain*, London, 1967

Norton, Philip, *Dissension in the House of Commons 1974-79*, London, 1980

Olson, Mancur, *The Logic of Collective Action*, Cambridge, Mass, 1971

Ovenden, K., *The Politics of Steel*, London, 1979

Panitch, L., *Social Democracy and Industrial Militancy, The Labour Party, the Trade Unions and Incomes Policy 1945-74*, London, 1976

Parker, Sir Peter, *The New Industrial Policy*, Stamp Memorial Lecture, 1977

Parkin, F., *Class, Inequality and Political Order*, London, 1971

Parris, H., *Government and the Railways in Nineteenth Century Britain*, London, 1965

Parris, H., *Constitutional Bureaucracy: the development of British Central Administration since the Eighteenth Century*, London, 1969

Parry, Geraint, *Political Elites*, London, 1969

Pateman, Carol, *Participation and Democratic Theory*, London, 1970

Perroux, F., *Le Corporatisme*, Paris, 1944

Phelps-Brown, E. H., The National Economic Development Organisation, *Public Administration*, Vol. 41, 1963, pp. 239-46

Pike, F. B. and Stritch, T. (eds.), *The New Corporatism*, London, 1977

Plamenatz, John., *Democracy and Illusion*, London, 1973

Plowden, W., *The motor car and politics in Britain*, London, 1973

Policy Studies Institute, *Relations between Trade Unions and Political Parties*, London, 1978

Political and Economic Planning, *Reshaping Britain: a programme of economic and social reform*, London, 1974

Pollard, S., *The Development of the British Economy 1914-1967*, London, 1973

Pollitt, Christopher, The Central Policy Review Staff, 1970-74, *Public Administration*, Vol. 52, 1974, pp. 375-94

Radice, Giles, *Community Socialism*, Fabian tract No. 464, London, 1979

Rawls, John, *A Theory of Justice*, Cambridge, Mass., 1971

Regeneration of British Industry, The, Cmnd. 5710, HMSO, London, 1974

Richardson, J. J. and Jordan, A. G., *Governing under Pressure*, London, 1979

Ridley, F. F., The Job Creation Programme: administrative problems of implementation, *Public Administration*, Vol. 58, 1980, pp. 261-86

Robinson, Ann, *Parliament and Public Expenditure*, London, 1978

Rogow, A. A., *The Labour Government and British Industry 1945-51*, Oxford, 1955

Roll, Eric, *The World After Keynes*, London, 1968

Roll, Eric, *The Uses and Abuses of Economics*, London, 1978

Rose, R., *The Problem of Party Government*, London, 1976

Rose, R. and Peters, G., *Can Government Go Bankrupt?*, London, 1979

Rose, R., Do Parties Make a Difference, London, 1981

Roth, Andrew, *The Business Background of MPs*, London, 1967

Rush, Michael, *The Selection of Parliamentary Candidates*, London, 1969

Sainsbury, David, *Government and Industry: a new partnership*, London, 1981

Scase, R. (ed.), *Industrial Society: class, cleavage and control*, London, 1977

Schmitter, P. C. and Lehmbruch, G. (eds.), *Trends Towards Corporatist Intermediation*, Beverly Hills/London, 1979

Schumpeter, J. A., *Capitalism, Socialism and Democracy*, London, 1943

Self, P. and Storing, H. H., *The State and the Farmer*, London, 1962

Self, P., Administrative Theories and Politics, London, 1972

Shanks, Michael, *Planning and Politics*, London, 1977

Shonfield, A., *Modern Capitalism*, London, 1965

Skidelsky, R. (ed.), *The End of the Keynesian Era*, London, 1977

Smith, T. A., *Anti-Politics: Consensus, Reform and Protest in Britain*, London, 1972

Smith, T. A., *The Politics of the Corporate Economy*, London, 1979

Stewart, M., *The Jekell and Hyde Years: Politics and Economic Policy since 1964*, London, 1977

Study of Parliament Group, Memorandum of evidence to the Select Committee on Procedure, HC 588-III, pp. 1–21

Taylor, Robert, *The Fifth Estate: Britain's unions in the seventies*, London, 1978

Taylor, Robert, The new watchdogs of Parliament, *New Society*, Vol. 55, No. 948, 15 January, 1981

Tivey, Leonard, *The Nationalised Industries since 1960*, London, 1973

Trades Union Congress *The Trade Union Role in Industrial Policy*, London, 1977

Trevithick, J. A., *Inflation: a guide to the crisis in economics*, London, 1977

Trade Unions and Political Parties, *Government and Opposition*, Vol. 3, No. 4, 1978

Turner, Graham, *Business in Britain*, London, 1971

Tyrrell, R. Emmett Jr. (ed.), *The Future That Doesn't Work: Social Democracy's Failures in Britain*, London, 1977

Tyrrell, George, The Politics of a Hived-off Board: the Advisory Conciliation and Arbitration Service, *Public Administration*, Vol. 58, 1980, pp. 225–33

Vernon, Ray, *Sovereignty at Bay*, London, 1971

Vernon, Ray (ed.), *Big Business and the State: changing relations in Western Europe*, London, 1974

Walkland, S. A., *The Legislative Process in Great Britain*, London, 1968

Walkland, S. A., Parliament and the Economy in Britain, *Parliamentary Affairs*, Vol. XXXII, No. 1, 1979, pp. 6–19

Walkland, S. A. (ed.), *The House of Commons in the Twentieth Century*, London, 1979

Walkland, S. A. and Ryle, M., (eds.), *The Commons Today*, London, 1981

Warnecke, S. and Suleiman, E. (eds.), *Industrial Policies in Western Europe*, London, 1976

Watkinson, Viscount, *Blueprint for Industrial Survival*, London, 1976

Webb, S. and Webb, B., *A Constitution for the Socialist Commonwealth of Great Britain*, London, 1920

Wigham, E., *The Power to Manage*, London, 1973

Wilson, Sir Harold, *The Governance of Britain*, London, 1976

Winch, D., *Economics and Policy*, London, 1969

Winkler, J. T., Law, state and economy: the Industry Act 1975 in perspective, *British Journal of Law and Society*, Vol. II, No.2, 1975, pp. 103–28

Wiseman, H. V., *Parliament and the Executive*, London, 1966

Wootton, Graham, *The Politics of Influence*, London, 1966

Wootton, Graham, *Pressure and Politics in Contemporary Britain*, London, 1978

Worswick, G. D. N. and Ady, P. H. (eds.), *The British Economy 1945-50*, Oxford, 1952

Worswick, G. D. N. and Ady, P. H. (eds.), *The British Economy in the 1950s*, Oxford, 1962

Wright, Maurice, Public Expenditure in Britain: the crisis of control, *Public Administration*, Vol. 55, 1977, pp. 143-70

Young, S., *Intervention in the Mixed Economy*, London, 1974

Zysman, John, *Political Strategies for Industrial Order: State, Market and Industry in France*, Berkeley, California, 1977

Official Publications

Command Papers

Cmnd 6527 Employment Policy, London, 1944

Cmnd 1432 Control of Public Expenditure, Plowden Report on the
            Machinery of Government, London, 1961
Cmnd 2764 The National Plan, London, 1965
Cmnd 3638 The Civil Service, 7 vols., London, 1968, 1969
Cmnd 4641 Government Organisation for Defence Procurement and
            Civil Aerospace, London, 1970
Cmnd 5710 Regeneration of British Industry, London, 1974
Cmnd 6315 An Approach to Industrial Strategy, London, 1975
Cmnd 6706 Committee of Inquiry on Industrial Democracy, London,
            1977
Cmnd 7937 Committee to Review the Functioning of Financial
            Institutions, Report, London, 1980

House of Commons Papers

HC 109 House of Commons Industry and Trade Committee, First
         Report (Imports and Exports), Session 1980-81
HC 163 House of Commons Treasury and Civil Service
         Committee, Monetary Policy, Session 1980-81
HC 588 House of Commons Select Committee on Procedures, First
         Report, Session 1977-78
HC 596 House of Commons Select Committee on Expenditure,
         Report on Chrysler (UK) Ltd., Session 1975-76
HC 617 House of Commons Select Committee on Expenditure,
         Report on the Motor Vehicle Industry, Session 1974-75
HC 712 House of Commons Treasury and Civil Service
         Committee, Civil Service Manpower Reductions, Session
         1979-80
HC 713 House of Commons Treasury and Civil Service
         Committee, Monetary Control, Session 1979-80

Index